Modeling for Sustainable Management in Agriculture, Food and the Environment

Editors

George Vlontzos
Department of Agriculture Crop Production
and Rural Environment
University of Thessaly, Volos, Greece

Yiannis Ampatzidis
Agricultural and Biological Engineering Department
University of Florida, Immokalee, FL, USA

Basil Manos
Department of Agricultural Economics
Aristotle University of Thessaloniki, Thessaloniki, Greece

Panos M. Pardalos
Department of Industrial and Systems Engineering
University of Florida, Gainesville, FL, USA

CRC Press
Taylor & Francis Group
Boca Raton London New York

CRC Press is an imprint of the
Taylor & Francis Group, an **informa** business

A SCIENCE PUBLISHERS BOOK

First edition published 2022
by CRC Press
6000 Broken Sound Parkway NW, Suite 300, Boca Raton, FL 33487-2742

and by CRC Press
2 Park Square, Milton Park, Abingdon, Oxon, OX14 4RN

© 2022 Taylor & Francis Group, LLC

CRC Press is an imprint of Taylor & Francis Group, LLC

Reasonable efforts have been made to publish reliable data and information, but the author and publisher cannot assume responsibility for the validity of all materials or the consequences of their use. The authors and publishers have attempted to trace the copyright holders of all material reproduced in this publication and apologize to copyright holders if permission to publish in this form has not been obtained. If any copyright material has not been acknowledged please write and let us know so we may rectify in any future reprint.

Except as permitted under U.S. Copyright Law, no part of this book may be reprinted, reproduced, transmitted, or utilized in any form by any electronic, mechanical, or other means, now known or hereafter invented, including photocopying, microfilming, and recording, or in any information storage or retrieval system, without written permission from the publishers.

For permission to photocopy or use material electronically from this work, access www.copyright.com or contact the Copyright Clearance Center, Inc. (CCC), 222 Rosewood Drive, Danvers, MA 01923, 978-750-8400. For works that are not available on CCC please contact mpkbookspermissions@tandf.co.uk

Trademark notice: Product or corporate names may be trademarks or registered trademarks and are used only for identification and explanation without intent to infringe.

Library of Congress Cataloging-in-Publication Data

Names: Vlontzos, George, 1971- editor. | Ampatzidis, Yiannis, editor. |
Manos, Basil, 1950- editor. | Pardalos, P. M. (Panos M.), 1954- editor.
Title: Modeling for sustainable management in agriculture, food and the
environment / George Vlontzos, Yiannis Ampatzidis, Basil Manos, Panos M.
Pardalos.
Description: First edition. | Boca Raton, FL : CRC Press, 2021. | Includes
bibliographical references and index. | Summary: "Modeling in
agriculture, food and environmental protection and management is
practiced widely. The interrelationship of these sectors necessitates
the need for methodologies and operational tools capable of increasing
effectiveness and efficiency, establishing at the same time the
sustainable utilization of inputs and natural resources. An integrated
approach by a multidisciplinary team of researchers is necessary. This
book introduces the readers to relevant methodological approaches and
applications, and outlines the challenges in the near future"-- Provided
by publisher.
Identifiers: LCCN 2021007106 | ISBN 9780367186678 (hardcover)
Subjects: LCSH: Sustainable agriculture--Computer simulation. |
Agricultural innovations. | Precision farming.
Classification: LCC S494.5.S86 M63 2021 | DDC 338.10285--dc23
LC record available at https://lccn.loc.gov/2021007106

ISBN: 978-0-367-18667-8 (hbk)
ISBN: 978-1-032-01311-4 (pbk)
ISBN: 978-0-429-19752-9 (ebk)

DOI: 10.1201/9780429197529

Typeset in Palatino Roman
by Innovative Processors

Preface

The recent developments in computer science, data mining and big data analytics have formulated a new framework in agriculture, food production and environmental protection. The continuous challenge of researchers is to extract new data patterns and utilize them for decision making purposes. On the other hand, managers, policy makers, and practitioners have to be familiarized with such methodologies, in order to be able to establish efficient and effective working groups for the tasks to be resolved. This book emphasizes on the complexity obtained by the interrelationship of agriculture, food production and process and environmental issues. It reveals also the significant potential of modelling during various problem solving cases being treated in these sectors, illustrating at the same time the new challenges to be met in the near future. Consumer awareness for important issues of food production and processing practices is continuously increasing and the necessity for advanced behavioral tools follows the same trend. Furthermore, the value chain management challenge is becoming one of the most crucial tasks due to the increased importance of new parameters like the origin of products, their environmental footprint the enhancement of local production etc. The book addresses these topics in a holistic approach, merging modelling with advanced marketing practices in a coherent and innovative manner, being an effective tool in a continuously demanding world.

It consists of seven chapters, presenting a series of up to date research findings in a readers' friendly way, trying to familiarize them with terms and technologies applied to agriculture and food production.

The first chapter presents the recent technologies applied for achieving circular economy goals. The target of sustainable development is closely interrelated with the principles of circular economy, being this more feasible to be reached by the adoption of thriving technologies like Internet of Things, Data Mining, Artificial Intelligence, etc.

The second chapter analyses various techniques for simplifying data mining in precision agriculture. This approach of farming is not only promising, but up to now has offered significant improvements on inputs' utilization and increase of productivity.

The third chapter focuses on the outcomes of applying computerized technologies for modelling land use and land cover changes. This specific natural resource is not only absolutely necessary for farming, but quite frequently it is considerably exposed to incorrect farming practices leading to soil degradation, especially in sensitive habitats, like the Mediterranean basin.

The forth chapter presents an empirical study on assessing the interaction of conventional farming and satisfying sustainability goals on an environmentally sensitive habitat. The use of modelling for quantifying the impact of various parameters of such multidimensional relations offers new insights on formulating and applying policies and actions tailored to specific local needs and challenges.

The fifth chapter illustrates alternative techniques and technologies for increasing the efficiency of applied crop protection protocols and practices. These technologies can be modified on ready to use mechanical agricultural equipment, offering improved services towards the more general concept of precision farming.

The sixth chapter emphasizes on the utility of remote sensing and the goals obtained by their application. This is a useful tool to analyze the vegetation dynamic on local, regional, or global scales and to determine the impact of climate on vegetation.

Finally, the seventh chapter clarifies the findings of the EURAKNOS project. This, aims to collate and allow access to data related to the agricultural production in Europe that is made available by Thematic Networks.

We hope that this book will be of interest to a broader audience, as well as practitioners. We strongly believe that modern farming is a multitasking process, requesting interdisciplinary approaches to meet feasible solutions on controversial issues on the production level, as well as satisfying continuously changing consumer concerns about, food safety, security, and environmental protection of rural areas.

George Vlontzos
Yiannis Ampatzidis
Basil Manos
Panos M. Pardalos

Contents

Preface   iii

1. New Technologies Contribution on the Agrifood Sector for Achieving Circular Economy Goals   1
   Christina Kleisiari, Leonidas-Sotirios Kyrgiakos, Panos Pardalos, and George Vlontzos

2. Dimensionality Reduction Techniques for High-dimensional Data in Precision Agriculture   28
   Mostafa Reisi-Gahrooei, James A. Whitehurst, Yiannis Ampatzidis and Panos Pardalos

3. Modelling Land Use and Land Cover Changes in the Mediterranean Agricultural Ecosystems   40
   Javier Martínez-Vega, Samir Mili and Marta Gallardo

4. Farmers' Perceptions Towards Social-economic Sustainability: A Case Study of the Karla Basin   74
   Chatzipetrou Chrysafo-Anna, Christos T. Nakas and George Vlontzos

5. Advanced Crop Protection Techniques and Technologies   112
   Athanasios T. Balafoutis, Charikleia K. Kavroumatzi, Michail Moraitis, Konstantinos Vaiopoulos, Nikos Mylonas, I. Tsitsigiannis, Yiannis Ampatzidis, Dimitrios, Spyros Fountas, Dionysis Bochtis

6. Remote Sensing in Agricultural Production Assessment   172
   Nicolas R. Dalezios and Ioannis N. Faraslis

7. Integrating Agriculture-related Data Provided by Thematic Networks into a High Impact Knowledge Reservoir   199
   Hercules Panoutsopoulos, Borja Espejo Garcia, Philip E.G. Verbist, Spyros Fountas, Pieter Spanoghe and Christopher Brewster

8. A Multicriteria DEA Model for Estimating the Efficiency of
   Agricultural Production Process 227
   Anna Kalioropoulou, Basil Manos and Thomas Bournaris

Index 240

CHAPTER

1

New Technologies Contribution on the Agrifood Sector for Achieving Circular Economy Goals

Christina Kleisiari[1]*, Leonidas-Sotirios Kyrgiakos[2], Panos Pardalos[3], and George Vlontzos[4]

[1,2] Ph.D. Student, Department of Agriculture, Crop Production and Rural Environment, University of Thessaly, Volos, Greece

[3] Distinguished Professor, Department of Industrial and Systems Engineering, University of Florida, Gainesville, United States

[4] Assistant Professor, Department of Agriculture, Crop Production and Rural Environment, University of Thessaly, Volos, Greece

Introduction

It is a fact that global population of the planet is growing rapidly, and so is the increase in demand for agricultural products. According to a recent research (Swaminathan and Bhavani 2013), the amount of food produced should double in the next 15 years in order to provide self-sufficiency and meet the needs of an ever-growing population. The projected increase in demand for feed to support livestock production is analogous. In addition, population growth will also increase the demand for certain commodities such as textiles and clothing products that lead to an increased demand for agricultural raw materials such as cotton and flax as well. However, correspondingly in recent years there has been a steady decline of available resources used in the production process. Furthermore, according to a report published by Food and Agriculture Organization of the United

---

*Corresponding author: chkleisiari@uth.gr

Nations (FAO 2013), there is a worldwide increase in the price of energy as well as an increase in the price of plant protection products, a decrease in the amount of irrigation water available and a deterioration in the quality of the land available for cultivation. All of these problems are exacerbated by climate change and extreme weather. The main way for agricultural production to meet these challenges successfully, is to make the most of available knowledge, technology and innovation with a view to protect the environment.

Circular economy is an idea created at the end of the industrial period as a result of the over-exploitation of natural resources as well as the enormous environmental impact of human actions on planet Earth. The linear flow of energy that has been prevalent for many years, and still largely exists today, intensifies the exploitation of natural resources and leads to quantitative and qualitative degradation. It is clear that the prevalence of linear energy flow in a circular form of use has led mankind to tackle a set of environmental problems that have a major impact on agriculture, such as soil, water and air pollution as well as the greenhouse effect. It has been shown that 70% of water consumption and up to 30% of greenhouse gas emissions come from processes taking place at various stages of the agri-food sector (Aleksandrowicz et al. 2016). However, this situation can be easily improved by the widespread use of renewable energy at all stages of the agri-food chain (e.g. solar panels, wind turbines, biogas plants, use of food residues for soil fertilization, etc.) and the enhanced application of new technologies to promote the principles of circular economy.

In recent years, with the aim of achieving the goals of circular economy, the adoption of digital technologies by agricultural production has become very intense, contributing to a more sustainable food production system. Developments in AI, the IoT and other technology applications are currently being used in both rural production and throughout the value chain, as they provide solutions to address certain challenges such as the need for greater anticipation of accuracy, waste reduction and overall supply chain management (OECD 2019). It has been shown by numerous previous studies that technology-driven circular economy starts from the beginning of a product's lifecycle (production, cultivation) and can be applied to all stages of it, including its consumption (Mor et al. 2015).

In general, the benefits of precision farming can be divided into three main areas: (a) the economy, (b) the environment, and (c) society. From an economic point of view, the introduction of more rational decision-making systems in agriculture brings significant economic benefits, offering the possibility of increasing the profit margin and overall profitability without increasing the cost of cultivation. It is estimated that there is a possibility of increasing the productivity of agriculture by 70% by 2050 with the implementation of Internet of Things systems (Sarni et al. 2019). According to Myklevy et al. (2016), an average farm where new technologies are applied, can increase its yield by up to 1.75% while reducing energy costs and the use of water and agrochemicals.

In terms of the environment, precision farming methods have undeniable benefits for reducing environmental impacts and risks (Aubert et al. 2012). Indeed, there is now clear research evidence that the use of precision farming methods leads to a reduction in environmental degradation, including an increase in fuel efficiency resulting in a reduction in the carbon footprint of the environment (Balafoutis et al. 2017). It has also been shown that the adoption of these systems has significant benefits in reducing nitrate leaching in crops, proving that precision agriculture can reduce groundwater contamination and soil erosion (Silva et al. 2011).

The following case studies and applications of modern technological means help to achieve the basic objectives of the circular economy at all stages of the agri-food chain.

Technology Applications in the Field

The proper and 'smart' design of agricultural products, based on applying the most efficient way of exploiting the available resources in the production method, is the first and foremost stage of agricultural production where the circular economy can be applied. It aims to reduce as much as possible the production of waste from agricultural activity while increasing the profit for the producer (Toop et al. 2017). As mentioned earlier, producers nowadays, and in the near future, are facing the challenge of cultivating more, with the use of as limited inputs and water as possible, while at the same time having to cope with adverse weather conditions caused by climate change. Additionally, they have to adapt to the ever-increasing demand for food and meet diverse and ever-changing consumer preferences. A feasible means to achieve these goals is through the adoption of new technological methods and innovations in agricultural production.

Biotechnology–Genetic Improvement

Applications of plant biotechnology and genetic engineering in agriculture have led to the creation of new varieties of plants with improved characteristics, while at the same time contributing significantly to environmental protection. In order to achieve economic and environmental sustainability in a farm production system, innovative processes need to be developed and significant obstacles overcome. The technological advances of recent years have led to the development of a new generation of plant improvement techniques (Wieczorek and Wright 2012). Recent techno-economic analyzes have shown that biotechnological processes give the opportunity of recycling and upgrading CO_2 emissions into high-value end-products, while utilizing each component of the original biomass in an integrated management framework, are leading to the development of a sustainable and circular bio-economy (OECD 2019). Thus, through advances in biotechnology, it is possible to automate large-scale plant phenotypes, in the field or in a greenhouse, using digital systems. This technology is called *phenomics* and helps to understand the interaction between a plant and its environment. It is a very useful tool for crop management and can be applied with the use of optical sensors. Biochemical and anatomical properties of the crop are sketched without requiring a conventional visit of an expert to the field (Mahlein 2016).

Environmental pollution can be decreased through biotechnology contribution, developing new species with a greater series of defense mechanisms to biotic and abiotic factors, limiting the use of agrochemicals. Moreover, biotechnology is responsible for giving handful of information to pharmacy industry about plant or animal mechanisms, in the effort of creating more environmentally friendly products with higher efficiency rates. Replacing some crops with new varieties that require less irrigation water and less fertilizer quantities has direct environmental benefits. After discovering that certain genes can be transferred to some plant species attracting or even repelling insects, new varieties have been established having a "natural" insect protection system that does not require the application of pesticides (War et al. 2012).

In this context, vegetation zones on field borders can conserve biodiversity, enhancing surviving rates of local populations in extreme weather conditions like winter temperatures. Their survival is not only crucial in terms of preserving native species for maintaining a gene bank, but these organisms also contribute to biological control of undesirable pests, eliminating biocides usage. Margin zones can be cultivated with more favorable target plants for the most common pests of the surrounding area, acting as an indicator about field population. It seems that type of flower on field borders plays a significant role for pest control, with nectar-producing plants preserving more efficiently local populations than random indigenous plants within field (Balzan and Moonen 2014).

Genetically modified crop cultivation, as an application of biotechnology, has produced very significant benefits for producers worldwide, as it can lead to higher yields at lower production costs compared to the cultivation of the corresponding conventional varieties. In particular, in 1983 the first transgenic plant with new enhanced features was created. It was a tobacco plant that was resistant to certain herbicides (Zerbini et al. 2014). It was successfully created a few years later (1990) and the first genetically modified cotton (Bt cotton) that, with the help of the bacterium *Bacillus thurigiensis*, produced a substance with very effective insecticidal activity. This was followed by genetically modified soybeans that were highly resistant to herbicides and developed by Monsanto.

According to US Food and Drug Administration (FDA), the first GM-food was first launched in 1994, referring to a tomato with late ripening effect (Bawa and Anilakumar 2013). Nowadays, there is a growing number of such products with improved characteristics, and new varieties of GM crops and foods are being introduced into the so-called "new generation" of Genetically Modified Products with even more improved properties. This leads to a large number of countries on a global scale where GM plants are grown and then used as food or feed.

The most important contribution of GM crops, declared by their supporters, is that they minimizes the risk of an upcoming food crisis by contributing to both increased food production and meeting the nutritional needs of Earth's ever-growing population. From the GM crop cultivation point of view, this activity can positively affect producers' income by using improved and more resistant varieties, and reducing the production costs resulting from the limited use of plant protection products and fertilizers (Buiatti et al. 2013). More precisely, GM crops are more resistant to certain adverse weather conditions (e.g. drought and extreme temperatures) but also to pesticides, which means that they require less cultivation activities, compared with the conventional ones and thus increases the crop yield while reducing production costs (Oliver 2014). It has been scientifically proven that GM crops which are resistant to the herbicide glyphosate allow weed control and facilitate crop control using this particular herbicide (Cerdeira and Duke 2006; Brookes and Barfoot 2012). The reported data on the use of certain environmental indicators on pesticide use in terms of quantity, environmental impact and cost reduction found a very significant reduction in greenhouse gas emissions resulting from the replacement of conventional crops with GM ones, as the latter had lower requirements for pesticides and agricultural practices requiring the use of machinery. In particular, it was found that the increase in GM soybean cultivation by approximately 5 million hectares in the United States from 1996–2009 resulted in a significant 65% reduction in the use of agricultural machinery for farming. An overall reduction of fuel consumption by approximately 12% is estimated for the same period with a relative reduction in greenhouse gas emissions.

In addition, limited use of chemical pesticides is able to reduce environmental pollution, while at the same time creating products with improved characteristics and better nutritional value compared to conventional, non-modified foods, despite the concerns of many consumers. Taking for example the GM soybeans case, despite consumer concerns about its food safety, the European Food Safety Authority (EFSA) decided that GM soybeans could be considered as safe and nutrient-equivalent as non- genetically modified soybeans as regards the adverse effects that could have on human and animal health and the effects that their use can have on the environment (Naegeli et al. 2019).

On the other hand, there are several concerns about GM food and feed consumption, mainly related to economic, social, environmental and food safety and bioethics issues. Due to lack of information about new food-related products entering the market every day and accompanying technologies for their improvement, there are many concerns from the consumers' side regarding their health. Some researchers have expressed concerns about the potential risk of biodiversity disruption and damage to plant and animal organisms by growing GM plants. It has been shown that many GM crops secrete toxins into the soil through their root system. The cumulative effects of these toxins can have negative results on both soil and aquatic ecosystems, and they can accumulate in different tissue types of living organisms, causing long-term problems. According to a research (Waltz E 2011), large populations of a butterfly species have been eliminated from GM corn pollen. It is also expected that a large percentage of traditional varieties will be reduced and may even face extinction danger. Lu and Yang (2009), studied the transfer of transgenic from rice to its wild relatives through gene flow and its ecological consequences, expressing concern about possible genetic pollution that can be defined as the uncontrolled spread of GMOs in the environment and can be a risk factor for agricultural ecosystems. GMOs have the ability to mutate, proliferate and propagate with other organisms as well as migrate, causing disruption or even damage to natural ecosystems balance.

Furthermore, those who oppose GM plants and GM foods argue that their consumption can lead to adverse effects on human health. After all, since the first entry of GM food into the market, it has not been long since it became clear whether or not there are any effects from their use. Even the reckless use of GM plants by humans and animals may have a detrimental effect on their health. A few years ago, for instance, it was discovered that genetic modification of a particular type of soybean that had been preceded by the introduction of certain genes from walnuts caused an allergic shock to consumers who had a history of walnut allergy (Maghari and Ardekani 2011). Despite strict legislation enacted by various countries around the world regarding the introduction of GMOs and various types of checks through the whole supply chain so as to avoid any potential danger, numerous citizen groups oppose GMOs expressing security concerns about human health and environmental protection.

Utilization of Renewable Energy Sources/Waste Management

The uncontrolled use of conventional sources of energy during the agricultural production process results in high economic and environmental costs. Replacing them with renewable energy sources is considered an urgent need and should be done globally and to a greater extent. Focusing on mitigating climate change with the assistance of readily available technological means, the utilization of solar energy,

New Technologies Contribution on the Agrifood Sector   **7**

geothermal energy and biomass have been greatly simplified (Chel and Kaushik 2011).

Intensification of agriculture has led to decreased water reserves and increased water pollution. Reclaimed water is a smart solution for decreasing water amounts for irrigation purposes. Heavy metal concentration has been studied both in soil and plants, in order to examine reclaimed water use effects in agriculture (S. Lu, Wang, and Pei 2016). Samples have been taken in 2011 and 2014, resulting in a slight increase, but still under national maximum residue level. Environmental effects of reclaimed water should be extensively investigated (e.g. soil, crop type, combination with biocides, influence in microorganisms etc.) as it is a very promising practice for reusing water, minimizing by this way the negative externalities of agriculture in the environment.

New technologies have been established as well, using sensors and wireless networks in order to improve decision making processes, eliminating energy and water loss (Chappell et al. 2013, Lea-Cox 2012). The Decision Support System (DSS) combines weather, land and crop type datasets with a view to accomplish greater accuracy on open-field crop irrigation (Mastrorilli and Zucaro 2016). Monitoring water on a systematic basis provides all the data needed for implementing water use models with higher certainty levels (Wada et al. 2013).

Combining the aforementioned food security issue with energy resources there is a rising question about the amount of energy that can be used for minimizing agricultural impacts and preserve great food production. Energy Return On Investment (EROI) analysis investigates the fraction of amount of energy that is returned back to society to the amount of energy spent for the production of this unit (Hall et al. 2009). EROI has been implemented in the agricultural sector as well, explaining energy efficiency and flows on main crops, comparing differences with the industrial sector as well (Hall et al. 2009). Assessing agricultural energy consumption efficiency, Data Envelopment Analysis is the dominant methodology approach due to the fact that it can depict environmental consequences of energy inputs and pinpoint the most efficient decision making units (DMUs) out of existing ones and not a theoretical optimal level (Łozowicka 2020).

Mineral fertilizers demand high energy amounts during the production procedure and transportation to the field. Literature review reveals that acidification, eutrophication, land use, global warming and consumption of non-renewable sources (gas, oil, and coal) are the fundamental factors of negative environmental effects caused by fertilizers (Skowrońska and Filipek 2014). Life Cycle Assessment (LCA) was the key analysis used in the majority of previously reviewed papers, proofing its significance on evaluation of fertilizer production but the survey concludes that there are still doubts about globalizing results that have been locally obtained.

8   *Modeling for Sustainable Management in Agriculture, Food and the Environment*

Intergovernmental Panel on Climate Change using climate models predicts that mean earth temperature will increase around 1,5°C and it will not exceed more than 2°C (IPCC 2018). Furthermore, 4 different scenarios (optimistic to pessimistic scale) are presented about the influence of CO_2 amounts in the environment until 2100. Innovation, new technology, fossil fuel alternation to biofuels and change of current habits are the main factors that construct these final scenarios. Another point suggests that crop yield will be slightly interfered from temperature increase, without great production loss.

Fossil fuels are used in agriculture as well. It is a nonrenewable source of energy with their burning emissions worsening the greenhouse effect. Fossil fuels should be replaced by biofuels as a renewable type of energy but this can be complex on a rapid population growth concept. Food vs fuel is an increasing topic, while magnitude of arable land is the restricting factor (Rosillo-Calle 2012, Thompson 2012, Timilsina 2012). Moreover, biofuels are still less energy efficient than fossil fuels and alternation of current equipment and technology is needed for achieving maximum energy output without operational problems. Plant breeders attempt to develop new varieties with thicker cell walls and endurance in extreme environmental conditions (cold, drought, high temperatures etc.), producing adaptive and resilient cultivars that can be cultivated even on degraded land (Murphy et al. 2011). Thus, the cultivation of energy crops is affected by many factors such as policy framework, commodity futures, available capital and environmental conditions (Borras et al. 2016).

Gas emissions from livestock account for 14.5% of total human activity. Feed production and enteric fermentation are the main contributors to greenhouse gas (GHG) emissions in the agricultural sector with beef cattle accounting for 65% of emissions (Gerber et al. 2013). Main emitted gases are: methane-(CH_2) =44%, nitrous oxide-(N_2O) =29% and carbon dioxide-(CO_2) =27% of sector's emissions. Attempts have been made for increasing fat content on animal feed and enabling animal genomics so as to reduce livestock emissions (Grainger and Beauchemin 2011). Methane can be used for electric energy production on biogas plants, as an alternative to conventional electric production units.

Solid waste management can contribute to the mitigation of environmental consequences of livestock emissions, leading to a sustainable increase of arable land productivity. Biogas plants are an innovative solution for converting animal waste into reusable energy. Combinations of thermal treatment practices with bacteria species and type of manure are implemented in order to achieve maximum productivity. Examining energy flows and input energy through corn biomass achieved to enhance by 62% the total energy output implementing deep digest processing. (Maksimov et al. 2017). Another paper focused on the material origin (manure of beef, chicken, swine and plant residues) assessing methane production. A mixture of chicken and swine manure was the most efficient, concluding in 32% more methane. Authors underline that there is still a lot of gap until reaching highest profitability from biogas plants (Wandera et al. 2018). As World Bank indicates, 70% of water is used for agricultural purposes (World Bank, 2017). Computational problems arise for water use estimates due to lack of datasets not only in agriculture but in the domestic and industrial sector as well (Flörke et al. 2013). Climate change will stress more water supplies, rising population will have higher requirements of water consumption while agriculture will demand higher water proportions for irrigation purposes (Flörke et al. 2018). As AQUASTAT suggests there is a 5.1% pressure on fresh water due to irrigation globally (AQUASTAT 2012), accounting for water deficit in agricultural sector.

Irrigation systems have changed dramatically the last 50 years, from sprinklers to water reels and water pipes for land fields and from conventional to circular water systems for greenhouses. All methods tend to decrease evapotranspiration (loss of water from leaf surface and ground to the atmosphere) and increase water availability for plants. Increasing interest for water use efficiency has been noted, as bibliography suggests (Velasco-Muñoz et al. 2018). Underground water abstraction is a common practice for farmers in order to irrigate their crops. Unfortunately, there is a very poor legislation framework about the amount of water that an individual can abstract. Gleeson and Richter survey reveals that farmers can take advantage from underground water banks in an environmental friendly way, by introducing a new index — Environmental Flow Response Time (EFRT) (Gleeson and Richter 2018). It states that by it, authorities should monitor water resources on a monthly basis in order to identify the underwater stream and propose water use changes accordingly.

Biocides use have resulted in higher crop yields. They are manufactured in a way that they are soluble in water so as to be absorbed from the outer surface and move through the inner structures of organisms. Their physicochemical properties make them easily water soluble, moving from agricultural fields through water flows to rivers and even sea ecosystems, influencing negatively water quality and living organisms. Constructed wetlands can efficiently minimize runoff water from the field's surface. As Vymazal and Březinová's (2015) literature review indicates, there are many field surveys, highlighting that wetlands are a necessity for preserving water quality in natural sources. Absorption rate from wastelands varies for different pesticide chemical groups but this practice is an effective barrier for preventing chemical expansion in food chain.

Precision Agriculture

Sustainability and parallel conservation of natural resources is the main objective for achieving long-term supply of goods and services coming from agriculture (Zhang 2013). The close and inseparable relationship between rural development and the protection of the natural environment is evident, making clear the great need for continuous research on appropriate farming systems serving sustainable development (Darnhofer et al. 2012). The terms of sustainability and sustainable development are nowadays an essential ingredient for assessing a region's development. However, sustainability is a multidimensional concept which has created difficulties for scientists who have tried at times to give a clear explanation. There have been many international efforts to measure sustainability, yet only few of them have an integrated approach that takes into consideration all three key aspects of sustainability: environment, economy and community. Therefore, it was considered necessary to introduce some indicators that would help to gather, group and better interpret and quantify all these aspects (Singh et al. 2012).

Indicators relating to the environmental dimension of sustainability are relevant to the use of pesticides, nutritional balance, energy, water use and irrigation practices and land management. There are a plethora of methods used by agriculture in order to protect the climate, protect biodiversity and wise use of water resources and soils (Wezel et al. 2014). Very positive results have emerged from the application of precision farming (Schader et al. 2014) and the biological control of parasite (Roberts et al. 2013; van Lenteren et al. 2018). Precision agriculture is a crop management system based on the spatial and temporal variability of crop and soil factors within a field. Precision farming through the application of certain technologies enables producers to maximize their yields while minimizing the resources they use. At the same time it contributes greatly to reducing the negative environmental impacts resulting from conventional farming practices.

It has been shown that in many cases the transition to a robotic cropping system can make plant production more efficient and sustainable (Ramin Shamshiri et al. 2018). A typical example is the application of technology in greenhouses engaged in the production of fruits and vegetables. Very modern methods have been developed to fully automate greenhouse crops that function as a way to reduce costs while improving quality. The technology used to monitor plant growth, as well as the robot collectors, are such mechanisms.

A. Automation/Robotics

Many different types of robots are now used for more accurate crop monitoring, plant protection automation, and easier harvesting of certain species. By 2023, it is estimated that drones using artificial intelligence will be widely used in agricultural production. Many types of high mass tractors are slowly giving way to robots, with benefits to be achieved to increase crop efficiency, reducing soil compaction and reducing the amount of fuel and fertilizer required (Reddy et al. 2016). Drones (UAVs) capable of mapping entire farms or parts of them using innovative remote sensing and digital orthophotography methods have begun to be increasingly used in the application of precision farming technologies. Then, the algorithm very accurately calculates the viability of the crop and the needs for fertilization and plant protection with real-time accuracy, since even a possible infestation of diseases or insects is detected very early (Urbahs and Jonaite 2013). Robotics can be used also to replace the time-consuming and costly traditional methods of harvesting vegetables (e.g. lettuce, tomato, and broccoli). Robotic systems with cameras, lasers and automatic sprinklers are also used in the field of plant protection for more efficient use of pesticides (Ahmed et al. 2016). Equally important is the contribution of robotics to livestock breeding, in particular to dairy cows but also to chickens and swine with the aim of improving the welfare of livestock and increasing productivity with respect to the environment (Holloway 2007).

B. Sensors

Still another technological finding used extensively in agriculture are sensors of various kinds and properties. Some factors that are calculated with the help of sensors are humidity, wind speed and temperature. Sensors capable of evaluating the visual properties of plants beyond the visible range in different regions of the electromagnetic spectrum are also used for the valid and timely detection and diagnosis of diseases of a crop with the aim of immediately planning the plant protection procedures that should be followed (Mahlein 2016). The ever-increasing use of sensors by manufacturers has led to a significant reduction in equipment, installation and maintenance costs. The types of sensors mainly used in precision agriculture are thermal and spectral sensors and measure temperature, fluorescence and reflectivity.

The information obtained from the sensor measurements is transmitted through a communication system to another processing device. In precision farming systems, crop data collection by remote sensing for integrated crop management, and limited use of fertilizers, pesticides and water, is also important (Liaghat and Balasundram 2010). To make this process more efficient, the sensors should be positioned in specific locations in the field or in the greenhouse or applied to the tractor, robotic systems or satellites and, where appropriate, necessary information should be collected. Broadband sensors allow wireless sensors to create a Distributed Wireless Sensor Network (DWSN). Communication between the nodes in a wireless sensor network is implemented using RF (radio frequency), optical (e.g. infrared), ultrasonic and magnetic coupling

(Jawad et al. 2017). A DWSN network includes a data acquisition network and a data distribution network controlled by a management center. The use of RFs through wireless sensor networks finds utility in environmental monitoring. In more detail, they provide producers with information on possible adverse conditions (e.g. flood, frost) that threaten the crop so that all necessary measures need be taken.

A large class of sensors used in precision farming systems are sensors aimed at mapping production. Examples of such sensors are sensors used in combine harvesters customarily to detect qualitative characteristics of seeds (usually its flow and moisture content) to calculate harvesting time (Nelson, Trabelsi, and Lewis 2016) and also sensors used in cotton harvesters to calculate its flow (Sui et al. 2010). There are also sensors for calculating soil parameters (mainly for measuring soil electrical conductivity) that directly affect the productivity of the field. Indeed, according to Seifi et al. (2010) who calculated the electrical conductivity of cultivated soils, they observed that this measurement can detect if there is soil contamination. Finally, it is also worth mentioning sensor systems that have the capability to control and assist in the programming of variable dose input devices. This category includes sensors that control, for example, the stage at which a crop is found, and depending on their color, it can be understood whether there is a need for fertilization or not. Sensor systems are mounted on agricultural tractors and can record the different needs of the field for fertilizer or plant protection. The sensor then communicates with an artificial intelligence system to the tractor and automatically applies the required amount of fertilizer or pesticide where the problem is located (Colaço and Bramley 2018).

Lloret et al. (2011) used a wireless sensor network in Spain's vineyard. The system used worked with the ZigBee standard for connecting the nodes to one another, requesting limited capital and energy inputs. The grid consisted of 12 nodes and the sensors used measured environmental and territorial temperature and humidity as well as solar radiation. Low-power electronics and long-lasting batteries that can be combined with small photovoltaics or solar panels make it possible to minimize the cost of installing systems with wireless sensors to make them economically viable.

C. Cloud Computing

Producers in recent years have had greater access to large amounts of data as the cost of access to data centers has decreased. This makes it easier to collect, process and store the information they care about, while providing easy and fast access to the web and simple connectivity further enhances this prospect (cloud computing).

D. Blockchain

Finally, the growing use of the Internet, coupled with the indispensable infrastructure and encryption capabilities, makes it possible to capture and exchange information securely and transparently, with benefits for the blockchain (Mao et al. 2018). Distributed ledger technology (DLT), on which blockchain is based, is a database distributed over a multi-computer network rather than a central location. Tripoli and Schmidhuber (2018), when testing DLT technologies in agriculture to create "smart contracts" among stakeholders, concluded that the goals of sustainable development in agri-food sector can be easily achieved. Easy access to a large database can help improve supplies, enhance market transparency and prove cost-effective for the environment as it leads to an automated production process that contributes to environmental protection.

Storage–Transportation

Most of the technological breakthroughs used in agriculture are mainly concerned with the first stage of the value chain, i.e. the stage of production so as to provide a more integrated and sustainable management of the operation of farms globally, while maximizing yields. Definitely, in recent years there has also been an expansion of technological innovations to other stages of agricultural production such as the stage of distribution of agricultural products, retail trade and consumption. Therefore, various applications have been created that enable stakeholders to have a complete picture of the supply chain through tracking and tracing of agricultural products (Z. Li et al. 2017).

The term logistics in agricultural businesses is used to describe the process of designing and implementing and monitoring all the processes required for agricultural products from their production to their sale at the point of sale (X. Li 2014). New and innovative digital technologies have been integrated into the value chain and succeeded dramatic changes as transports and warehousing are now automated and integrated with high intelligence and efficiency. The majority of businesses worldwide have adopted such logistics technologies and achieved greater consumer satisfaction at the least possible cost. At the same time, the use of logistics technologies has proved to be very useful for the producers themselves who can increase their profits with proper planning as they now have complete information on their product demand.

The first stage of logistics with technological innovations is the receipt of goods for storage. For this purpose a Warehouse Management Subsystem (WMS) is commonly used providing the necessary barcodes, magnetic locations etc. In addition to using these systems, radio networks (RFnetworks), wireless terminals and radio IDs (RFIDs) are implemented

(Yan, Yiyun, and Xiaosheng 2008). These technologies minimize the cost of searching for products and a real-time image of the storage space is readily available. Salah et al. (2019) applied blockchain technology to trace soybeans at all stages of the supply chain, and succeeded in recording all actions and transactions carried out during the shipment storage and delivery of the final product by the consumer, providing greater reliability, efficiency and safety in everyone involved in this process.

The concept of reverse logistics is to further develop the logistics process as it is based on the principles of circular economy and environmental protection, having as its main objective the reusing of products. Reverse logistics starts when a product or a set of products returns to business either because they were defective or because their life cycle has ended or they have simply been unsold for a long time. It also includes packages returned to refill and resell. The main reasoning behind the promotion of reverse agricultural supply chain practices lies on both operational and environmental motives. The major incentive that drives a business to implement reverse logistics practices is to reduce the costs resulting from their production process while becoming more competitive. This can be achieved as a gain from input materials, because in many cases the residual value recovered from reused products and raw materials cost much less. At the same time, there is a significant environmental gain as the pollution of the environment is reduced due to a satisfactory reduction of waste, following a process of recycling, reusing, repairing and/or reshaping existing returned products. Thus, the business becomes more sustainable while benefiting even more as it acquires a greener image and improves its relationship with the consumer public (Bernon et al. 2018).

A typical example of businesses using reverse logistics are breweries that re-bottle used beer bottles and dairy units that accept returns of milk used for the production of dairy products, like cheeses. There are also specialized companies dedicated exclusively to reverse logistics that take advantage of the residual value of used foods and / or old or defective food packaging produced by other companies. Holmberg and Åquist (2018) used blockchain technology to detect dairy products at all stages of the supply chain and concluded that this technology leads to cost savings and environmental benefits in case of product recall. In particular, there was a very large difference in carbon footprint (calculated in equivalent CO_2 units) using blockchain technology compared to traditional transport without tracking technology.

The key to the proper and efficient operation of reverse logistics systems is the existence of good and valid information systems. It has been proven that most reverse supply chains using IoT based information systems have become more efficient. Such an information system collects all the necessary data and after processing the necessary information obtained it provides substantial assistance on the decision making process

New Technologies Contribution on the Agrifood Sector **15**

(Panigrahi et al. 2018). The creation of the database is done after their detailed logging in the PML (Physical Markup Language) and can then be easily managed by all members involved in a value chain. Any action taken on the product after its production is recorded at the same time through the radio frequency tag. Each product obtains a code from the object naming service (ONS) included in the same information system (Cheng and Choi 2010).

Finally, it is worth mentioning the term green logistics which includes all technologies that help reduce the energy footprint of logistics and reverse logistics. Calculation and the effort to reduce the carbon footprint are now issues of concern to businesses worldwide and the green supply chain is in line with the laws and policies of many countries. These technologies enhance the viability of a business by designing a supply chain that is environmentally friendly and at the same time generates financial gain due to reduced fuel, energy and packaging materials use (Kumar 2015). Green logistics include practices that save energy and minimize the use of environmentally hazardous materials at all stages of supply. Thus, when referring to a green supply chain we mean the green product production, green storage, green transport and distribution and the reverse supply chain process mentioned earlier.

Considering that much of the distribution of agricultural products is done by road transportation, a wide range of software packages have been created to help route optimization and avoid unnecessary itineraries, achieving up to a 20% reduction in transport costs which in turn leads to reduced fuel consumption and therefore the reduction of greenhouse gas emissions (Golden et al. 2008). The storage of agricultural products has high energy requirements especially when it comes to storing fresh fruits and vegetables where constant levels of temperature, humidity and ventilation must be maintained. For this reason, automated storage systems have been created that not only preserve food for a longer period of time, but also enable the digital control of the goods and the management of warehouse conditions (Jedermann et al. 2014). The Smart Container consists of a set of sensors designed to automatically measure humidity and air temperature in real time, and can also provide information on the state of ripeness of fruits or vegetables resulting from measuring the level of ethylene emitted. According to Lang et al. (2011), their implementation may result in fewer losses during transport and consequently reduced CO_2 emissions.

Consumption

Consumers in recent years have become increasingly interested in the composition and origin as well as the conditions from which the food they consume was produced. The increased use of digital services by producers

16 *Modeling for Sustainable Management in Agriculture, Food and the Environment*

has led to the creation of databases providing information consumers can refer to. Recent researches have shown that more and more consumers are placing greater emphasis on the viability of the products they choose to consume and are beginning to adopt more environmentally friendly consumption patterns while showing great interest in the origin of the products to be consumed. Consumers have the opportunity to contribute directly and effectively, through their everyday consumer decisions, to solving environmental problems. So when the consumer behavior of a large proportion of the population tends to choose products being produced under environmentally friendly methods, many businesses automatically have to adopt more environmentally friendly practices and apply them in their production process (Joshi and Rahman 2015).

New technologies provide opportunities for regenerative and local food development. With the rise of food technology and state-of-the-art technology and economic operators, a new range of food and agricultural solutions emerge: innovations in the creation of complex, efficient and consistent organic fertilizers, improved traceability technologies and the application of AI to the production and promotion of agricultural products (Ellen MacArthur Foundation 2018). The implementation of an organized traceability system helps to record and maintain all information related to the route followed by a product from the original supplier to the consumer. Traceability helps to ensure the quality of food arriving at points of sale, to easily find the historical origin of the products, and to find those responsible in the event of a problem in the food chain (Ringsberg 2014). The growing use of smartphones and tablets makes information search easy to access.

E-marketing that has been in people's lives for decades has now been used to market agricultural products. Regarding the use of technology to promote agricultural products, eligible actions are their promotion by electronic means (e.g. agricultural business website), electronic media advertising and e-commerce. Traditional agricultural trade is hampered by high transaction costs, low transaction efficiency, too many links to product circulation, disadvantages that are greatly reduced in e-commerce activity. Moreover, e-commerce of agricultural products improves both producer and consumer access to the market regardless of geographical location.

Limiting Factors

As technology acceptance model (Davis et al. 1989) suggests there are multiple stages before the final decision of actual use from the end-user. Literature review of Antolini et al. (2015), reveals major factors affecting implementation of new technologies in the agricultural sector. Demographic, agro-environmental and individual characteristics have been taken into account in order to extend the fitting of the previously mentioned model to the agriculture field. Due to the fact that farming is dependent on a series of environmental factors involved that affect yield and total revenue, one of the primary issues of technology adoption in agriculture is the farmers' trust in new technologies (Jayashankar et al. 2018). Despite sensor evolution and use of multidisciplinary platforms, modeling of individual parameters and their combinations affecting the growing crop remains a hard task, due to high variability of all factors involved. Kernecker et al. (2020) have investigated two target groups of farmer, those who implement new technologies and those who do not in 7 EU countries, concluding that there is a generally positive image about new technologies in agriculture but there is a lack of their implementation in the field, because they are not persuaded enough about the upcoming benefits. In the same survey, agricultural experts were more optimistic about new technologies, meaning that education can be a determining factor in technology acceptance in agriculture. Apart from education factor, Läpple et al. (2015) have revealed that farm size has a positive correlation with smart technology use, concluding that there is a need of defining «innovation» so as to be properly assessed in future survey.

Literature review of Tabas et al. (2011) shapes 5 limiting factors for innovation adoption in SMEs such as economic status, policy support and individual factors regarding structure and personnel of the enterprise. An applied survey of technological barriers in agriculture revealed 6 different factors, similar to those of the previous survey (Long et al. 2016). The greater difference is the inclusion of consumer and market needs as a new factor, but authors highlight the absence of field surveys in the developed countries which demonstrate different socio-economic characteristics. Farmer cooperatives seem to have a great influence on technology adoption to their members, but as Abebaw and Haile (2013) suggest innovation implementation should be promoted from farmers' cooperatives infrastructure and gradually be commonly accepted by all members.

The agricultural cooperatives that make the most of the available technological tools, proceed to the automation of many processes (from the production to the sale of their produced products), while now it is possible to expand mass sales through the internet and utilize electronic trading services and software applications facilitating these processes. Furthermore, there is the opportunity to process and utilize the information and data that arise both from the internal-corporate processes and from the productive activities of the cooperative itself. Thus, a cooperative that adopts digital technologies of sustainable agriculture, is prepared to face any change in the market and to contribute to smart growth by providing innovative proposals to needs that often are not satisfied by other corporations. The operation of agricultural cooperatives that apply new technologies is often developmental leading to an increase in the level of productivity of the factor of production used and the production of new products of higher quality but also reducing production and distribution costs (Del Corso et al. 2015).

However, when it comes to technological innovation, not all members need to be involved. In particular, it has been shown that when only a small proportion of producers invest in the application of new technologies, they create a dynamic competitive advantage that is able to strengthen their market position. As Grimal and Kephaliacos (2000) have stated, in this way the perfect competition is created that results in a short-term or long-term change in the technical-productive example that will be followed by all the producers.

Conclusions

Technological applications in the agri-food sector aim to increase crop yields while reducing production costs while also focusing on minimizing energy consumption and reducing the ecological footprint of the agricultural production system. It should be emphasized that the dominant means of transferring all the above-mentioned innovations to those who need them (consumers) from those who produce them (producers) are the so-called 'innovation partnerships' between the academic community and the research centers, cooperatives and individual producers, but also of the manufacturing industries, traders and chains of agricultural products and finally consumers. Enhancing research and innovation in the primary sector is a financial priority of the new Common Agricultural Policy (CAP), and governments around the world should adopt laws and policies that promote and implement advanced technologies such as artificial intelligence in agricultural production and will serve the long-term viability of agricultural systems based on the application of the principles of circular economy. Producers worldwide need to understand that the shift to smarter farming and investment in technology can bring multiple benefits to themselves and the environment. Definitely, appropriate training is required not only from producers but also from all the stakeholders in the supply chain so that precision applications can be used in a more efficient way. Proper implementation of digital farming will improve plant protection programs in the context of sustainable agriculture as well as the effectiveness of weed/insect/disease control. It will reduce production costs and meet the ever-increasing requirements of environmental legislation. The need to cooperate in the field of agrotechnology is imperative for all of the above since we are called upon to produce more, qualitatively and quantitatively, with less natural resources and inputs.

Sustainability plays a key role for mitigating environmental consequences, preserving at the same time the existing economy and people's welfare. Sustainability in agricultural systems should not be a theoretical index but a practical approach, measuring results of specific actions. Success or failure of a series of actions cannot be evaluated unbiased, if there is no data to compare. Implementation of a proper policy is of great importance so as to ensure sustainability that benefits both humans and the environment. As environmental problems affect the whole planet, international cooperation is needed to cope with them. Lack of information of factors effect technology adoption in developed countries combined with the limitations mentioned above for the advancement of these technologies, can be eliminated through improved and coordinated training of farmers, their inclusion into cooperatives and economic magnitude of enterprises. The International Environmental Legislation Framework set the goals to be achieved in relation with specific environmental problems. Beyond that, it is up to each government to fulfill their commitments by implementing specific policies relevant to these objectives. As previously mentioning, despite sensitivity of society to environmental issues, there is a lack of motives, both from government and market side, which decreases expression rates of environmentally friendly behavior from consumers.

In this context, it is clear that precision agriculture and the so-called "smart agriculture" have been increasingly applied over the years, creating new data in agricultural work and causing constant change in the agricultural sector. The resulting modernized farming models have a variety of benefits for agricultural production, both in creating more simplified field work and in optimizing the production process with the main goal of increasing the efficiency of input use while increasing production and increasing of profit for the farmer. At the same time, there are very important benefits for the natural environment, as the application of new technologies in the primary sector contributes significantly to the viability of the industry as a whole and to sustainable development. However, despite the extremely significant benefits, the degree of adoption of precision agriculture is still extremely limited, at least in the least developed agricultural countries. With the main goal of transforming agriculture into a more productive and long-term sustainable sector, it is necessary to activate all stakeholders and systematize the efforts for education and training of farmers. Particularly beneficial for the promotion of smart agriculture can be the targeting of more specific rural population groups, such as young and highly educated or skilled farmers, who in a collaborative framework can jointly support the modernization of the sector.

Future research following this review could examine the role played by various stakeholders in promoting smart farming practices, such as producers, research institutes, government agencies, educational institutions, private companies and agricultural cooperatives. In addition, future research should further analyze all the factors that shape farmers' attitudes towards new technologies, in order to find a way to apply them on a larger scale, which will strengthen the circular economy through agriculture.

References

Abebaw, D. and M.G. Haile. 2013. The impact of cooperatives on agricultural technology adoption: Empirical evidence from Ethiopia. Food Policy. https://doi.org/10.1016/j.foodpol.2012.10.003.

Ahmed, H., A.S. Juraimi and S.M. Hamdani. 2016. Introduction to robotics agriculture in pest control: A review Pertanika Journal of Scholarly Research Reviews. 2(2), 80-93.

Aleksandrowicz, L., R. Green, E.J.M. Joy, P. Smith and A. Haines. 2016. The impacts of dietary change on greenhouse gas emissions, land use, water use, and health: A systematic review. PLoS ONE. https://doi.org/10.1371/journal.pone.0165797.

Antolini, L.S., R.F. Scare and A. Dias. 2015. Adoption of precision agriculture technologies by farmers: A systematic literature review and proposition of an integrated conceptual framework. IFAMA World Conference Scientific Research Symposium.

AQUASTAT. 2012. Irrigation Water Requirement and Water Withdrawal by Country. 2012.

Aubert, B.A., A. Schroeder and J. Grimaudo. 2012. IT as enabler of sustainable farming: An empirical analysis of farmers' adoption decision of precision agriculture technology. Decision Support Systems 54(1), 510–520.

Balafoutis, A., B. Beck, S. Fountas, J. Vangeyte, T. Wal, T I. Soto and V. Eory. 2017. Precision agriculture technologies positively contributing to GHG emissions mitigation, farm productivity and economics. Sustainability 9(8), 1339.

Balzan, M.V. and A.C. Moonen. 2014. Field margin vegetation enhances biological control and crop damage suppression from multiple pests in organic tomato fields. Entomologia Experimentalis et Applicata 150(1), 45–65. https://doi.org/10.1111/eea.12142.

Bawa, A.S. and K.R. Anilakumar. 2013. Genetically modified foods: Safety, risks and public concerns – A review. Journal of Food Science and Technology. https://doi.org/10.1007/s13197-012-0899-1.

Bernon, M., B. Tjahjono and E.F. Ripanti. 2018. Aligning retail reverse logistics practice with circular economy values: An exploratory framework. Production Planning and Control. https://doi.org/10.1080/09537287.2018.1449266.

Borras, S.M., J.C. Franco, S.R. Isakson, L. Levidow and P. Vervest. 2016. The rise of flex crops and commodities: Implications for research. Journal of Peasant Studies 43(1), 93–115. https://doi.org/10.1080/03066150.2015.1036417.

New Technologies Contribution on the Agrifood Sector　　　　　　　**21**

Brookes, G. and P. Barfoot. 2012. Global impact of biotech crops: Environmental effects, 1996-2010. GM Crops & Food. https://doi.org/10.4161/gmcr.20061.

Buiatti, M., P. Christou and G. Pastore. 2013. The application of GMOs in agriculture and in food production for a better nutrition: two different scientific points of view. Genes and Nutrition. https://doi.org/10.1007/s12263-012-0316-4.

Cerdeira, A.L. and S.O. Duke. 2006. The current status and environmental impacts of glyphosate-resistant crops: A review. Journal of Environmental Quality 35, 1633-1658.

Chappell, M., S.K. Dove, M.W. Iersel, P.A. Thomas and J. Ruter. 2013. Implementation of wireless sensor networks for irrigation control in three container nurseries. HortTechnology 23(6), 747–753.

Chel, A. and G. Kaushik. 2011. Renewable energy for sustainable agriculture. Agronomy for Sustainable Development. https://doi.org/10.1051/agro/2010029.

Cheng, T.C.E. and T.M. Choi. 2010. Innovative Quick Response Programs in Logistics and Supply Chain Management. https://doi.org/10.1007/978-3-642-04313-0.

Colaço, A.F. and R.G.V. Bramley. 2018. Do crop sensors promote improved nitrogen management in grain crops? Field Crops Research. https://doi.org/10.1016/j.fcr.2018.01.007.

Darnhofer, I., D. Gibbon and B. Dedieu. 2012. Farming Systems research into the 21st century: The new dynamic. Farming Systems Research, November 2015, 1–490. https://doi.org/10.1007/978-94-007-4503-2.

Davis, F.D., R.P. Bagozzi and P.R. Warshaw. 1989. User acceptance of computer technology: A comparison of two theoretical models. *Management Science*. https://doi.org/10.1287/mnsc.35.8.982.

Del Corso, J.P., C. Kephaliacos and G. Plumecocq. 2015. Legitimizing farmers' new knowledge, learning and practices through communicative action: Application of an agro-environmental policy. Ecological Economics 117, 86–96. https://doi.org/10.1016/j.ecolecon.2015.05.017

Ellen MacArthur Foundation. 2018. Cities and Circular Economy for Food. Ellen Macarthur Foundation.

FAO. 2017. Water for Sustainable Food and Agriculture Water for Sustainable Food and Agriculture. http://www.fao.org/3/i7959e/i7959e.pdf

Flörke, M., E. Kynast, I. Bärlund, S. Eisner, F. Wimmer and J. Alcamo. 2013. Domestic and industrial water uses of the past 60 years as a mirror of socio-economic development: A global simulation study. Global Environmental Change 23(1), 144–156. https://doi.org/10.1016/j.gloenvcha.2012.10.018.

Flörke, M., C. Schneider and R.I. McDonald. 2018. Water competition between cities and agriculture driven by climate change and urban growth. Nature Sustainability 1(1), 51–58. https://doi.org/10.1038/s41893-017-0006-8.

Gleeson, T. and B. Richter. 2018. How much groundwater can we pump and protect environmental flows through time? Presumptive standards for conjunctive management of aquifers and rivers. River Research and Applications 34(1): 83–92. https://doi.org/10.1002/rra.3185.

Golden, B., S. Raghavan and E. Wasil. 2008. The vehicle routing problem: Latest advances and new challenges. Operations Research/Computer Science Interfaces Series. https://doi.org/10.1007/978-0-387-77778-8.

Grainger, C. and K.A. Beauchemin. 2011. Can enteric methane emissions from ruminants be lowered without lowering their production? Animal Feed Science and Technology 166–167, 308–320. https://doi.org/10.1016/j.anifeedsci.2011.04.021.

Grimal, L. and C. Képhaliacos. 2000. Internalization of external effects versus decrease of externalities: From end of pipe technologies to cleaner technologies. International Journal of Sustainable Development 3(3), 239–256.

Hall, C.A.S., S. Balogh and D.J.R. Murphy. 2009. What is the minimum EROI that a sustainable society must have? Energies 2(1), 25–47. https://doi.org/10.3390/en20100025.

Holloway, L. 2007. Subjecting cows to robots: Farming technologies and the making of animal subjects. Environment and Planning D: Society and Space. https://doi.org/10.1068/d77j.

Holmberg, A. and R. Åquist. 2018. Blockchain technology in supply chain: A case study of the possibilities and challenges with an implementation of a blockchain technology supported framework for traceability. The Journal of International Scientific Researches. https://www.semanticscholar.org/paper/Blockchain-technology-in-food-supply-chains-%3A-A-of-Holmberg-%C3%85quist/9fec814ef3c09683ab5949e8bdf2d79c811dc871#citing-papers

IPCC. 2018. Global Warming of 1.5°C. Summary for Policymakers, 33.

Jawad, H.M., R. Nordin, S.K. Gharghan, A.M. Jawad and M. Ismail. 2017. Energy-efficient wireless sensor networks for precision agriculture: A review. Sensors (Switzerland). https://doi.org/10.3390/s17081781.

Jayashankar, P., S. Nilakanta, W.J. Johnston, P. Gill and R. Burres. 2018. IoT adoption in agriculture: The role of trust, perceived value and risk. Journal of Business and Industrial Marketing. https://doi.org/10.1108/JBIM-01-2018-0023.

Jedermann, R., M. Nicometo, I. Uysal and W. Lang. 2014. Reducing food losses by intelligent food logistics. Philosophical Transactions of the Royal Society A: Mathematical, Physical and Engineering Sciences. https://doi.org/10.1098/rsta.2013.0302.

Joshi, Y. and Z. Rahman. 2015. Factors affecting green purchase behaviour and future research directions. International Strategic Management Review. https://doi.org/10.1016/j.ism.2015.04.001.

Kernecker, M., A. Knierim, A. Wurbs, T. Kraus and F. Borges. 2020. Experience versus expectation: Farmers' perceptions of smart farming technologies for cropping systems across Europe. Precision Agriculture. https://doi.org/10.1007/s11119-019-09651-z.

Kumar, A. 2015. Green logistics for sustainable development: An analytical review. IOSRD International Journal of Business 1(1), 07-13.

Lang, W., R. Jedermann, D. Mrugala, A. Jabbari, B. Krieg-Brückner and K. Schill. 2011. The 'Intelligent Container' – A cognitive sensor network for transport management. IEEE Sensors Journal. https://doi.org/10.1109/JSEN.2010.2060480.

Läpple, D., A. Renwick and F. Thorne. 2015. Measuring and understanding the drivers of agricultural innovation: Evidence from Ireland. Food Policy. https://doi.org/10.1016/j.foodpol.2014.11.003.

Lea-Cox, J.D. 2012. Using wireless sensor networks for precision irrigation scheduling, problems, perspectives and challenges of agricultural water management. *In*: Genetic Engineering – Basics, New Applications and Responsibilities, 2: 64. InTech. https://doi.org/10.5772/32009.

Lenteren, J.C. van, K. Bolckmans, J. Köhl, W.J. Ravensberg and A. Urbaneja. 2018. Biological control using invertebrates and microorganisms: Plenty of new opportunities. BioControl 63(1), 39–59. https://doi.org/10.1007/s10526-017-9801-4.

Li, X. 2014. Operations management of logistics and supply chain: Issues and directions. Discrete Dynamics in Nature and Society. https://doi.org/10.1155/2014/701938.

Li, Z., G. Liu, L. Liu, X. Lai and G. Xu. 2017. IoT-based tracking and tracing platform for prepackaged food supply chain. Industrial Management and Data Systems. https://doi.org/10.1108/IMDS-11-2016-0489.

Liaghat, S. and S.K. Balasundram. 2010. A review: The role of remote sensing in precision agriculture. Department of Agriculture Technology, Faculty of Agriculture. American Journal of Agricultural and Biological Sciences 5(1), 50-55.

Lloret, J., I. Bosch, S. Sendra and A. Serrano. 2011. A wireless sensor network for vineyard monitoring that uses image processing. Sensors. https://doi.org/10.3390/s110606165.

Long, T.B., V. Blok and I. Coninx. 2016. Barriers to the adoption and diffusion of technological innovations for climate-smart agriculture in Europe: Evidence from the Netherlands, France, Switzerland and Italy. Journal of Cleaner Production. https://doi.org/10.1016/j.jclepro.2015.06.044.

Łozowicka, A. 2020. Evaluation of the efficiency of sustainable development policy implementation in selected EU member states using DEA: The ecological dimension. *Sustainability*. https://doi.org/10.3390/su12010435.

Lu, B.R. and C. Yang. 2009. Gene flow from genetically modified rice to its wild relatives: Assessing potential ecological consequences. Biotechnology Advances. https://doi.org/10.1016/j.biotechadv.2009.05.018.

Lu, S., J. Wang and L. Pei. 2016. Study on the effects of irrigation with reclaimed water on the content and distribution of heavy metals in soil. International Journal of Environmental Research and Public Health 13(3). https://doi.org/10.3390/ijerph13030298.

Maghari, B.M. and A.M. Ardekani. 2011. Genetically modified foods and social concerns. Avicenna Journal of Medical Biotechnology Jul-Sep, 3(3), 109–117.

Mahlein, A.K. 2016. Plant disease detection by imaging sensors – Parallels and specific demands for precision agriculture and plant phenotyping. Plant Disease. https://doi.org/10.1094/PDIS-03-15-0340-FE.

Maksimov, M.M., V.O. Davydov, G.V. Krusir and O.B. Maksimova. 2017. Increasing of process energy efficiency of biogas plants production processing. Odes'kyi Politechnichnyi Universytet Pratsi 2429(3(53)), 43–53. https://doi.org/10.15276/opu.3.53.2017.06.

Mao, D., Z. Hao, F. Wang and H. Li. 2018. Innovative blockchain-based approach for sustainable and credible environment in food trade: A case study in

Shandong Province, China. Sustainability (Switzerland). https://doi.org/10.3390/su10093149.

Mariani, J. and J. Kaji. From dirt to data: The second green revolution and IoT. Deloitte Insights. Available online: https://www2.deloitte.com/insights/us/en/deloitte-review/issue-18/second-greenrevolution-and-internet-of-things.html#endnote-sup-9 (accessed on 27 July 2020)

Mastrorilli, M. and R. Zucaro. 2016. Towards sustainable use of water in rainfed and irrigated cropping systems: Review of some technical and policy issues. AIMS Agriculture and Food 1(3), 294–314. https://doi.org/10.3934/agrfood.2016.3.294.

Mor, R.S., S. Singh, A. Bhardwaj and L.P. Singh. 2015. Technological implications of supply chain practices in agri-food sector – A review. International Journal of Supply and Operations Management Int J Supply Oper Manage. 2(2), 720-747.

Murphy, R., J. Woods, M. Black and M. McManus. 2011. Global developments in the competition for land from biofuels. Food Policy 36(Suppl. 1), S52–S61. https://doi.org/10.1016/j.foodpol.2010.11.014.

Myklevy, M., P. Doherty and J. Makower. 2016. The New Grand Strategy. St. Martin's Press: New York, NY, USA, p. 271.

Naegeli, H., J.L. Bresson, T. Dalmay, I.C. Dewhurst, M. Epstein, L.G. Firbank, P. Guerche, J. Hejatko, F.J. Moreno, E. Mullins, F. Nogue, N. Rostoks, J.J.S. Serrano, G. Savoini, E. Veromann, F. Veronesi, F. Alvarez, A.F. Dumont, N. Papadopoulou, M. Ardizzone,Y. Devos, A. Gennaro, J.A. Ruiz Gomez, A. Lanzoni, F.M. Neri, K. Paraskevopoulos, T. Raffaello and G. De Sanctis. 2019. Assessment of genetically modified soybean MON 87708 × MON 89788 × A5547-127, for food and feed uses, under regulation (EC) No 1829/2003 (Application EFSA-GMO-NL-2016-135). EFSA Journal. https://doi.org/10.2903/j.efsa.2019.5733.

Nelson, S.O., S. Trabelsi and M.A. Lewis. 2016. Microwave sensing of moisture content and bulk density in flowing grain and seed. Transactions of the ASABE. https://doi.org/10.13031/trans.59.11377.

OECD. 2019. Bio-economy and the sustainability of the agriculture and food system: Opportunities and policy challenges. OECD Food, Agriculture and Fisheries Papers, No. 136, no. 2018: 104. https://doi.org/https://doi.org/10.1787/d0ad045d-en.

Oliver, M.J. 2014. Why we need GMO crops in agriculture. Missouri Medicine Nov-Dec, 111(6), 492–507.

Panigrahi, S.K., F.W. Kar, T.A. Fen, L.K. Hoe and M. Wong. 2018. A strategic initiative for successful reverse logistics management in retail industry. Global Business Review. https://doi.org/10.1177/0972150918758096.

Ramin, S., Redmond, C. Weltzien, I.A. Hameed, I.J. Yule, T.E. Grift, S.K. Balasundram, L. Pitonakova, D. Ahmad and G. Chowdhary. 2018. Research and development in agricultural robotics: A perspective of digital farming. International Journal of Agricultural and Biological Engineering 11(4), 1–11. https://doi.org/10.25165/j.ijabe.20181104.4278.

Reddy, N.V., A.V.V.V. Reddy, S. Pranavadithya and J. Jagadesh Kumar. 2016. A critical review on agricultural robots. International Journal of Mechanical Engineering and Technology 7(4), 183-188.

New Technologies Contribution on the Agrifood Sector

Ringsberg, H. 2014. Perspectives on food traceability: A systematic literature review. Supply Chain Management. https://doi.org/10.1108/SCM-01-2014-0026.

Roberts, R.K., J.A. Larson, B.C. English and J.C. Torbett. 2013. Farmer perceptions of precision agriculture for fertilizer management of cotton. *In*: Precision Agriculture for Sustainability and Environmental Protection. https://doi.org/10.4324/9780203128329.

Rosillo-Calle, F. 2012. Food versus fuel: Toward a new paradigm—The need for a holistic approach. ISRN Renewable Energy 2012, 1–15. https://doi.org/10.5402/2012/954180.

Salah, K., N. Nizamuddin, R. Jayaraman and M. Omar. 2019. Blockchain-based soybean traceability in agricultural supply chain. IEEE Access. https://doi.org/10.1109/ACCESS.2019.2918000.

Schader, C., J. Grenz, M.S. Meier and M. Stolze. 2014. Scope and precision of sustainability assessment approaches to food systems. Ecology and Society 19 (3). https://doi.org/10.5751/ES-06866-190342.

Seifi, M.R., R. Alimardani and A. Sharifi. 2010. How can soil electrical conductivity measurements control soil pollution? Research Journal of Environmental and Earth Sciences 2(4), 235-238.

Silva, C.B., M.A.F.D. de Moraes and J.P. Molin. 2011. Adoption and use of precision agriculture technologies in the sugarcane industry of São Paulo state, Brazil. Precision Agriculture 12(1), 67–81.

Singh, R.K., H.R. Murty, S.K. Gupta and A.K. Dikshit. 2012. An overview of sustainability assessment methodologies. Ecological Indicators 15(1), 281–299. https://doi.org/10.1016/j.ecolind.2011.01.007.

Skowroñska, M. and T. Filipek. 2014. Life cycle assessment of fertilizers: A review. International Agrophysics 28(1), 101–110. https://doi.org/10.2478/intag-2013-0032.

Sui, R., J.A. Thomasson and S.D. Filip. 2010. Cotton-harvester-flow simulator for testing cotton yield monitors. International Journal of Agricultural and Biological Engineering. https://doi.org/10.3965/j.issn.1934-6344.2010.01.044-049.

Swaminathan, M.S. and R.V. Bhavani. 2013. Food production and availability – Essential prerequisites for sustainable food security. Indian Journal of Medical Research. https://doi.org/10.1142/9789813200074_0025.

Swinton, S.M. and J. Lowenberg-Deboer. 2001. Global adoption of precision agriculture technologies, who, when and why. pp. 557–562. *In*: G. Grenier and S. Blackmore (Eds.), European Conference on Precision Agriculture. Montpellier, France.

Tabas, J., M. Beranová and J. Vavřina. 2011. Barriers to development of the innovation potential in the small and medium-sized enterprises. Acta Universitatis Agriculturae et Silviculturae Mendelianae Brunensis. https://doi.org/10.11118/actaun201159070447.

Talebpour, B., U. Türker and U. Yegül. 2015. The role of precision agriculture in the promotion of food security. International Journal of Agricultural and Food Research, 4(1), 1–23.

The State of the World's Land and Water Resources for Food and Agriculture: Managing Systems at Risk. 2013. https://doi.org/10.4324/9780203142837.

Thompson, P. 2012. The agricultural ethics of biofuels: The food vs. fuel debate. Agriculture 2(4), 339–358. https://doi.org/10.3390/agriculture2040339.

Timilsina, G. 2012. Ask the experts: The food versus fuel debate. Biofuels 3(6), 635–648. https://doi.org/10.4155/bfs.12.59.

Toop, T.A., S. Ward, T. Oldfield, M. Hull, M.E. Kirby and M.K. Theodorou. 2017. AgroCycle – Developing a circular economy in agriculture. Energy Procedia. https://doi.org/10.1016/j.egypro.2017.07.269.

Tripoli, M. and J. Schmidhuber. 2018. Emerging opportunities for the application of blockchain in the agri-food industry agriculture. Food and Agriculture Organization of the United Nations, no. August. https://www.researchgate. net/profile/Josef_Schmidhuber/publication/327287235_Emerging_ Opportunities_for_the_Application_of_Blockchain_in_the_Agri-food_ Industry/links/5b86ced4299bf1d5a7310c38/Emerging-Opportunities-for-the-Application-of-Blockchain-in-the-.

Urbahs, A. and I. Jonaite. 2013. Features of the use of unmanned aerial vehicles for agriculture applications. Aviation. https://doi.org/10.3846/16487788.20 13.861224.

van Lenteren, J.C., K. Bolckmans, J. Köhl, W.J. Ravensberg and A. Urbaneja. 2018. Biological control using invertebrates and microorganisms: plenty of new opportunities. BioControl 63, 39–59. https://doi.org/10.1007/s10526-017-9801-4

Velasco-Muñoz, J.F., J.A. Aznar-Sánchez, L.J. Belmonte-Ureña and M.J. López-Serrano. 2018. Advances in water use efficiency in agriculture: A bibliometric analysis. Water 10(4), 377. https://doi.org/10.3390/w10040377.

Vymazal, J. and T. Březinová. 2015. The use of constructed wetlands for removal of pesticides from agricultural runoff and drainage: A review. Environment International 75, 11–20. https://doi.org/10.1016/j.envint.2014.10.026.

Wada, Y., D. Wisser, S. Eisner, M. Flörke, D. Gerten, I. Haddeland, N. Hanasaki, Y. Masaki, F.T. Portmann, T. Stacke, Z. Tessler and J. Schewe. 2013. Multimodel projections and uncertainties of irrigation water demand under climate change. Geophysical Research Letters 40(17), 4626–4632. https://doi. org/10.1002/grl.50686.

Waltz E. 2011. GM crops: Battlefield. Nature, 2011. https://doi. org/10.4135/9781446201091.n17.

Wandera, S.M., W. Qiao, D.E. Algapani, S. Bi, D. Yin, X. Qi, Y. Liu, J. Dach and R. Dong. 2018. Searching for possibilities to improve the performance of full scale agricultural biogas plants. Renewable Energy 116, 720–727. https://doi. org/10.1016/j.renene.2017.09.087.

War, A.R., M.G. Paulraj, T. Ahmad, A.A. Buhroo, B. Hussain, S. Ignacimuthu and H.C. Sharma. 2012. Mechanisms of plant defense against insect herbivores. Plant Signaling and Behavior. https://doi.org/10.4161/psb.21663.

Wezel, A., M. Casagrande, F. Celette, J.F. Vian, A. Ferrer and J. Peigné. 2014. Agroecological practices for sustainable agriculture: A review. Agronomy for Sustainable Development 34(1), 1–20. https://doi.org/10.1007/s13593-013-0180-7.

Wieczorek, A.M. and M.G. Wright. 2012. History of agricultural biotechnology: How crop development has evolved. Nature Education Knowledge 3(10), 9.

World Bank. 2017. Annual freshwater withdrawals, agriculture. https://data.worldbank.org/indicator/er.h2o.fwag.zs

Yan, B., Y. Chen and X. Meng. 2008. RFID technology applied in warehouse management system. *In*: Proceedings – ISECS International Colloquium on Computing, Communication, Control, and Management, CCCM 2008. https://doi.org/10.1109/CCCM.2008.372.

Zerbini, F.M., F.N. da Silva, G.P.C. Urquiza and M.F. Basso. 2014. Transgenic plants. *In*: Biotechnology and Plant Breeding: Applications and Approaches for Developing Improved Cultivars. https://doi.org/10.1016/B978-0-12-418672-9.00008-8.

Zhang, F. 2013. Solutions for Sustainable Agriculture and Food Systems Thematic Group 7 of the SDSN (Sustainable Agriculture and Food Systems) Comprises, no. September 2013.

CHAPTER

2

Dimensionality Reduction Techniques for High-dimensional Data in Precision Agriculture

Mostafa Reisi-Gahrooei[1]*, James A. Whitehurst[1], Yiannis Ampatzidis[2]* and Panos Pardalos[1]

[1] Department of Industrial and Systems Engineering, University of Florida
[2] Department of Agricultural and Biological Engineering, University of Florida

High Dimensional Data

High-dimensionality of data refers to a situation in which each data point lies in a high-dimensional space. A high-dimensional space is the one with a large number of coordinates (e.g., >100). When dealing with high-dimensional data, machine learning algorithms may fail due to two major challenges. First, high-dimensional datasets usually exhibit high correlations among variables, which can cause severe model overfitting and high out-sample generalization errors if not adequately treated. Second, in many cases the number of available samples are small and are not enough to perform sensible learning without particular consideration. The second problem is known as the small N, large p problem, where N refers to the sample size and p refers to the number of variables. These aforementioned problems are tightly related. The first problem if treated appropriately is the blessing of dimensionality and provides a solution to both challenges. That is, the correlation among variables in a high-dimensional dataset can be exploited to significantly reduce the dimension of data to a level that it is smaller than the sample size. At the same time, it alleviates the overfitting problem as a smaller number

---

*Corresponding authors: mreisigahrooei@ufl.edu and i.ampatzidis@ufl.edu

of model parameters is needed to be learned. Algorithms and techniques that are mapping high-dimensional data to a smaller space are called dimensionality reduction algorithms. These algorithms have massive applications in different areas, including manufacturing, healthcare, and agriculture.

Types of Dimensionality Reduction Algorithms

Unsupervised Dimensionality Reduction

Unsupervised dimensionality reduction algorithms are those that are not exploiting available labels or values associated to the data points. Two major unsupervised dimensionality reduction algorithms are principal component analysis and autoencoders.

Principal component analysis (PCA)

Principal Component Analysis (PCA) is the basis of many machine learning methods and has a wide range of applications in various fields of studies, including biology, image processing, material science, and agriculture (Kallithraka et al. 2001, Novembre and Stephens 2008, Rajan 2005, Sinelli, Limbo, Torri, Di Egidio, and Casiraghi 2010; Vasilescu and Terzopoulos 2002, Wagner and Castner 2001, Yeung and Ruzzo 2001). PCA generates a low-dimensional descriptor of high-dimensional data such that the minimum amount data variation is lost. That is, when performing PCA, important information (measured by data variation) is extracted and represented by a new small set of uncorrelated variables called principal component scores or PC scores. The PC scores are linear projections of the original data points on vectors called principal components (PCs). The PCs are directions in the data space along which the dataset has maximum variability. In other words, the first principal component is the direction with the maximum data variability, the second PC is the direction with the second largest data variability, and so on. Figure 1 illustrates the principal components of a two-dimensional dataset. The projections of data points on each PC give the corresponding PC score. The PCs are usually obtained by minimizing the reconstruction error, meaning the deviation of the original data from the one reconstructed from the reduced dimension data points. The key advantage of PCA is that the transpose of the mapping that performs dimensionality reduction reconstructs the data. PCA is considered an unsupervised dimensionality reduction because it does not take advantage of any labels or output values that might be available. This may reduce the power of PCA when it is being used as an input to other machine learning algorithms such as regression or classification methods.

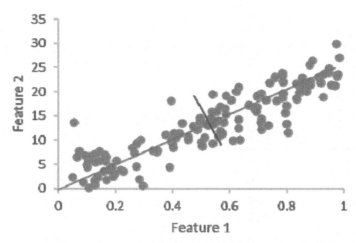

Figure 1: Feature 1 and Feature 2 for 150 observations. The lines represent the first and second principal components

Auto-encoders

Auto-encoders belong to the class of neural network algorithms. These algorithms find a small set of features that can reconstruct the original data with minimum error. Auto-encoders can be transformed to PCA if linear activation functions are used and right constraints are imposed on the model weights. In general, and unlike PCA, the weights in an Auto-encoder are not orthogonal and the encoding and decoding weights are different from each other. That is, the same set of weights that maps the data into a smaller space is not the same as the ones that reconstruct the data. An auto-encoder performs the following operations:

$$C = f(X)$$

$$Z = g(C)$$

Where Z is the decoded version of original data X and C is a vector of features after dimensionality reduction. Figure 2 illustrates an example of an Auto-encoder. One limitation of Auto-encoder is that it does not quantify how much information each feature may carry. Another lamentation is that it may require a large amount of data. Nevertheless, with novel data augmentation techniques this issue can be resolved.

Supervised Dimensionality Reduction

Supervised approaches are those that take the data label or other information into consideration when performing dimensionality reduction. That is, they aim to preserve the input-output relationship while reducing the

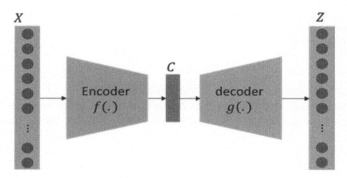

Figure 2: Illustration of encoder-decoder functions

input dimensionality. Examples of supervised dimensionality reduction algorithms are canonical correlation analysis (CCA) and partial least square (PLS) analysis and supervised autoencoder.

Canonical Correlation Analysis

Canonical correlation analysis is a linear subspace learning method that finds linear transformations of the input and output vectors in a way that the transformed variables have maximum correlation. Let $X = (X_1; X_2; ...; X_n)$ be an input vector of size n and $Y = (Y_1; Y_2; ...; Y_m)$ be an output vector of size m. The CCA searches for transformation vectors $a = (a_1; a_2; ...; a_n)$ and $b = (b_1; b_2; ...; b_m)$ such that the correlation between random variables $U_1 = a^T X$ and $V_1 = b^T Y$ is maximized. U_1 and V_1 are called first canonical variables. This process can be continued for $k = \min\{n, m\}$. That is, CCA results in at most independent canonical variables for inputs and outputs. One can take $p_x \leq k \leq n$ of canonical variables say $U = (U_1, U_2, ..., U_{px})$ as the transformed vector of inputs and take $p_y \leq k \leq n$ of canonical variables say $V = (V_1, V_2, ..., V_{py})$.

Partial Least Square Analysis

Similar to CCA, partial least square analysis performs dimensionality reduction by taking the relationship between the inputs and the outputs into consideration. Unlike the PCA that finds a projection of the data that maximizes the variability without considering the output values, PLS finds a projection of the input space that aims to maximize a combined measure of within input variability and between input and output correlation. PLS is suitable for situations when the sample size is small but number of variables is large, and variables are highly correlated.

Supervised Autoencoder

Supervised Autoencoders aim to simultaneously reconstruct the inputs and estimate the outputs. Let X be the vector of inputs and Y be the vector of outputs. Then the supervised autoencoder estimates mappings f, g, and h such that

$$C = f(X); Zg(C); \text{ and } Y \approx h(C)$$

where Z is the decoded version of original data X and C is a vector of features after dimensionality reduction. This goal is achieved by minimizing a combined objective function that includes two components:

$$J = |G(C) - X| + I \lambda |Y - h(C)|,$$

where, l is a tuning parameter, and $|.|$ is a norm of a vector. Figure 3 depicts an example of a supervised autoencoder.

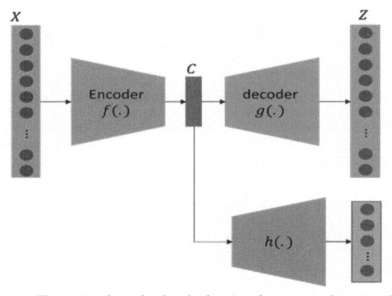

Figure 3: Illustration of encoder-decoder functions for supervised autoencoder

Yield Prediction Studies Using Dimensionality Reduction

Literature Review

One of the major application of data mining in agriculture (Mucherino, Papajorgji, and Pardalos 2009, Mucherino, Papajorgji, and Pardalos, Data mining in agriculture 2009) is yield prediction, which is valuable for many crop management practices. Improved accuracy enables informed nutrient adjustment, market planning, harvest preparation, high-throughput

Dimensionality Reduction Techniques for High-dimensional Data... **33**

plant phenotyping, and precision agriculture (Raun et al. 2001, Hansen, Jorgensen, and Thomsen 2002, Maimaitijiang et al. 2020, Ampatzidis, Vougioukas, Whiting, and Zhang 2014). Many methods for data collection and algorithms have been proposed to predict yield. Popular prediction methods include reflectance measurements to determine vegetation indices, such as the normalized difference vegetation index (NDVI) (Raun et al. 2001, Hansen, Jorgensen, and Thomsen 2002, Chen et al. 2019). NDVI methods that are satellite driven can however be inconsistent for yield prediction (Aghighi, Azadbakht, Ashourloo, Shahrabi, and Radiom, 2018). In addition to canopy reflectance, hyperspectral cameras can provide more complex information about crops (Aguate et al. 2017, Águila, Efremenko and Trautmann 2019). With the use of canopy reflectance and hyperspectral image data, dimensionality reduction methods, like those mentioned in this chapter, have proven to be valuable in agriculture study and prediction (Gilbertson and van Niekerk 2017, Aguate et al. 2017, Raun et al. 2001, Hansen, Jorgensen and Thomsen 2002, Maimaitijiang et al. 2020, Tan et al. 2020, Guo et al. 2020).

Compared to popular methods of using vegetation indices, the use of dimensionality reduction with high dimension data such as spectral image data generally provides more information and enables better prediction (Aguate et al. 2017, Maimaitijiang et al. 2020, Tan et al. 2020). The caveat and potential downside to dimension reduction methods is the possibility of lost information as big data is transformed into significantly fewer components (Aguate et al. 2017). Despite this potential downside, Partial Least Squares (PLS) is frequently cited as a valuable method for dimensionality reduction because of its supervised nature (Tan et al. 2020, Aguate et al. 2017, Hansen, Jorgensen, and Thomsen 2002, Maimaitijiang et al. 2020). In many cases, methods such as PLS or auto-encoders outperform the use of unsupervised principal components as feature inputs (Tan et al. 2020, Guo et al. 2020).

Case Study

To demonstrate the effectiveness of dimensionality reduction methods, presented in this section is a case study of winter wheat yield prediction using spectral imaging data captured by a hexacopter unmanned aerial vehicle (UAV) (Matrice 600 Pro, DJI, Shenzehen, China) equipped with a hyperspectral sensing system, Pika L 2.4 (Resonon, Bozeman, MT). The hyperspectral sensing system covers a 400–1000 nm range divided in 150 bands. For spectral data collection, a front overlap of 85% and side overlap of 70% were used. Data were collected at an altitude of 60.96 m (200 ft) above the ground. A white calibration tarp was placed in the region of data collection to be used to calibrate the hyperspectral data collected.

The dataset analyzed contained 143 plots with various attributes including yield, genotype, and spectral data. Yield, grain number per meter squared and cellular membrane thermostability (to predict heat tolerance) were collected and studied as responses variables.

Data

For each plot, there are 150 frequencies of spectral image data captured. This data is highly correlated and larger in dimension than the number of observations. Four rounds of UAV flights collected four sets of data using the hyperspectral camera. The average curves for these flights are shown in Fig. 4. With this in mind, it is necessary to use dimensionality reduction as linear regression with 150 highly correlated predictors, performed very poorly.

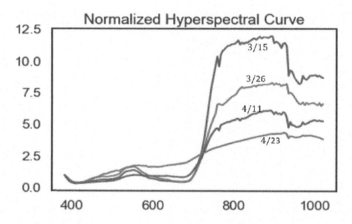

Figure 4: Normalized Average Reflectance Curve by Flight

Methodology

Model performance was measured using a standardized mean square error (SMSE) to compare between response variables and mean absolute percentage error (MAPE).

$$\text{SMSE} = \frac{\Sigma(y-\hat{y})^2}{n\Sigma y^2} = \frac{MSE}{\Sigma y^2}$$

$$\text{MAPE} = \frac{1}{n}\Sigma\left|\frac{y-\hat{y}}{y}\right|$$

5-fold cross validation was used for 30 iterations to randomly split the data into test and train groups and measure average error in terms

Dimensionality Reduction Techniques for High-dimensional Data... **35**

of both performance metrics. Table 1 shows the list of all models tested compared to the control group, a linear regression model using NDVI as the predictor.

Brief Descriptions of Models

Linear Regression

We use each observed frequency of a spectral curve to predict yield using linear regression. Results for this model are not shown because it performed very poorly compared to the models listed.

Linear Regression: NDVI: We use the calculated NDVI values as the predictor to predict yield using linear regression.

Clusters: Data points were clustered together based on genotype into 9 clusters and these clusters were used as dummy variables to predict yield using linear regression.

Table 1. List of models tested

Algorithm	Model Description	Inputs
Linear Regression	Linear - NDVI (Control)	NDVI
Linear Regression	Clusters	$Cluster_i$ " i ' (1,9)
Ridge Regression	Ridge	$Frequency_i$ " i ' (1,150)
Linear Regression	PCA - Linear	PCA_1, PCA_2
Linear Regression	PCA - Interaction	PCA_1, PCA_2, PCA_1*PCA_2
Linear Regression	PCA - 2nd Order Polynomial	PCA_1, PCA_2, PCA_1^2, PCA_2^2
Linear Regression	PCA - 2nd Order Polynomial & Interaction	PCA_1, PCA_2, PCA_1*PCA_2, PCA_1^2, PCA_2^2
Linear Regression	PCA - 3rd Order Polynomial	PCA_1, PCA_2, PCA_1^3, PCA_2^3
Linear Regression	PCA - 3rd Order Polynomial & Interaction	PCA_1, PCA_2, PCA_1*PCA_2, PCA_1^3, PCA_2^3
Linear Regression	PCA - 2nd Order Polynomial & Clusters	PCA_1, PCA_2, PCA_1^2, PCA_2^2, $Cluster_i$ " i ' (1,9)
Partial Least Squares	PLS - 1 Component	$Frequency_i$ " i ' (1,150)
Partial Least Squares	PLS - 2 Components	$Frequency_i$ " i ' (1,150)
Trees Regression	Trees - PCA	PCA_1, PCA_2
Trees Regression	Trees - Hyperspectral	$Frequency_i$ " i ' (1,150)
Canonical Correlation Analysis	CCA	$Frequency_i$ " i ' (1,150)

Ridge Regression

Similar to Linear Regression, we use each observed frequency of the spectral curve to predict yield but the model parameters are penalized to account for correlation between frequencies.

PCA (Principal Components Analysis)

We take the first two PCA scores as the inputs into a linear regression model. Multiple models are listed in the table that also add polynomial and interaction terms of the PCA scores to account for nonlinearity.

Partial Least Squares Regression

We use each observed frequency of a spectral curve to predict yield using partial least squares regression. The model reduces these frequencies into reduced features that are used to predict yield. The models were optimally tuned to predict yield using one or two features.

Trees Regression

Decision trees are used both with PCA scores as inputs and the full range of hyperspectral data. In both cases, the models were tuned to have an optimal maximum depth of 1 in order to reduce overfitting.

Canonical Correlation Analysis

We use each observed frequency of a spectral curve to train the model using canonical correlation analysis. The CCA scores are then used to fit the model and predict wheat yield.

Results

In general, dimension reduction methods outperformed other methods such as clustering, ridge regression and trees regression using the spectral image data as an input. This can be seen in the Fig. 5 for wheat yield prediction with distribution of the 30 averages for each model. Models are indexed identically for both charts and ordered by MAPE values. It is evident that models using principal components analysis outperformed non dimensionality reduction methods.

Very similar results are seen when looking at how these models predict cellular membrane thermostability (CMT) in Fig. 6. We see dimensionality reduction methods outperform the other models in terms of accuracy and precision.

Dimensionality Reduction Techniques for High-dimensional Data...

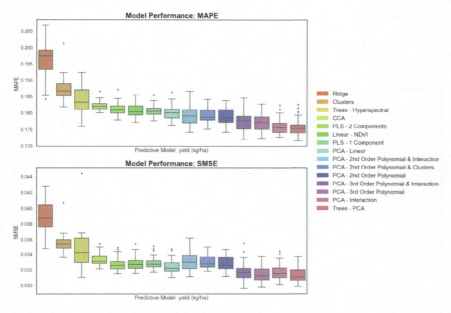

Figure 5: Boxplots of a) MAPE and b) SMSE for yield by model given 30 random sets for 5-fold cross validation

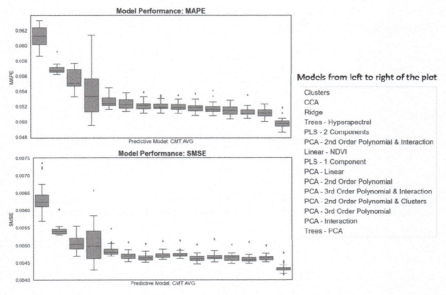

Figure 6: Boxplots of a) MAPE and b) SMSE for CMT by model given 30 random sets for 5-fold cross validation

Conclusion

With advancement in sensing technology, HD data (e.g., images) can vastly be collected and used for crop yield prediction and health management. Nevertheless, extracting useful information from these highly complex datasets is challenging and requires advanced machine learning and statistical learning techniques. Dimensionality reduction approaches are proven to be extremely useful when dealing with HD data. In this chapter, examples of both unsupervised (i.e., PCA and autoencoders) and supervised (i.e., CCA, PLS, and supervised autoencoders) dimension reduction approaches are provided. The applicability of these dimensionality reduction techniques has been shown in a case study of estimating crop yield based on spectral data. This case study demonstrated the power of dimensionality reduction to outperform other models such as ridge regression, clustering, or trees regression prior to any dimensionality reduction. Although, there is risk of lost information (if not tuned properly), in this example this loss was minimal as methods such as PCA outperformed other methods. The provided case study, in conjunction with existing literature cited in this chapter, demonstrates significant value in using dimensionality reduction methods for yield prediction.

References

Aghighi, H., M. Azadbakht, D. Ashourloo, H.S. Shahrabi and S. Radiom. 2018. Machine learning regression techniques for silage maize yield prediction using time-series images of Landsat 8 OLI. IEEE Journal of Selected Topics in Applied Earth Observations and Remote Sensing 11(12), 1–15.

Aguate, F.M., S.P. Trachsel, J. Burgueño, J. Crossa, M. Balzarini, D. Gouache and G. de los Campos. 2017. Use of hyperspectral image data outperformans vegetation indices in prediction of maize yield. Crop Science 57(5), 2517–2524.

Águila, A., D.S. Efremenko and T. Trautmann. 2019. A review of dimensionality reduction techniques for processing hyper-spectral optical signal. Light & Engineering 27(3), 85–98.

Ampatzidis, Y.G., S.G. Vougioukas, M.D. Whiting and Q. Zhang. 2014. Applying the machine repair model to improve efficiency of harvesting fruit. Biosystems Engineering 120, 25–33.

Chen, Z., Y. Miao, J. Lu, L. Zhou, Y. Li, H. Zhang and C. Liu. 2019. In-season diagnosis of winter wheat nitrogen status in smallholder farmer fields across a village using unmanned aerial vehicle-based remote sensing. Agronomy 9(10), 619.

Gilbertson, J.K. and A. van Niekerk. 2017. Value of dimensionality reduction for crop differentiation with multi-temporal imagery and machine learning. Computers & Electronics in Agriculture 142, 50–58.

Guo, J., H. Li, J. Ning, W. Han, W. Zhang and Z.-S. Zhou. 2020. Feature dimension reduction using stacked sparse auto-encoders for crop classification with multi-temporal, quad-pol SAR data. Remote Sensing 12(2), 321.

Hansen, P.M., J. Jorgensen and A. Thomsen. 2002. Predicting grain yield and protein content in winter wheat and spring barley using repeated canopy reflectance measurements and partial least squares regression. Journal of Agricultural Science 139(3), 307–318.

Kallithraka, S., I. Arvanitoyannis, P. Kefalas, A. El-Zajouli, E. Soufleros and E. Psarra. 2001. Instrumental and sensory analysis of Greek wines: Implementation of principal component analysis (PCA) for classification according to geographical origin. Food Chemistry 73(4), 501–514.

Maimaitijiang, M., V. Sagan, P. Sidike, S. Hartling, F. Eposito and F.B. Fritschi. 2020. Soybean yield prediction from UAV using multimodal data fusion and deep learning. Remote Sensing of Environment, 237, 111599.

Mucherino, A., P. Papajorgji and P.M. Pardalos. 2009. A survey of data mining techniques applied to agriculture. Operational Research, 9(2), 121–140.

Mucherino, A., P. Papajorgji and P.M. Pardalos. 2009b. Data Mining in Agriculture. New York: Springer-Verlag New York.

Novembre, J. and M. Stephens. 2008. Interpreting principal component analyses of spatial population genetic variation. Nature Genetics 40(5), 646–649.

Rajan, K. (2005). Materials informatics. Materials Today 8(10), 38–45.

Raun, W.R., J.B. Solie, G.V. Johnson, M.L. Stone, E.L. Lukina, W.E. Thomason and J.S. Schepers. 2001. In-season prediction of potential grain yield in winter wheat using canopy reflectance. Agronomy Journal 93(1), 131–138.

Sinelli, N., S. Limbo, L. Torri, V. Di Egidio and E. Casiraghi. 2010. Evaluation of freshness decay of minced beef stored in high-oxygen modified atmosphere packaged at different temperatures using NIR and MIR spectroscopy. Meat Science 86(3), 748–752.

Tan, C., X. Zhou, P. Zhang, Z. Wang, D. Wang, W. Guo and F. Yun. 2020. Predicting grain protein content of field-grown winter wheat with satellite images and partial least square algorithm. PLoS ONE, 15(3), e0228500

Vasilescu, M.A. and D. Terzopoulos. 2002. Multilinear analysis of image ensembles: TensorFaces. pp. 447–460. European Conference on Computer Vision. Copenhagen, Denmark.

Wagner, M. and D.G. Castner. 2001. Characterization of absorbed protein films by time-of-flight seocndary ion mass spectrometry with principal component analysis. Langmuir 17(15), 4649–4660.

Yeung, K.Y. and W.L. Ruzzo. 2001. Principal component analysis for clustering gene expression data. Bioinformatics 17(9), 763–774.

CHAPTER

3

Modelling Land Use and Land Cover Changes in the Mediterranean Agricultural Ecosystems

Javier Martínez-Vega[1], Samir Mili[1]* and Marta Gallardo[2]

[1] Institute of Economics, Geography and Demography, Spanish National Research Council, Albasanz 26-28, 28037 Madrid, Spain

[2] Department of Geography, National Distance Education University, Paseo de la Senda del Rey 7, 28040 Madrid, Spain

Introduction

Land[1] use changes are among major drivers of global environmental change (Verburg et al. 2015) and the second largest contributor to atmospheric carbon dioxide after fossil fuel combustion (Fuchs et al. 2013). Environmental effects of land use such as greenhouse gas emissions, water use and pollution, biodiversity loss and soil erosion, are substantial from local to global scales (Kuemmerle et al. 2016).

In the European Union (EU) where croplands occupy 21.5% of the total land surface (Eurostat 2017), many land transitions have taken place due to changes in farming and management systems affecting land use patterns (e.g. fallow land, abandoned, reactivated and reforested land)

---

[1] Land is defined in this chapter as the terrestrial portion that accommodates the natural resources (soil, near-surface air, vegetation and other biota, and water), the ecological processes, topography, and human settlements and infrastructure that operate within that system (IPCC 2019).

---

*Corresponding author: samir.mili@cchs.csic.es

Modelling Land Use and Land Cover Changes in the Mediterranean... **41**

(Fuchs et al. 2013). Major land use change trajectories in Europe also have been associated to the globalization of agricultural markets and the transition from rural to urban societies (van Vliet et al. 2015).

In this context, few farmers remain unaffected by national and global markets (Grau et al. 2013). Agricultural policies, in particular the Common Agricultural Policy (CAP), play a key role in determining whether or not European land is utilized for agricultural productions and the type of cultivated products.

Price falls in agricultural products provoke bankruptcy of many farms and disruption in the rural structure and environment (Rabbinge and von Latesteijn 1992). Landowners and managers facing increased agricultural market competition have resorted mostly to one of three active management strategies: intensification, extensification, and afforestation (Navarro and Pereira 2012). At the same time there have been also processes of farmland abandonment (Munroe et al. 2013) and rewilding.

Intensification is typically prompted by a combination of underlying enablers where technological drivers (e.g. mechanization, digitalization) and institutional drivers (e.g. subsidies, land use programs) are the most frequently reported. Sustainable intensification of agricultural production is expected to be an important pathway for achieving future food security while protecting the environment (Thomson et al. 2019).

In contrast, the disintensification of agricultural land manifested as contraction, partly caused by farmers abandoning their land but also partly by conversion to urban land and natural areas, reflects institutional choices, farmer characteristics (e.g. attitude and motivation, age, household welfare) and economic drivers (e.g. off-farm employment, globalization of agricultural markets, urbanization) (van Vliet et al. 2015). European farmland today is being partially abandoned, especially in remote areas (Navarro and Pereira 2012) and in mountain and semiarid areas (Lasanta et al. 2017). This process is correlated with the national and international economy, biophysical limitations, soil degradation, climate factors and other variables such as farmer's age, farm size and chances for continuity (Lasanta et al. 2017). The CAP played a role in land abandonment when it subsidized set-aside land or land retirement between 1988 and 2008 to control productions and reduce crop surpluses (Lasanta et al. 2017).

Moreover, results of recent modelling studies suggest that there will likely be significant levels of farmland abandonment in Europe over the next 20–30 years (Renwick 2013), but also significant intensification of crop production and grazing (Malek et al. 2018). In addition, the contribution of agriculture to GDP and employment in Europe will continue decreasing (Navarro and Pereira 2012).

Meanwhile, in the Mediterranean region, existing climate models project a consistent tendency toward warmer weather condition and greater occurrence of extreme hot events, interrelated with a general tendency toward less precipitations (Fader et al. 2016, García-Ruiz et al. 2011, Malek et al. 2018). Severe droughts experienced in former times every 100 years will recur every 10 years in northern Mediterranean countries (García-Ruiz et al. 2011).

Also, water scarcity in the Mediterranean is projected to increase under climate change prospects (Iglesias et al. 2011) and will become the predominant concern for Mediterranean farmers (Harmanny and Malek 2019). Changes in water resources are particularly relevant in areas where water availability is a limiting factor for economic development, such as Southeast Spain and the Ebro Depression, where the expansion of irrigated areas and urbanization have caused increasing water supply difficulties (García-Ruiz et al. 2011, Fader et al. 2016).

Adaptation strategies in the Mediterranean basin include water management for irrigation, sustainable resource management (more nature-based strategies such as organic farming or the use of groundcover to control soil erosion), technological developments such as mechanization of farm production practices, cultivation practices (e.g. crop diversification and rotation), and farm management which include financial and administrative practices such as insurance and diversification of household income (Harmanny and Malek 2019).

In Spain 21.3% of the whole land is covered by croplands (Eurostat 2017). Despite their decreasing intensity, internal agriculture conversions are still the second major driver of change in the Spanish landscape. The most frequent internal agriculture flow is the conversion from arable land to vineyards and orchards. Conversions from arable to permanent irrigated perimeters were very frequent between 2000 and 2006, but have almost disappeared from the landscape between 2006 and 2012. In this period, 59% of the artificial land was previously arable land and permanent crops (EEA 2017). Land abandonment processes started during the early decades of the 20th century and increased during the 1950s and 1960s (Lasanta et al. 2017). There is an increasing contrast between marginal and highly productive areas (i.e. between extensification and intensification). This is the most evident characteristic of the spatial organization of population and activities (García-Ruiz et al. 2011).

In this context, the present contribution explores the processes of land use and land cover (LULC) changes affecting the Mediterranean agricultural ecosystems, taking southern Spain (regions of Andalusia and Murcia) as a representative case study. As in other Mediterranean areas, agricultural ecosystems in these regions play a strategic role from socioeconomic and environmental standpoints. At the same time, they are increasingly vulnerable to human activities, water scarcity, and climate change. LULC is a powerful driver of sustainable landscape development, conservation and management. Analysis of LULC change facilitates the design of policies to balance competing uses, development pressures and conservation obligations.

Specifically, this chapter intendeds to (i) portraying the main driving factors of environmental, social or economic nature that have led to these changes, (ii) explaining the influence of LULC changes on the spatial pattern of the morphology of agricultural ecosystems and their environmental consequences, and (iii) informing the decision-making process of managers responsible for sectoral and territorial policies at different scales from local and regional to national and European.

The methodological approach applied consists of performing cartographic modelling of LULC changes using CORINE Land Cover (CLC) maps for 2006 and 2018, taking into account the 44 classes of level 3. Cross-tabulation techniques have been used. Descriptive statistics of land uses (persistence, gains, losses, total change, net change, annual change rate) have been calculated. Moreover, the LULC change processes have been geographically localized and correlated with their driving factors using logistic regression modelling. Some of these factors are environmental and biophysical (topography, climate, soils, aquifers, designation of protected areas) whilst others are socioeconomic (accessibility, agricultural and environmental policies, among others). GUIDOS software has been used to compute a fragmentation index of the agrarian landscape that will help to understand some ecological implications of the LULC changes within the agricultural semi-natural ecosystems of the study area.

Study Area and Data Sets

Study Area

The study area comprises the regions of Andalusia and Murcia located in Spanish southern peninsular (Fig. 1). Both regions are illustrative examples of the Mediterranean basin and other regions of the world with similar climate and analogous biophysical characteristics. They jointly occupy an area of 98,924 km^2 equivalent to 19.55% of the total national area. Both are peripheral regions, situated between the Spanish Plateau and the sea corridor of the Gulf of Cadiz-Gibraltar-Alboran-Mediterranean. Thus, they connect the north with the south (Europe-Africa) and the east with the west (Mediterranean-Atlantic). Their relief is the result of tectonic forces between the plates of Europe and Africa. From geomorphological standpoint, Andalusia is composed of four units: the Hercynian massif of Sierra Morena separated from the Spanish Plateau, to the north; the Alpine Baetic mountain ranges, to the southeast; and the open alpine pit towards the Atlantic, in the center, drained by the Guadalquivir River. The Mediterranean coast of the south and southeast of the peninsula, resulting from the sinking of the Alboran plate (Ortega 1991), is located

Figure 1. Study area: Andalusia and Murcia, two Mediterranean regions located in the south of mainland Spain.

on the outer edge of the Baetic mountain ranges. In the Region of Murcia, the Baetic mountain ranges alternate with the depressions, cuvettes and corridors, filled with tertiary and quaternary materials (Calvo and López-Bermúdez 1992). The basin of the Campo de Cartagena-Mar Menor is the most extensive.

Mediterranean climate predominates in both regions with different nuances (García-Couto 2011). According to the Köppen-Geiger climate classification, the center and the west of the study area have a temperate climate with dry and hot summer (Csa). In the Baetic mountain ranges the Csb climate—temperate climate with dry and fresh summer—predominates, and the Mediterranean continental type (Dsc and Dsb) prevails in the highest areas of the Sierra Nevada. In the southeast, the warm steppe climate (BSh) and the hot-desertic and cold climates (BWh and BWk, respectively) mark an important geographical influence.

The southeast is the most arid area in Europe. However, the transfer of water between the Tajo and Segura river basins (Garrido et al. 2006) and the presence of large aquifers under the study area (Spanish Government 2019) compensate partially the surface water shortage and the high evapotranspiration. The intensively irrigated farms in this area increasingly demand more water and arouse a complex socio-economic and environmental debate (Grindlay et al. 2011, Ibor et al. 2011, Martínez-

Modelling Land Use and Land Cover Changes in the Mediterranean...　　**45**

Granados et al. 2011, Lopez-Gunn et al. 2012, Swyngedouw 2013, Melgarejo et al. 2014, Martínez-Álvarez et al. 2017, Kochskämper et al. 2018, Aldaya et al. 2019).

The study area also is one of the most populous areas of Spain. It accommodates over 21% of the national population with a density close to 100 inhab/km^2 (Table 1). Most of the population is concentrated around the provincial capitals, especially in the metropolitan area of Seville and in the Cadiz-Algeciras-La Linea de la Concepcion conurbation, and in the Mediterranean and Atlantic coastlines, with average densities of 500 and 9,000 inhab/km^2, respectively. In contrast, a large part of the mountain territories is depopulated. Thirty-two percent of the municipalities of the nine provinces forming the study area have a density of less than 20 inhab/km^2 and some indeed are at 5 inhab/km^2.

Table 1. Demographic and territorial characteristics of the study area

	Area (km^2)	*%*	*Population (inhab)*	*%*	*Density (inhab/km^2)*
Andalusia	87,588	17.31	8,408,975	18.07	96.00
Murcia	11,314	2.23	1,472,991	3.16	130.19
Study area	98,902	19.55	9,881,966	21.24	99.92
Spain	505,981	100.00	46,528,024	100.00	91.95

Source: Spanish Statistical Office (INE), 2018.

In both regions the employment in the agricultural sector is rather relevant, tripling the national average (Table 2). The two regions concentrate 20% of the utilized agricultural area and about 30% of farms in the whole of Spain.

The agricultural sector contributed 5.1% of GDP in Andalusia and 5.3% in Murcia in 2016, doubling the national average. The strength of the sector has allowed both regions to be among the major fruits and vegetables suppliers to European markets. The whole agri-food system represents 10% of the regional GDP in Andalusia and 21.4% in Murcia.

The proportion of agricultural area in Murcia and in Andalusia exceeds 50% of their total areas. In both regions there has been a large expansion of greenhouse crops and irrigated lands, being the Spanish regions with the highest proportion of surface area occupied by these uses. Agricultural area in Andalusia has recorded an increase due to the development of the primary sector (OSE 2006). This process has also affected protected areas where the two National Parks of Andalusia (Doñana and Sierra Nevada) have experienced a slight increase in agricultural uses (Hewitt et al. 2016).

Other related trends have been reported in both regions over the last decades. In Andalusia, between 1956 and 1980, farming areas have grown greatly in the most fertile zones (the valley bottoms), while in mountain and coastal ranges, agriculture and livestock farming decreased (Fernandez Ales et al. 1992). Between 1956 and 2007, wetlands and water surfaces have lost 22 percent of their extension, transformed into agricultural and forest areas (Bermejo Pérez et al. 2011). Until 1999, built-up areas and infrastructures increased 281 percent, focused intensively in certain provinces located in the coast. During the last half century, the coastal strip of 2 km wide has grown up to 700 percent, in particular the province of Granada with an increase in artificial areas above 800 percent (Bermejo Pérez et al. 2011). In the previous decade, almost 70% of the agricultural area was occupied by rainfed crops, mainly herbaceous crops and olive groves. Irrigated crops have increased in recent years and account for about 18% of agricultural area, mostly planted by corn, barley, alfalfa, potato, tomato, beet and cotton, but also olive and citrus groves (Bermejo Pérez et al. 2011).

Net returns affect positively the probability of reconversion to herbaceous crops and olive farming, and negatively the probability of choosing grassland uses. Net subsidies have a positive effect in all cases, increasing the probability of choosing herbaceous crops, fruit trees, olive trees, grassland and hardwood forest uses. Moreover, being in a protected area decreases the probability of moving from herbaceous to olive and of remaining in grasslands (Oviedo et al. 2017).

In Murcia, despite the relative loss of weight of the agriculture in the economy, the agri-food sector has maintained a high degree of competitiveness, based greatly on the irrigation expansion. More than a half of its territory is dedicated to agriculture (56.2%), mainly irrigated crops and fruit trees. Competition on land in the coastal zone has forced a move of the agricultural activity towards forest border areas. Accordingly, the main cause of forest loss in the region is the conversion to agricultural land. Murcia has one of the lowest proportions of wooded forest areas of Spain (OSE 2006).

Data Sets

In order to map the dependent variable (LULC changes) land use-land cover maps of the CLC project corresponding to the initial and the final study years (v18.5 of 2006 and 2018) have been downloaded (http://centrodedescargas.cnig.es/CentroDescargas/index.jsp, last accessed 15 October 2020).

In addition, in accordance with the available data, geographical characteristics of the study area, literature and expert judgments, the following driving factors have been selected (Table 3). These include biophysical factors—linked to orography, climate, soil, hydrology,

Table 2. Some socioeconomic characteristics of agriculture in the study area

	Agricultural holdings (no)[1]	Utilised agricultural area, uaa (ha)[1]	Persons employed in agriculture (% of the total employed)[2]	GDP (thousand €)[3]	GDP per capita (€)[3]
Andalusia	242,324	4,399,491	9.37	160,811,516	19,132
Murcia	29,101	377,362	13.40	31,258,596	21,134
Study Area	271,425	4,776,853	10.02	192,070,112	20,133
Spain	933,059	23,229,753	4.31	1,270,463,136	24,721

Sources: 1) INE 2019a. Survey on the structure of agricultural holdings; 2) INE 2019b. INEbase, Employment in agriculture; 3) INE 2019c. INEbase, Territorial statistics.

Table 3. Selected driving factors

Variable	Type[1]	Source
Elevations (E)	C	CNIG, Digital Elevation Models DTM200 http://centrodedescargas.cnig.es/CentroDescargas/index.jsp
Slopes (S)	C	CNIG, Digital Elevations Model DTM200 http://centrodedescargas.cnig.es/CentroDescargas/index.jsp
Average temperature (T) 1970-2000	C	WorldClim v2, http://worldclim.org/version2
Annual precipitation (P) 1970-2000	C	WorldClim v2, http://worldclim.org/version2
Edaphic limitations For Agriculture (Limagr)	B	European Soil Database v2.0, Pedotransfer Rules Database v2.0 https://esdac.jrc.ec.europa.eu/ESDB_Archive/ESDBv2/fr_intro.htm
Aquifers (Aq)	B	MITECO, Groundwater perimeters in Spain. https://sig.mapama.gob.es/redes-seguimiento/

(Contd.)

Table 3. Selected driving factors

Variable	Type[1]	Source
Protected areas (Pa)	B	MITECO, Nationally Designated Protected areas and Natura Net 2000 areas, https://www.miteco.gob.es/es/biodiversidad/servicios/banco-datos-naturaleza/servidor-cartografico-wms-/ EUROPARC-ESPAÑA, Biosphere Reserves, ZEPIM and RAMSAR Zones, http://www.redeuroparc.org/observatorio/descargas
Wildland fires (Wf)	B	European Forest Fire Information System – EFFIS (San-Miguel-Ayanz et al. 20120) (http://effis.jrc.ec.europa.eu) of the European Commission Joint Research Centre.
Population density (Pd)	C	Spanish Statistical Office, Demography and population http://www.ine.es/dyngs/INEbase/es/categoria.htm?c=Estadistica_P&c id=1254734710984
Distance to population entities (Dp)	C	CNIG, CORINE Land Cover 2018 http://centrodedescargas.cnig.es/CentroDescargas/locale?request_locale=en
Distance to highways and roads (Dro)	C	CNIG, National Topographic Base at 1:500,000 BCN500 http://centrodedescargas.cnig.es/CentroDescargas/locale?request_locale=en
Distance to rivers and reservoirs (Dr)	C	CNIG, National Topographic Base at 1:500,000 BCN500 http://centrodedescargas.cnig.es/CentroDescargas/locale?request_locale=en
Distance to coast line (Dc)	C	CNIG, National Topographic Base at 1:500,000 BCN500 http://centrodedescargas.cnig.es/CentroDescargas/locale?request_locale=en

1. C=Continuous; B=Binary (yes/no)

biodiversity, forest fires—as well as demographic and accessibility variables.

Methods

The research has followed the workflow depicted in Fig. 2. ArcGIS v10.3 (ESRI Inc.) has been used for the vectorial treatment of downloaded data and chiefly for the analysis of LULC changes. The Land Change Modeler (LCM), module of IDRISI-Selva (Eastman 2012), has been applied for the analysis of correlations between the driving factors and the spatial distribution of LULC changes. Finally, GUIDOS-MSPA (Soille and Vogt

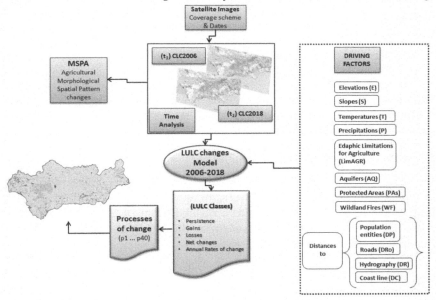

Figure 2. Methodological flow diagram of the study.

2009) has been employed for the analysis of the spatial pattern of the agricultural landscape and the processes of advancement on the one hand, and fragmentation, on the other hand.

LULC changes

CLC data has been used as the longest, most accurate and comparable source of LULC data accessible for the whole country (Pérez-Hoyos and García-Haro 2013). LULCs from level-3 CLC data have been compared at two time points: 2006 and 2018. To simplify comparisons, polygons below 0.5 hectare have been omitted and the 44 CLC level 3 LULC classes

50 *Modeling for Sustainable Management in Agriculture, Food and the Environment*

have been grouped in 30 classes. The aggregations affected artificial surfaces, wetlands and marine waters (classes 1, 4 and 5.2). However, the maximum disaggregation in the agricultural and forest ecosystems has been maintained. Cross-tabulation matrices (Pontius et al. 2004) were designed to obtain statistics of LULC changes between 2006 and 2018. Following Rodríguez-Rodríguez et al. (2019)—albeit with more detail and focus on agriculture—40 processes of change have been examined (Table 4).

Considering the period of time studied, the following descriptive statistics have been calculated for each LULC change process: class persistence, gains, losses, absolute and relative change, and net change. In addition, the annual rate of change (*rt*) of each LULC change process has been computed using the following equation according to Rodríguez Eraso et al. (2013):

$$rt = \frac{1}{t_2 - t_1} \times Ln\left(\frac{A_2}{A_1}\right) \times 100$$

Where A_1 and A_2 are the areas (in hectares) of the assessed LULC class in the initial year (t_1) and final year (t_2), respectively. This equation is a variant of the used by Puyravaud (2003).

Explanatory Factors of LULC Changes

In order to analyze the relationships between the dependent and independent variables in the LCM framework, the CLC2006 and CLC2018 maps have been transformed into a raster format of 50×50 m pixel size. Also, the maps that represent each of the driving factors have been rasterized with the same spatial resolution.

To calculate the distances to different elements and entities (population centers, roads, rivers and reservoirs and coast line), the Euclidean distance that computes the direction in degrees toward the closest element of interest has been used for each cell analyzed on the raster map. In case of communication routes, the highways and the main and the secondary roads have been extracted from the cartographic base. For hydrography, the first, second and third order rivers have been selected. In addition, the bodies of reservoirs, lakes and lagoons have been added. For the calculation of distances to population entities, the urban, industrial, commercial and transport areas have been pooled together. Part of driving factors is binary, indicating the presence/absence in each cell of the analyzed variable, while others provide continuous values on a given scale.

To examine the relationships between land uses and the explanatory variables, the V Cramer coefficient (Cramér 1946) has been calculated for each of the land uses, where 1 indicates a perfect association and 0

Table 4. Cross-tabulation matrix between LULC classes of 2006 (in rows) and 2018 (in columns). LULC change processes are indicated with a mixed alphabetic and color code

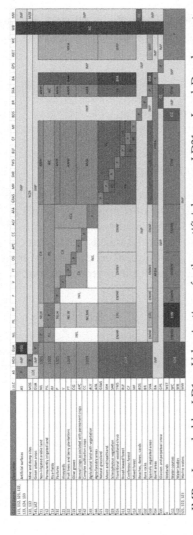

P – Persistence, IMP – Improbable, LD1 – Urbanization of other artificial zones, LD21 – Land Development on non-irrigated herbaceous crops, LD22 – Land Development on permanently irrigated land, LD23 – Land Development on non-irrigated woody crops, LD24 – Land Development on mixed agricultural areas, LD3 – Land Development of forest and natural areas, LD4 – Land Development of wetlands and water bodies, MZR – Mining zones restoration, EGU – Expansion of green urban areas, RC – Reservoirs construction, CR – Crops reconversion, RCE – Rainfed crops extensification, INIL – Intensification of non-irrigated arable lands, ENIHF – Expansion of non-irrigated herbaceous crops on forests, ENIWF – Expansion of non-irrigated woody crops on forests, EMAF – Expansion of mixed agricultural areas on forests, ENIHW – Expansion of non-irrigated herbaceous crops on wetlands, ENIWW – Expansion of non-irrigated woody crops on wetlands, EMAW – Expansion of mixed agricultural areas on wetlands, NILH – New irrigated land on non-irrigated herbaceous crops, NILW – New irrigated land on non-irrigated woody crops, NILMA – New irrigated land on mixed agricultural areas, EIFL – Expansion of irrigation on forest lands, EIW – Expansion of irrigation on wetlands, FR – Forest regression, BAA – Burned agricultural areas, BFA – Burned forest areas, CC – Climatic Change, CVW – Colonization of vegetation on wetlands, ANIH – Abandonment of non-irrigated herbaceous crops, ANIW – Abandonment of non-irrigated woody crops, AMA – Abandonment of mixed agricultural areas, RIL – Reconversion of irrigated land in rainfed crops, AIC – Abandonment of irrigated crops, FS – Forest succession, ARBA – Agricultural restoration of burned areas, FRBA – Forest restoration of burned areas, WRA – Wetlands restoration on agricultural areas, WRF – Wetlands restoration on forest lands.

indicates that there is no association. Subsequently, logistic regressions have been performed to investigate the relationship between the probability of occurrence of the selected land uses (dependent variables) and the predictors (independent variables). A sampling proportion of 20% was used. Dependent variables have values of 0 and 1 (absence/presence). ROC (Receiving Operating Characteristic) has also been computed to inspect the goodness of fit of the model. The logistic regression equation is defined as:

$$P(Y-1 \mid X) = \frac{e^{\sum_{i=0}^{i=n} B_i X_i}}{1 + e^{\sum_{i=0}^{i=n} B_i X_i}}$$

Where P is the probability of the dependent variable being 1, X_i are the independent variables $(X_0 = 1$ for the constant term) and B_i the variable parameters.

Agricultural Morphological Spatial Pattern Changes

An index that assesses the fragmentation of agricultural habitats and temporal variations in terms of their size and spatial pattern has been calculated (Chuvieco et al. 2013). This is the Agricultural Habitat Fragmentation Index (AHFI) that helps to understand a series of ecological implications of LULC changes within agricultural ecosystems of the study area as well as their exchanges with the rest of the territorial matrix.

$$\text{AHFI} = \frac{\sum_{j=1}^{k} np_{ji} w_j}{\sum_{j=1}^{k} np_{ji}}$$

Where k is the number of fragmentation categories, np_{ji} is the number of pixels of category j in the ecoregion i, and w_j is the weight of category j of fragmentation.

Taking into account the level 1 of the CLC legend, maps CLC2006 and CLC2018 have been reclassified in binary format. Classes 1, 3, 4 and 5 have been combined and considered as background while class 2 has been considered as a single objective category linked to agricultural ecosystems of the regions of Andalusia and Murcia.

The MSPA algorithm (Soille and Vogt 2009) classifies each pixel according to its geometric position in the analyzed matrix, differentiating seven entities: (1) cores, (2) islets, (3) perforations, (4) edges, (5) loops, (6) bridges, and (7) branches. The index has a range from 1 (highest fragmentation) to 2 (lowest fragmentation). It allocates a different weight to each of the entities mapped according to the relationships between resilience and spatial coherence (Opdam et al. 2003, 2006). There is a continuous gradation from the agrarian core (greatest weight) to the islets (lowest weight). The index relates the number of pixels of each category or fragmentation entity and their weights.

Results

Overall it has been found that both regions under study have experienced significant LULC changes. It can be asserted that agricultural ecosystems have been major protagonists in this process and have been involved as the origin or destination of changes.

LULC Patterns and Processes of Change in Mediterranean Agricultural Ecosystems

Detailed analysis of the LULC changes at class and process level can be found in Appendix 1, where all descriptive statistics are depicted (persistence of each class, gains, losses, absolute and relative change, net change and annual rate of change) in hectares and in percentage with respect to the total area of both regions (about ten million hectares), and with respect to the total area that has undergone changes (about one million hectares).

Nearly 89.4% of the territory of Andalusia and Murcia has not undergone changes in land uses between 2006 and 2018. The rest (10.6%) has shown some change. In this latter portion, changes that are unlikely, due perhaps to interpretation errors, barely reach 0.20% of the total area.

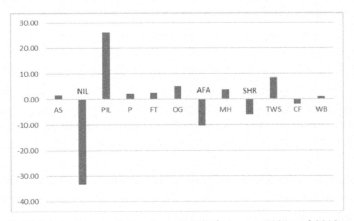

Figure 3. Main net changes in land use (>1%), between 2006 and 2018 at regional level. AS – Artificial surfaces, NIL – Non-irrigated arable land, PIL – Permanently irrigated land, P – Pastures, FT – Fruit trees and berry plantations, OG – Olive groves, AFA – Agro-forestry areas, MH – Moors and heathland, SHR – Sclerophylous vegetation, TWS – Transitional woodland-shrub, CF – Coniferous forest, WB – Water bodies. *Source*: CLC2006 and 2018.

Taking into account the net changes (Fig. 3) among the agricultural land uses, it can be underlined the remarkable growth of irrigated land and a more moderate increase of olive groves and fruit trees. Conversely, the negative net change in dry arable crops and agroforestry areas (meadows) is worth noting.

Among the main processes of land use change (Fig. 4), the NILHs that concentrate about 29% of the change surface area stand out. Geographically, they extend through the middle and lower valley of the Guadalquivir, the main river that drains much of Andalusia (Fig. 5), where the slopes are scarce, the soils have no limitations for agriculture and there are extensive underground aquifers. ENIHF is a process of agronomic interest which is differential between both regions. It represents the advance of the agricultural frontier on old scrub spots or on soils with sparse vegetation.

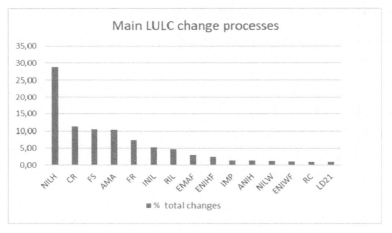

Figure 4. Main LULC change processes (as a percentage of the total change) at regional level. NILH – New irrigated land on non-irrigated herbaceous crops, CR – Crops reconversion, FS – Forest succession, AMA – Abandonment of mixed agricultural areas, FR – Forest regression, INIL – Intensification of non-irrigated arable lands, RIL – Reconversion of irrigated land in rainfed crops, EMAF – Expansion of mixed agricultural areas on forests, ENIHF – Expansion of non-irrigated herbaceous crops on forests, IMP – Improbable, ANIH – Abandonment of non-irrigated herbaceous crops, NILW – New irrigated land on non-irrigated woody crops, ENIWF – Expansion of non-irrigated woody crops on forests, RC – Reservoirs construction, LD21 – Land Development on non-irrigated herbaceous crops. *Source*: CLC2006 and 2018.

The new olive groves mainly occupy the hills of the province of Jaen, and are largely prompted by the agro-environmental support of the CAP. However, fruit trees are dominating in Murcia. It could be argued that, to a certain extent, there has been a geographical specialization of this process.

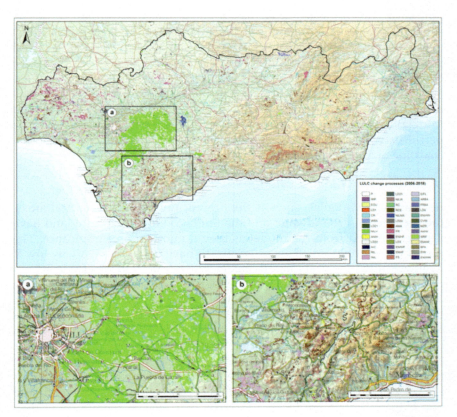

Figure 5. Geographical distribution of main LULC change processes at regional level. a) Detailed view of the "NILH New irrigated land on non-irrigated herbaceous crops" change process in the surroundings of Seville, Spain. b) Detailed view of the "AMA Abandonment of mixed agricultural areas" change process in the Sierra de Grazalema and Serranía de Ronda (Malaga, Spain).
Source: CLC2006 and 2018. Codes from Table 4.

On the contrary, the AMA and ANIH processes are worth highlighting. Both affect approximately 12% of the total area of change. The most extensive patches are located in areas of poor accessibility, on the slopes of the main mountain areas (Sierra Morena, Grazalema, Sierra Nevada and Cazorla), and the marginal soils with limitations for agriculture.

Similarly, forest succession (FS) affects more than 10% of the surface change. The abandonment of traditional agriculture and livestock has led to transitions from scrub to wooded scrub and to wooded. The patch that extends in the Sierra Nevada National Park and its surroundings is very significant. A possible cause for this evolution is that the conservation

56 *Modeling for Sustainable Management in Agriculture, Food and the Environment*

policy of this protected area has favored the transformation of the subarbustive scrub to moors and heathland. The inverse process (FR) affects approximately 80,000 hectares. The substitution of holm oaks and pine forests with bushes is probably the result of forest fires that have occurred previously in the area.

Finally, over 30,000 hectares of former farmland have become new urban areas, infrastructure (highways and airport, such as Corbera in Murcia) and recreational areas (golf courses). They are located in the peri-urban areas of the big cities (Seville, Cadiz and Malaga) and in the coastline of Mediterranean and Gulf of Cadiz.

Major Drivers of LULC Changes

Boolean-type variables, such as the presence of protected natural areas, the presence of groundwater and the limitation of agricultural land have been eliminated from the model as they do not obtain significance. The rest of the variables, with a *p value* <0.001, have obtained relatively low V Cramer values, the vast majority being between 0.3 and 0.1 (Table 5).

Table 6 depicts the results of the logistic regressions. As can be seen, artificial-type uses are related to distance variables to the main transport routes, urban centers and the coast. Irrigated and non-irrigated crops are associated with proximity to transport routes, but are far from urban centers. In addition, they are located in areas of low slope. Irrigated crops are located in areas with low altitude, while rainfed crops, heterogeneous agriculture and permanent crops are located at higher altitude. All crops are associated to locations with higher temperatures. Irrigated and non-irrigated crops are located in areas that receive more rainfall than permanent crops and areas of heterogeneous agriculture. Forest uses— pastures and meadows, scrubs and woods—are located far away from transport infrastructure and urban centers associated with areas of greater slope, the former being located in areas of higher altitude. Wetlands and bodies of water are related to the proximity to the coast and water courses, in areas of low altitude and low slope. The areas of heterogeneous agriculture, pastures and natural meadows have obtained poorer predictions, with lower AUC (area under the curve)—ROC between 0.66 and 0.67. Probably, its geographical distribution in small patches spread throughout the territory does not help in the characterization of a clear pattern.

Agricultural Morphological Spatial Pattern Changes

In the regions of Andalusia and Murcia as a whole, the $AHFI_{2006}$ has been equivalent to 1.5227 while in 2018 it has been reduced to 1.5164. Accordingly, the increase in fragmentation of agricultural ecosystems has been relatively small. Overall, the agricultural matrix remains

Table 5. V Cramer coefficients

Land use	DH	DRo	DC	DR	DP	E	S	P	T
Overall V	0.1396	0.1089	0.1153	0.0918	0.3134	0.2085	0.1996	0.1722	0.2123
Artificial surfaces	0.2320	0.1254	0.2380	0.0860	0.8781	0.1804	0.1101	0.0969	0.1776
Non-irrigated arable land	0.0257	0.0782	0.0597	0.0931	0.0713	0.1493	0.1951	0.1153	0.1484
Irrigated arable land	0.1882	0.0902	0.0564	0.1200	0.1600	0.3871	0.3525	0.2321	0.4117
Permanent crops	0.1418	0.1777	0.1371	0.0430	0.2149	0.2155	0.1450	0.2096	0.2007
Heterogeneous agriculture	0.2099	0.0295	0.0781	0.0412	0.0745	0.1754	0.1203	0.1240	0.1745
Open spaces with little or no vegetation	0.0443	0.0595	0.1063	0.0401	0.0504	0.1785	0.1119	0.2211	0.1703
Pastures and natural grasslands	0.0326	0.0280	0.0520	0.0668	0.0489	0.0739	0.0853	0.2022	0.0699
Shrubs	0.1235	0.1580	0.0930	0.0234	0.1699	0.1812	0.2837	0.1291	0.1894
Forest	0.1453	0.1576	0.0545	0.0538	0.1924	0.2121	0.2562	0.1916	0.2485
Wetlands and water bodies	0.0502	0.0853	0.1249	0.1923	0.0749	0.1988	0.1741	0.1383	0.1693

DH=Distance to highways; DRo=Distance to roads; DC=Distance to coast line; DR=Distance to rivers and reservoirs; DP=Distance to population entities; E=Elevations; S=Slopes; P=Average precipitation; T=Average temperature.

Table 6. Logistic regression results

Driving factors	Artificial surfaces	Non-irrigated arable land	Irrigated arable land	Permanent crops	Heterogeneous agriculture	Open spaces with little or no vegetation	Pastures and natural grasslands	Shrubs	Forest	Wetlands and water bodies
Constant	-0.02761680	-9.86133198	-11.06831320	-20.27563090	-2.98880780	-2.44185751	-2.10976608	-1.97872475	-1.47470606	0.70965413
DH	-0.00002045		-0.00003962		0.00005177					
DRo		-0.00005937		-0.00008217			0.00001780	0.00003988	0.00002701	0.00013386
DC	-0.00001159		0.00001212	0.00006041	0.00001073	-0.00007290				-0.00006659
DR		0.00001283								-0.00018978
DP	-0.00239433	0.00002498	0.00002837	-0.00009405				0.00005689	0.00008827	
E	-0.00061253	0.00246952	-0.00029234	0.00470892	0.00002772	0.00225073	0.00068514	-0.00032786	-0.00055055	-0.00229758
S		-0.14423413	-0.23541679	-0.01210174	-0.0407198	0.01789873	0.01833291	0.05393672	0.04085806	-0.24251891
P		0.00306331	0.00013906	-0.00227537	-0.00060358	-0.00395505	-0.00382761	0.00051961	0.00231777	-0.00034390
T		0.37599127	0.60718537	1.05121701	0.03121866	0.04483425	0.04700157	-0.04585128	-0.15702617	-0.06991155
ROC	0.9568	0.7280	0.8731	0.7433	0.6712	0.8116	0.6637	0.7297	0.7598	0.9024

DH=Distance to highways; DRo=Distance to roads; DC=Distance to coast line; DR=Distance to rivers and reservoirs; DP=Distance to population entities; E=Elevations; S=Slopes; P=Average precipitation; T=Average temperature.

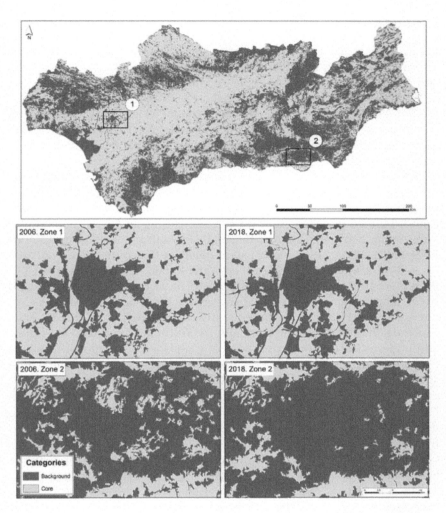

Figure 6. Agricultural Morphological Spatial Pattern in Andalusia and Murcia in 2018 (above). In zone 1 (Seville and its surroundings) urban sprawl and the development of new road infrastructure have fragmented agricultural ecosystems. In zone 2 (province of Almeria), forest areas have invaded and fragmented the agricultural areas.
Source: CLC2006 and 2018.

similar. However, these regional results hide substantial local differences, associated with the different LULC change processes that predominate in each zone (Fig. 6).

Discussion

It can be asserted that at regional scale CLC is a reliable geographic information source. It facilitates the monitoring of agricultural land uses, and the detection of the processes of change that favor the increase of agricultural income and also those that are not highly sustainable. Despite the limitations of this source and the errors detected (Diaz Pacheco and Gutiérrez 2013), and the change in methodology (García-Álvarez and Camacho 2017), it remains a standard cartographic series available at European level.

However, while CLC captures a series of changes relatively well (e.g. urbanization), estimates remain uncertain for other relevant LULC change processes, for instance agricultural abandonment and deforestation, which cannot be distinguished from forest clear-cutting in CLC. There is also a mismatch between CLC and the CAPRI (Common Agricultural Policy Regionalized Impact) cropland extent database (Kuemmerle et al. 2016).

On a continental scale, there are other alternatives to CLC. Pflugmacher et al. (2019) have elaborated on a new pan-European land cover map from multi-temporal images of Landsat 8 and the LUCAS database, which they have subsequently compared with CLC 2012. They conclude that CORINE substantially overestimated seasonal croplands and underestimated the proportions of grasslands. On a global scale, the Climate Change Initiative-Land Cover (CCI-LC) map is available with a spatial resolution of 300 m. and a 1992–2015-time series (https://www. esa-landcover-cci.org/). Liu et al. (2018) have compared this product with FAOSTAT data. Meier et al. (2018) have also compared statistical data to the Global Map of Irrigated Areas (GMIA) with an irrigation map derived from remote sensing data (CCI-LC, NDVI-SPOT, and NDVI-MERIS). Global results show an irrigation area 18% larger than existing approaches based on statistical data.

In any event, the CLC source used evidences some conflicting processes derived from the expansion of irrigation as noticed by other authors. Custodio et al. (2016) point out the socioeconomic advantages of the exploitation of underground aquifers in the southeast of the Iberian Peninsula. However, they also call attention to the unsustainability of agriculture based on the exploitation of these water resources, the mismatch of this model under the EU Water Framework Directive and the ethical problems derived from the expansion of these land uses. In the southwest of Andalusia, one of the most striking LULC changes has been the expansion of intensive irrigated agriculture over 70% of Doñana, one of the most important wetlands in Europe (Zorrilla-Miras et al. 2014). This transformation has caused severe environmental impacts such as the destruction of natural habitats and significant loss of ecosystem services.

Sánchez-Picón et al. (2011) also emphasize the relationship between the expansion of intensive greenhouse agriculture in the southeast of Andalusia and Murcia and the depletion of underground aquifers. In the case of the region of Murcia, the persistence or the intensification of irrigation is worrisome taking into account the existing evidence of increased temperatures, decreasing precipitations and longer drought periods (Gil-Guirado and Pérez-Morales 2019).

The increase in irrigated agriculture strengthens the agricultural economy of the countries where it occurs and provides new development opportunities. However, its environmental impacts, such as the overexploitation of groundwater aquifers and the intrusion of seawater, are also of global concern (Jakeman et al. 2016). Irrigation expansion is a similar process in Egypt (Sharaky et al. 2019) and in other North African countries, as well as in other Mediterranean-type areas of the world such as Australia and California (Jakeman et al. 2016).

In line with the results of this study, both in the Mediterranean (Maneas et al. 2019) and elsewhere there is a notable advance in agricultural land at the expense of forestlands and wetlands (Clark et al. 2010, Shen et al. 2018, Polo-Akpisso et al. 2019), causing various environmental impacts. Hence, it is necessary to define the strategies of adaptation to the changes produced in order to implement the appropriate policies (Taffa Ariti et al. 2015). In the Mediterranean basin, Harmanny and Malek (2019) indicate that irrigated agricultural areas with better accessibility and areas with more water scarcity are those that are most likely to be globally adapted, both in terms of resource management and aspects related to technological development and production practices. According to their results, the irrigated areas of the coast of the region of Murcia and the lower basin of the Guadalquivir riverbank have the greatest spatial likelihood to incorporate all the adaptations.

In Spain, other studies have related the CAP aids with the expansion of almond tree cultivation in the region of Murcia (Romero et al. 2012). Given these changes in land use, they recommend soil conservation practices in marginal almond crops.

Admittedly, the abandonment of agricultural land has been witnessed worldwide, and also in the Mediterranean. In Turkey, Konukcu et al. (2017) point out that the abandonment of agricultural land in the Ergene River Basin between the years of 1990 and 2012 jeopardizes food security. This is one of the most productive areas of the country. In Spain, Rey Benayas et al. (2007) argue that the abandonment of agricultural land is mostly driven by socioeconomic factors, claiming also that this process offers two contrasted views. On the one hand, it implies loss of biodiversity, increased frequency and intensity of fires (Viedma et al. 2015), soil erosion and desertification, loss of cultural and aesthetic values, and reduction of diversity from the landscape. On the other hand, it involves active reforestation, water regulation, soil and nutrient cycle recovery, and the increase of biodiversity and wildlife.

Similarly, in the EU land abandonment is a relevant process that occurs mostly in less productive mountainous and remote areas with unfavorable conditions for agriculture (van der Zanden et al. 2017). In addition, this process and its budgetary compensations are a challenge that all of Europe is facing, according to the expected LULC change scenarios entailing agronomic, environmental and social perspectives. In the northeast of Spain, Vidal-Macua et al. (2018) point out that the main determinants of abandonment of non-irrigated agricultural land are related to topography. In the case of irrigated agriculture, the main determinant is linked to accessibility.

The land development process and its relationship with agriculture is another topic studied for decades. Heimlich and Anderson (2001) reference the advantages and disadvantages of this relationship. Other authors (Barbero-Sierra et al. 2013) point out that agriculture is one of the main agents of desertification in Spain, even though agricultural lands have been victims of the urbanization process as a result of a set of social and economic factors. According to these authors, between 1975 and 2008, half a million hectares of agricultural land have become new urban areas in Spain.

Other authors (García-Ayllón 2015, de Andrés et al. 2017) emphasize the worrisome relationship between urban expansion and natural coastal ecosystems. The latter receive increasing environmental pressure. Together with those of other regions, Andalusian and Murcian coastal ecosystems are among the most affected by this pressure in Spain.

Van den Berg et al. (2007) insist on an idea already known worldwide: the preference of the urban population to settle in new suburban areas in contact with nature, including forest areas. In Andalusia and Murcia this phenomenon has occurred in the peripheries of the main cities and on the mountain slopes located behind the coastal plains.

In the conversion between crops, the net change of olive groves by over 50,000 hectares in the study area is striking. For this outcome the quality standards as well as the sustainability and multifunctionality of protected designations of origin (PDOs) of olive oil have played a crucial role (Egea and Pérez and Pérez 2016, Farré-Ribes et al. 2019). About half of these PDOs are located in Andalusia.

From the ecological standpoint, there is widespread consensus that conventional agriculture entails growing environmental impacts, including biodiversity loss, reduction of soil quality by erosion and chemical use, and nutrient depletion (Thomson et al. 2019). Aware of these environmental impacts, the CAP is increasingly promoting agri-environmental measures and support (Buller et al. 2017, Science for Environment Policy 2017). Some actions are aimed at specific environmental objectives (protection of biodiversity, soil quality, water, landscape and air, mitigation of and adaptation to climate change) while others are multifunctional. Frequently, compensation measures have been implemented to addressing the loss of agricultural income resulting from the cease of unsustainable agricultural activities (Fornés et al. 2000, Esteban and Albiac 2012). More recently, further attention is being given to the role of agricultural and agroforestry ecosystems in the provision of ecosystem services and amenities (Campos et al. 2017).

Despite the increasing change in policy orientation, there are authors who point out that the European Commission, the European Parliament and the European Council have used the environmentalization as a justification strategy for the latest CAP reform (2014–2020), in parallel with an important productivist discourse to determine the policy measures (Erjavec and Erjavec 2015). In the same vein, SEO/ BirdLife-WWF Spain (2010) denounce the inconsistency of the perception of agri-environment aid in irrigated agriculture areas that have overexploited their underground aquifers and are vulnerable to nitrates. Interestingly, there is an ongoing debate on these issues at the political, scientific and citizen level.

At the global scale, political incentives for water saving technologies as well as the development of efficient public water conveyance systems may help to reduce water extractions today but also under future climate change (Fader et al. 2016). At the local scale, the characteristics of crops and how they are managed, especially in terms of tillage and agrochemical inputs, largely determine the environmental impact of agriculture (Thomson et al. 2019).

Regarding the analysis of the driving factors of land use changes, it is obvious that the results are moderately satisfactory. V Cramer values are relatively low, most of them being below 0.3. AUC-ROC values are higher (greater than 0.65), with poorer performance for land uses such as heterogeneous agriculture and pastures and natural grasslands. Best performance, beyond 0.9, was obtained for artificial surfaces and wetlands and water bodies. The latter can be associated to the scarcity of this land use in the study area. Although the explanatory variables used are limiting and determinant from biophysical viewpoint, the processes of change are also driven by government policies and other socio-economic, technological and psychological factors which are difficult to model in a GIS environment and therefore have not been taken into account. Another constraint in this regard has been the unavailability of suitable spatial resolution for variables such as precipitation and temperature. In the medium and long term it is unlikely to internalize the environmental costs

64 *Modeling for Sustainable Management in Agriculture, Food and the Environment*

of intensive irrigated agriculture in the financial accounts of agricultural holdings (Takatsuka et al. 2018). Thus, decision-making and its impact on the agricultural landscape distort a geographical distribution of land uses more in line with the capacity of use of the territory

Conclusions and Implications

Land-use change models allow to appreciate the trajectory of a location and its previous or subsequent implications (social, economic, political, and environmental). However, it should be recalled that they are a simplified representation of reality. Therefore, it is important to be aware of their limitations. The resolution used is a determining factor. Rindfuss et al. (2004) point out that the temporal resolution determines the dynamism that can be observed, the spectral resolution affects the discrimination of the state of the landscape and its condition, and the radiometric resolution controls the precision between the separation of land cover types and land uses. Likewise, it must be taken into consideration that the spatial and temporal resolution may not coincide with the biophysical and socio-economic data used. Regarding thematic resolution, the definition of the land use classes to be employed has an important effect on the results of the model, especially in models seeking to capture the process, not just the change (Conway 2009).

Furthermore, most of the studies on land-use changes are carried out at the pixel level (Gallardo 2018). A pixel, due to its regular shape, can never perfectly represent the curvatures of polygons. As highlighted by Rae et al. (2007), a considerable amount of information can be lost during the process of converting the information from vector to raster. All these factors must be taken into account when designing land-use change models and interpreting their results.

Agricultural systems in the study area have been the most dynamic segment in terms of LULC change. Over 81,000 hectares of agricultural land have changed their use status toward other non-agricultural uses in the two regions from 2006 to 2018. This has been the result of multiple processes of LULC change, including abandonment of marginal lands and reforestation of agricultural lands, urbanization and construction of infrastructures around large cities and on the Mediterranean and Atlantic coastal fringes, construction of reservoirs and irrigation infrastructures, and recovery of wetlands and other areas of environmental interest. At the same time, agricultural lands also have been the focus of inverse processes such as the intensification of cultivated land and the extension of irrigated crops. Indeed, within agricultural land uses, the major net change has been the remarkable growth of irrigated land, followed by important while more moderate increase in olive grove and fruit tree areas. In contrast, there has been a significant negative net change in rainfed arable crops and agroforestry areas.

These processes of change in LULC have implications for the environmental sustainability of regional agricultural ecosystems (fragmentation, loss of connectivity of agricultural habitats) as well as of other related ecosystems (reduction of coastal wetlands, overexploitation of coastal underground aquifers). They also have relevant consequences for the local agricultural and rural economy (rural employment and work conditions, production diversification and efficiency, productivity, profitability and competitiveness of the agri-food sector).

LULC evolutions are the footprints of natural events and human socio-economic choices, strategies and policies carried out over a territory. From this perspective, it can be asserted that there are worrisome transformations in land uses in the study area that should warn policy makers and land managers, and motivate new policy choices or a change of focus in existing strategies. In this respect, the following policy actions can be proposed: (i) increase of agro-environmental aids of the CAP while including adjustments to prevent and reduce the negative impacts induced by the expansion of intensive irrigated agriculture and cultivation in greenhouses; (ii) due consideration to climate change adaptation as changes in land conditions affect regional climate, particularly agriculture is threatened by increases in the occurrence of high temperature events and falling precipitations associated with climate change; (iii) increase and better target the support for the adaptation of farms to the changing environmental, technological and market challenges (climate change, digitalization, innovation, market access, risk management); (iv) better integration of the sustainable use and management of land in agricultural policies, addressing environmental goals as equal to production goals in the CAP; (v) better reflection of the environmental costs of land-degrading agricultural practices in policy design; (vi) convergence and further coherence of demographic, agri-livestock and forest policies to reduce and reverse the abandonment of agricultural land, promote the clearing of forests, and grant prevalence to forest fire prevention instead of extinction actions; (vii) strengthen urban policies to prevent the location of new urban developments in legally prohibited areas and in the areas most suitable for agriculture and biodiversity conservation.

These suggested potential actions are assisted by the growing evidence that in European regions, including the Mediterranean, a shift toward a more sustainable land management at local level aiming at jointly producing food and protecting the environment, can improve both magnitudes at the same time, compared to the prevailing tends of land polarization and agricultural intensification (Rega et al. 2019). The achievement of this balance needs a sound policy agenda focused on improving sustainable land management to prevent land degradation, and maintain log-term land productivity and environmental functions. In this respect, conservation agriculture, organic farming, agricultural diversification, and precision agriculture systems would be useful options. Likewise, the use of incentives such as payment for ecosystem services, and voluntary or compulsory standards and certification schemes for sustainable food production, can improve land management.

Moreover, holistic approaches mixing cross-cutting policies would be needed to tackle the complexity of challenges and the diversity of actors involved in addressing sustainable management of Mediterranean agricultural ecosystems. Coordination with other relevant sectors, such as transportation, health, water, energy and infrastructure, can increase co-benefits, reduce competition for land, and facilitate risk sharing and transfer mechanisms. The successful implementation of policy options also depends on the consideration of local environmental and socio-economic conditions, as well as the evaluation of potential synergies and trade-offs to balance the costs and benefits of specific strategies.

Acknowledgments

The authors would like to thank Pilar Echavarría from IEGD-CSIC for the support provided in data and map processing.

Appendix 1: Excel file available upon request from the authors.

References

Aldaya, M.M., E. Custodio, R. Llamas, M.F. Fernández, J. García, and M.A. Ródenas. 2019. An academic analysis with recommendations for water management and planning at the basin scale: A review of water planning in the Segura River Basin. Science of the Total Environment 662: 755–768. https://doi.org/10.1016/j.scitotenv.2019.01.266

Barbero-Sierra, C., M.J. Marques and M. Ruíz-Pérez. 2013. The case of urban sprawl in Spain as an active and irreversible driving force for desertification. Journal of Arid Environments 90: 95–102. https://doi.org/10.1016/j.jaridenv.2012.10.014

Bermejo Pérez, D., F. Cáceres Clavero and J.M. Moreira Madueño. 2011. Medio siglo de cambios en la evolución de usos de suelo de Andalucía (1956–2007). Junta de Andalucía, Sevilla: 175 pp. Available at: http://www.juntadeandalucia.es/medioambiente/portal_web/servicios_generales/doc_tecnicos/2011/evolucion_usos_suelo/cambios_usos_suelo.pdf [Accessed 02/10/2020].

Buller, H., Wilson G.A. and A. Holl. 2017. Agri-environmental Policy in the European Union. London, Routledge. https://doi.org/10.4324/9781315204390

Calvo, F. and F. López-Bermúdez. 1992. El medio físico. pp. 344–424. In: J. Bosque and J. Vilà [eds.] Geografía de España. Vol. 10, Planeta, Barcelona.

Modelling Land Use and Land Cover Changes in the Mediterranean... **67**

Campos, P., Mesa B., Álvarez A., Castaño FM. and F. Pulido. 2017. Testing Extended Accounts in Scheduled Conservation of Open Woodlands with Permanent Livestock Grazing: Dehesa de la Luz Estate Case Study, Arroyo de la Luz, Spain. Environments 4, 82. https://doi.org/10.3390/environments4040082

Chuvieco, E., S. Martínez, MV. Román, S. Hantson and L. Pettinari. 2013. Integration of ecological and socio-economic factors to assess global vulnerability to wildfire. Glob Ecol Biogeogr. 23(2), 245-258. doi:10.1111/geb.12095

Clark, M.L., T.M. Aide, H.R. Grau and G. Riner. 2010. A scalable approach to mapping annual land cover at 250 m using MODIS time series data: A case study in the Dry Chaco ecoregion of South America. Remote Sensing of Environment 114(1), 2816–2832. https://doi.org/10.1016/j.rse.2010.07.001

Conway, T.M. 2009. The impact of class resolution in land use change models. Computers, Environment and Urban Systems 33: 269–277. https://doi.org/10.1016/j.compenvurbsys.2009.02.001

Cramér, H. 1946. Mathematical Methods of Statistics. Princeton University Press, Princeton, USA.

Custodio, E., J.M. Andreu-Rodes, R. Aragón, T. Estrela, J. Ferrer, J.L. García-Aróstegui, M. Manzano, L. Rodríguez-Hernández, A. Sahuquillo and A. del Villar. 2016. Groundwater intensive use and mining in south-eastern peninsular Spain: Hydrogeological, economic and social aspects. Science of the Total Environment 559: 302–316. https://doi.org/10.1016/j.scitotenv.2016.02.107

de Andrés, M., J.M. Barragán and J. García Sanabria. 2017. Relationships between coastal urbanization and ecosystems in Spain. Cities 68, 8–17. https://doi.org/10.1016/j.cities.2017.05.004

Diaz-Pacheco, J. and J. Gutiérrez. 2013. Exploring the limitations of CORINE Land Cover for monitoring urban land-use dynamics in metropolitan areas. Journal of Land Use Science 9(3), 1–17.

Eastman, J.R. 2012. IDRISI Selva. Guía para SIG y procesamiento de imágenes. Clark University, Worcester.

European Environmental Agency [EEA]. 2017. Land Cover 2012. Spain Country fact sheet. European Environment Agency, 18 pp. Available at: https://www.eea.europa.eu/themes/landuse/land-cover-country-fact-sheets [Accessed 02/10/2020].

Egea, P. and L. Pérez y Pérez. 2016. Sustainability and multifunctionality of protected designations of origin of olive oil in Spain. Land Use Policy 58, 264–275. https://doi.org/10.1016/j.landusepol.2016.07.017

Erjavec, K. and E. Erjavec. 2015. 'Greening the CAP' – Just a fashionable justification? A discourse analysis of the 2014–2020 CAP reform documents. Food Policy 51: 53–62. https://doi.org/10.1016/j.foodpol.2014.12.006

Esteban, E. and J. Albiac. 2012. The problem of sustainable groundwater management: The case of La Mancha aquifers, Spain. Hydrogeology Journal 20, 851–863. https://doi.org/10.1007/s10040-012-0853-3

Eurostat. 2017. Key European Statistics. Brussels. Available at: https://ec.europa.eu/eurostat/

Fader, M., S. Shi, W. von Bloh, A. Bondeau and W. Cramer. 2016. Mediterranean irrigation under climate change: More efficient irrigation needed to

68 *Modeling for Sustainable Management in Agriculture, Food and the Environment*

compensate for increases in irrigation water requirements. Hydrology and Earth System Sciences 20: 953–973. https://doi.org/10.5194/hess-20-953-2016

Farré-Ribes, M., C. Lozano-Cabedo and E. Aguilar-Criado. 2019. The role of knowledge in constructing the quality of olive oil in Spain. Sustainability 2019, 11(15), 4029. https://doi.org/10.3390/su11154029

Fernandez Ales, R., A. Martin, F. Ortega and E.E. Ales. 1992. Recent changes in landscape structure and function in a Mediterranean region of SW Spain (1950–1984). Landscape Ecology 7, 3–18. https://doi.org/10.1007/BF02573953

Fornés, J., J.A. Rodriguez, N. Hernández and M.R. Llamas. 2000. Possible solutions to avoid conflicts between water resources development and wetland conservation in the "La Mancha Húmeda" Biosphere Reserve (Spain). Phys. Chem. Earth (B), 25(7–8), 623–627. https://doi.org/10.1016/S1464-1909(00)00075-7

Fuchs, R., M. Herold, P.H. Verburg and J.G.P.W. Clevers. 2013. A high-resolution and harmonized model approach for reconstructing and analyzing historical land changes in Europe. Biogeosciences, 10, 1543–1559. https://doi.org/10.5194/bg-10-1543-2013

Gallardo, M. 2018. Revisión y análisis de estudios de modelos de cambios de usos del suelo y de escenarios a futuro. Geographicalia, 70, 1–26. https://doi.org/10.26754/ojs_geoph/geoph.2018703278.

García-Álvarez, D. and M.T. Camacho. 2017. Changes in the methodology used in the production of the Spanish CORINE: Uncertainty analysis of the new maps. Int. J. Appl. Earth Obs. Geoinformation 63, 55–67. http://dx.doi.org/10.1016/j.jag.2017.07.001

García-Ayllón, S. 2015. La Manga case study: Consequences from short-term urban planning in a tourism mass destiny of the Spanish Mediterranean coast. Cities 43, 141–151 https://doi.org/10.1016/j.cities.2014.12.001

García-Couto, M.A. 2011. Iberian climate atlas: air temperature and precipitation (1971–2000). AEMET-IM. Available at: https://www.aemet.es/documentos/es/conocermas/publicaciones/Atlas-climatologico/Atlas.pdf [Accessed 09/10/2020].

García-Ruiz, J.M., I. López-Moreno, S.M. Vicente-Serrano, T. Lasanta-Martínez and S. Beguería. 2011. Mediterranean water resources in a global change scenario. Earth-Science Reviews 105, 121–139. https://doi.org/10.1016/j.earscirev.2011.01.006

Garrido, J., P. Martínez-Santos and M.R. Llamas. 2006. Groundwater irrigation and its implications for water policy in semiarid countries: The Spanish experience. Hydrogeology Journal 14: 340–349.

Gil-Guirado, S. and A. Pérez-Morales. 2019. Variabilidad climática y patrones termopluviométricos en Murcia (1863–2017). Técnicas de análisis climático en un contexto de cambio global. Investigaciones Geográficas 71, 27–54. https://doi.org/10.14198/INGEO2019.71.02

Grau, R., T. Kuemmerle and L. Macchi. 2013. Beyond 'land sparing versus land sharing': Environmental heterogeneity, globalization and the balance between agricultural production and nature conservation. Current Opinion in Environmental Sustainability 5, 477–483. https://doi.org/10.1016/j.cosust.2013.06.001

Modelling Land Use and Land Cover Changes in the Mediterranean... 69

Grindlay, A.L., M. Zamorano, M.I. Rodríguez, E. Molero and M.A. Urrea. 2011. Implementation of the European Water Framework Directive: Integration of hydrological and regional planning at the Segura River Basin, southeast Spain. Land Use Policy 28, 242–256. https://doi.org/10.1016/j.landusepol.2010.06.005

Harmanny, K.S. and Ž. Malek. 2019. Adaptations in irrigated agriculture in the Mediterranean region: An overview and spatial analysis of implemented strategies. Reg. Environ. Change 19, 1401–1416. https://doi.org/10.1007/s10113-019-01494-8

Heimlich, R.E. and W.D. Anderson. 2001. Development at the urban fringe and beyond: Impacts on agriculture and rural land. Agricultural Economic Report Number 803. Available at: http://ageconsearch.umn.edu/record/33943

Hewitt, R., F. Pera and F. Escobar. 2016. Cambios recientes en la ocupación del suelo de los parques nacionales españoles y su entorno. Cuadernos Geográficos 55, 46–84. Available at: http://revistaseug.ugr.es/index.php/cuadgeo/article/view/3130

Ibor, C.S., M.G. Mollá, L.A. Reus and J.C. Genovés. 2011. Reaching the limits of water resources mobilization: Irrigation development in the Segura river basin, Spain. Water Alternatives 4(3), 259–278. Available at: http://hdl.handle.net/10251/60080

Iglesias, A., L. Garrote, A. Diz, J. Schlickenrieder and F. Martin-Carrasco. 2011. Re-thinking water policy priorities in the Mediterranean region in view of climate change. Environmental Science & Policy 14, 744–775. https://doi.org/10.1016/j.envsci.2011.02.007

Intergovernmental Panel on Climate Change [IPCC]. 2019. Climate Change and Land—IPCC Special Report on Climate Change, Desertification, Land Degradation, Sustainable Land Management, Food Security, and Greenhouse gas fluxes in Terrestrial Ecosystems. Geneva, IPCC Press Office. Available at: https://www.ipcc.ch/report/srccl [Accessed 27/10/2020].

Jakeman, A.J., O. Barreteau, R.J. Hunt, J.D. Rinaudo and A. Ross (Eds). 2016. Integrated Groundwater Management: Concepts, Approaches and Challenges. SpringerOpen. https://link.springer.com/book/10.1007/978-3-319-23576-9

Kochskämper, E., N. Schütze and A. Ballester. 2018. Stakeholder and citizen involvement for Water Framework Directive implementation in Spain. Three case studies from Andalusia, Cantabria and Catalonia. pp. 64–89. *In:* E. Kochskämper, E. Challies, N.W. Jager and J. Newig. [eds.]. Participation for Effective Environmental Governance: Evidence from European Water Framework Directive Implementation. Routledge, London.

Konukcu, F., S. Albut and B. Alturk. 2017. Land use/land cover change modelling of Ergene River Basin in western Turkey using CORINE land use/land cover data. Agronomy Research 15(2), 435–443. https://agronomy.emu.ee/wp-content/uploads/2017/03/Vol15nr2_Konukcu.pdf

Kuemmerle, T., C. Levers, K. Erb, S. Estel, M.R. Jespen, D. Müller, C. Plutzar, J. Stürck, P.J. Verkerk, P.H. Verburg and A. Reenberg. 2016. Hotspots of land use change in Europe. Environmental Research Letters 11, 064020. https://doi.org/10.1088/1748-9326/11/6/064020

Lasanta, T., J. Arnáez, N. Pascual, P. Ruiz-Flaño, M.P. Errea and N. Lana-Renault. 2017. Space-time process and drivers of land abandonment in Europe. Catena 149, 810–823. http://dx.doi.org/10.1016/j.catena.2016.02.024

Liu, X., L. Yu, W. Li, D. Peng, L. Zhong, L. Li, Q. Xin, H. Lu, C. Yu and P. Gong. 2018. Comparison of country-level cropland areas between ESA-CCI land cover maps and FAOSTAT data. International Journal of Remote Sensing 39(20), 6631–6645, Available at: https://doi.org/10.1080/01431161.2018.1465 613 [Accessed 02/07/2020].

Lopez-Gunn, E., P. Zorrilla, F. Prieto and M.R. Llamas. 2012. Lost in translation? Water efficiency in Spanish agriculture. Agric. Water Manag. 108, 83–95. https://doi.org/10.1016/j.agwat.2012.01.005

Maneas, M., E. Makopoulou, D. Bousbouras, H. Berg and S. Manzoni. 2019. Anthropogenic changes in a Mediterranean coastal wetland during the last century—The case of Gialova Lagoon, Messinia, Greece. Water 11, 350. https://doi.org/10.3390/w11020350

Martínez-Alvarez, V., M.J. González-Ortega, B. Martin-Gorriz, M. Soto-García and J.F. Maestre-Valero. 2017. The use of desalinated seawater for crop irrigation in the Segura River Basin (south-eastern Spain). Desalination 422, 153–164. https://doi.org/10.1016/j.desal.2017.08.022

Martínez-Granados, D., J.F. Maestre-Valero, J. Calatrava and V. Martínez-Alvarez. 2011. The economic impact of water evaporation losses from water reservoirs in the Segura Basin, SE Spain. Water Resour. Manage. 25, 3153–3175, https://doi.org/10.1007/s11269-011-9850-x

Malek, Ž., P.H. Verburg, I.R. Geijzendorffer, A. Bondeau and W. Cramer. 2018. Global change effects on land management in the Mediterranean region. Global Environmental Change 50, 238–254. https://doi.org/10.1016/j.gloenvcha.2018.04.007

Meier, J., F. Zabel and W. Mauser. 2018. A global approach to estimate irrigated areas – A comparison between different data and statistics. Hydrol. Earth Syst. Sci., 22, 1119–1133. https://doi.org/10.5194/hess-22-1119-2018

Melgarejo, J., A. Molina and M.I. López. 2014. El memorándum sobre el trasvase Tajo-Segura. Modelo de resolución de conflictos hídricos. Revista Aranzadi de Derecho Ambiental 29, 23–48.

Munroe, D., D.B van Berkel, P.H. Verburg and J.F. Olson. 2013. Alternative trajectories of land abandonment: Causes, consequences and research challenges. Current Opinion in Environmental Sustainability 5: 471–476. http://dx.doi.org/10.1016/j.cosust.2013.06.010

Navarro, L.M. and H.M. Pereira. 2012. Rewilding abandoned landscapes in Europe. Ecosystems 15, 900–912. https://doi.org/10.1007/s10021-012-9558-7

Observatorio de la Sostenibilidad en España [OSE]. 2006. Cambios de ocupación del suelo en España. Implicaciones para la sostenibilidad. Mundi-Prensa, 485 pp. Madrid.

Ortega, F. 1991. El medio físico. pp. 33–109. In: J. Bosque and J. Vilà [eds.], Geografía de España. Vol. 8, Planeta, Barcelona.

Oviedo, J.L., A. Caparrós and P.J. Moreno Rodriguez. 2017. The effect of monetary and non-monetary drivers on agricultural and forest land-use change in Andalusia using logit models. International Conference on Regional Science. 25 pp. Sevilla, Universidad Pablo de Olavide. 15–17 November.

Pérez-Hoyos, A. and F.J. García-Haro. 2013. Land cover assessment in the Iberian Peninsula. Revista de Teledetección 40, 22–40. http://www.aet.org.es/?q=revista40-3

Pflugmacher, D., A. Rabe, M. Peters and P. Hostert. 2019. Mapping pan-European land cover using Landsat spectral-temporal metrics and the European LUCAS survey. Remote Sensing of Environment 221, 583–595. https://doi.org/10.1016/j.rse.2018.12.001

Polo-Akpisso, A., K. Wala, O. Soulemane, F. Foléga, K. Akpagana and Y. Tano. 2019. Assessment of Habitat Change Processes within the Oti-Keran-Mandouri Network of Protected Areas in Togo (West Africa) from 1987 to 2013 Using Decision Tree Analysis. Sci 2019, 1, 9. https://doi.org/10.3390/sci1010009.v1

Pontius Jr, R.G., E. Shusas and M. McEachern. 2004. Detecting important categorical land changes while accounting for persistence. Agriculture, Ecosystems and Environment 101: 251–268. https://doi.org/10.1016/j.agee.2003.09.008

Puyravaud, J.P. 2003. Standardizing the calculation of the annual rate of deforestation. Forest Ecology and Management 177, 593–596.

Rabbinge, R. and H.C. Van Latesteijn. 1992. Long-term options for land use in the European Community. Agricultural Systems 40, 195–210. https://doi.org/10.1016/0308-521X(92)90021-F

Rae, C., K. Rothley and S. Dragicevic. 2007. Implications of error and uncertainty for an environmental planning scenario: A sensitivity analysis of GIS-based variables in a reserve design exercise. Landscape and Urban Planning 79, 210–217. https://doi.org/10.1016/j.landurbplan.2006.01.001

Rega, C., J. Helming and M.L. Paracchini. 2019. Environmentalism and localism in agricultural and land-use policies can maintain food production while supporting biodiversity. Findings from simulations of contrasting scenarios in the EU. Land Use Policy, 87 (September 2019), 103986. https://doi.org/10.1016/j.landusepol.2019.05.005

Renwick, A., T. Jansson, P.H. Verburg, C. Revoredo-Giha, W. Britz, A. Gocht and D. McCracken. 2013. Policy reform and agricultural land abandonment in the EU. Land Use Policy 30, 446–457. http://dx.doi.org/10.1016/j.landusepol.2012.04.005

Rey Benayas, J.M., A.M. Martins, J.M. Nicolau and J.J. Schulz. 2007. Abandonment of agricultural land: An overview of drivers and consequences. CAB Reviews: Perspectives in Agriculture, Veterinary Science, Nutrition and Natural Resources 2, No. 057. Available at: https://www.cabdirect.org/cabdirect/abstract/20073206799 [Accessed 27/10/2020].

Rindfuss, R.R., S.J. Walsh, B.L.I. Turner, J. Fox and V. Mishra. 2004. Developing a science of land change: Challenges and methodological issues. PNAS 101, 13976–13981. https://doi.org/10.1073/pnas.0401545101

Rodríguez Eraso, N., D. Armenteras-Pascual and J. Retana Alumbreros. 2013. Land use and land cover change in the Colombian Andes: dynamics and future scenarios. Journal of Land Use Science 8(2), 154–174. https://doi.org/10.1080/1747423X.2011.650228

Rodríguez-Rodríguez, D., J. Martínez-Vega and P. Echavarría. 2019. A twenty-year GIS-based assessment of environmental sustainability of land use changes in and around protected areas of a fast developing country: Spain. Int. J. Appl. Earth Obs. Geoinformation 74, 169–179. https://doi.org/10.1016/j.jag.2018.08.006

Romero, A., C. Martínez and F. Belmonte. 2012. Cambios de usos del suelo en la Región de Murcia. El almendro como cultivo de referencia y su relación con los procesos de erosión. Nimbus 29–30, 607–626. Available at: https://dialnet.unirioja.es/servlet/articulo?codigo=4378263 [Accessed 27/10/2020].

San-Miguel-Ayanz, J., E. Schulte, G. Schmuck, A. Camia, P. Strobl, G. Libertà, C. Giovando, R. Boca, F. Sedano, P. Kempeneers, D. McInerney, C. Withmore, S. Santos de Oliveira, M. Rodrigues, T. Durrant, P. Corti, F. Oehler, L. Vilar and G. Amatulli. 2012. Comprehensive monitoring of wildfires in Europe: The European Forest Fire Information System (EFFIS). pp. 87–105. *In*: John Tiefenbacher [ed.]. Approaches to Managing Disaster – Assessing Hazards, Emergencies and Disaster Impacts. InTech, London.

Sánchez-Picón, A., J.A. Aznar-Sánchez and J. García-Latorre. 2011. Economic cycles and environmental crisis in arid southeastern Spain: A historical perspective. Journal of Arid Environments 75, 1360–1367. https://doi.org/10.1016/j.jaridenv.2010.12.014

Science for Environment Policy 2017. Agri-environmental schemes: Impacts on the agricultural environment. Thematic Issue 57. Commission DG Environment by the Science Communication Unit, UWE, Bristol. Available at: https://ec.europa.eu/environment/integration/research/newsalert/pdf/AES_impacts_on_agricultural_environment_57si_en.pdf [Accessed 07/10/2020].

Sociedad Española de Ornitología/BirdLife-World Wildlife Fund España [SEO/BirdLife-WWF España]. 2010. ¿Quién contamina cobra? Relación entre la política agraria común y el medio ambiente en España, 32 pp. Available at: http://awsassets.wwf.es/downloads/informe_wwf_y_seo__relacion_pac_y_ medio_ambiente__quien_contamina_cobra.pdf

Sharaky, A.M., E.S.A. El Abd and E.F. Shanab. 2019. Groundwater assessment for agricultural irrigation in Toshka Area, Western Desert, Egypt. pp. 347–387. *In*: A.M. Negm [eds]. Conventional Water Resources and Agriculture in Egypt. The Handbook of Environmental Chemistry, vol 74. Springer, Cham. https://link.springer.com/content/pdf/10.1007%2F978-3-319-95065-5.pdf

Shen, Q., G. Gao, F. Han, F. Xiao, Y. Ma, S. Wang and B. Fu. 2018. Quantifying the effects of human activities and climate variability on vegetation cover change in a hyper-arid endorheic basin. Land Degradation & Development 29, 3294–3304. https://doi.org/10.1002/ldr.3085

Soille, P. and P. Vogt. 2009. Morphological segmentation of binary patterns. Pattern Recognit Letters 30(4), 456–459. https://doi.org/10.1016/j.patrec.2008.10.015

Spanish Government, 2019. Las masas de agua y las unidades hidrogeológicas. MITECO, Madrid. Available at: https://www.miteco.gob.es/es/agua/temas/estado-y-calidad-de-las-aguas/aguas-subterraneas/masas-agua/ [Accessed 09/10/2020].

Spanish Statistical Office [INE]. 2018. España en cifras (Spain in figures) 2018. 60 pp. Madrid. Available at: https://www.ine.es/prodyser/espa_cifras/2018/2/ [Accessed 11/10/2020].

Spanish Statistical Office [INE]. 2019a. Survey on the structure of agricultural holdings. Available at: http://www.ine.es/dyngs/INEbase/es/operacion.htm?c=Estadistica_C&cid=1254736176854&menu=ultiDatos&idp=1254735727106 [Accessed 11/10/2020].

Spanish Statistical Office [INE]. 2019b. INEbase, Employed in agriculture. Available at: https://www.ine.es/jaxiT3/Tabla.htm?t=3977&L=0 [Accessed 11/10/2020].

Modelling Land Use and Land Cover Changes in the Mediterranean... 73

Spanish Statistical Office [INE]. 2019c. Territorial statistics. Available at: http://www.ine.es/FichasWeb/ RegComunidades.do [Accessed 11/10/2020].

Swyngedouw, E. 2013. Into the Sea: Desalination as hydro-social fix in Spain. Annals of the Association of American Geographers 103(2): 261–270. https://doi.org/10.1080/00045608.2013.754688

Takatsuka, Y., M.R. Niekus, J. Harrington, S. Feng, D. Watkins, A. Mirchi, H. Nguyen and M.C. Sukop. 2018. Value of irrigation water usage in South Florida agriculture. Science of the Total Environment 626, 486–496. https://doi.org/10.1016/j.scitotenv.2017.12.240

Taffa Ariti, A., J. van Vliet and P.H. Verburg. 2015. Land-use and land-cover changes in the Central Rift Valley of Ethiopia: Assessment of perception and adaptation of stakeholders. Applied Geography 65, 28–37. http://dx.doi.org/10.1016/j.apgeog.2015.10.002

Thomson, A.M., E.C. Ellis, H.R. Grau, T. Kuemmerle, P. Meyfroidt, N. Ramankutty and G. Zeleke. 2019. Sustainable intensification in land systems: Trade-offs, scales and contexts. Current opinion in Environmental Sustainability 38, 37–43. https://doi.org/10.1016/j.cosust.2019.04.011

van den Berg, A.E., T. Hartig and H. Staats. 2007. Preference for nature in urbanized societies: Stress, restoration, and the pursuit of sustainability. Journal of Social Issues 63(1), 79–96.

van der Zanden, E.H., P.H. Verburg, C.J.E. Schulp and P.J. Verkerk. 2017. Trade-offs of European agricultural abandonment. Land Use Policy 62, 290–301. https://doi.org/10.1016/j.landusepol.2017.01.003

Van Vliet, J., H.L.F. de Groot, P. Rietveld and P.H. Verburg. 2015. Manifestations and underlying drivers of agricultural land use change in Europe. Landscape and Urban Planning 133, 24–36. http://dx.doi.org/10.1016/j.landurbplan.2014.09.001

Verburg, P.H., N. Crossman, E.C. Ellis, A. Heinimann, P. Hostert, O. Mertz, H. Nagendra, T. Sikor, K.H. Erb, N. Golubiewski, R. Grau, M. Grove, S. Konaté, P. Meyfroidt, D.C. Parker, R.R. Chowdhury, H. Shibata, A. Thomson and L. Zhen. 2015. Land system science and sustainable development of the earth system: A global land project perspective. Anthropocene 12: 29–41. http://dx.doi.org/10.1016/j.ancene.2015.09.004

Vidal-Macua, J.J., M. Ninyerola, A. Zabala, C. Domingo-Marimon, O. Gonzalez-Guerrero and X. Pons 2018. Environmental and socioeconomic factors of abandonment of rainfed and irrigated crops in northeast Spain. Applied Geography 90: 155–174. https://doi.org/10.1016/j.apgeog.2017.12.005

Viedma, O., N. Moity and J.M. Moreno. 2015. Changes in landscape fire-hazard during the second half of the 20th century: Agriculture abandonment and the changing role of driving factors. Agriculture, Ecosystems and Environment 207, 126–140. http://dx.doi.org/10.1016/j.agee.2015.04.011

Zorrilla-Miras, P., I. Palomo, E. Gómez-Baggethunc, B. Martín-López, P.L. Lomas and C. Montes. 2014. Effects of land-use change on wetland ecosystem services: A case study in the Doñana marshes (SW Spain). Landscape and Urban Planning 122, 160–174. https://doi.org/10.1016/j. landurbplan.2013.09.013

CHAPTER

4

Farmers' Perceptions Towards Social-economic Sustainability: A Case Study of the Karla Basin

Chatzipetrou Chrysafo-Anna[1]*, Christos T. Nakas[2] and George Vlontzos[3]

[1] Phd Candidate at the University of Thessaly, School of Agricultural Sciences, Department of Agriculture Crop Production and Rural Environment, Laboratory of Biometry, Fytokoy Str, 384 46 N. Ionia, Magnisia Volos, Greece

[2] Professor, Laboratory of Biometry, University of Thessaly, School of Agricultural Sciences, Department of Agriculture Crop Production and Rural Environment

[3] Assistant Professor, Laboratory of Agricultural Economics, University of Thessaly, School of Agricultural Sciences, Department of Agriculture Crop Production and Rural Environment

Introduction

The future of agriculture has always been a major concern for policy-makers in the European Union. Every European country consists of a minimum of 44% rural areas and farmers are at the heart of rural communities (European Commission 2016). Land management and food production are derived from a set of national and European priorities. Common Agricultural Policy (CAP) is the EU's key in ensuring food security, sustainable use of natural resources, social cohesion and citizens' prosperity (European Commission 2017b). Europe has become the larger global importer and exporter of agri-food for 2017 (European Commission 2018). Nevertheless, in many cases, anonymous sale and joined collection of products led farmers' perceptions and efforts unnoticed and unvalued (Luhmann and Theuvsen 2017).

---

*Corresponding author: cchatzipetrou@agr.uth.gr

Farmers' Perceptions Towards Social-economic Sustainability... **75**

As European objectives for the period 2014–2020 promote smart, sustainable and inclusive growth, the need to highlight local farmer perception and knowledge is more imperative than before (Eurostat 2017, Davis and Schirmer 1987). To achieve a sustainable change means to modify and embody change at first in even simple behavior (Davis and Schirmer 1987, Falconer 2000). In addition, agro-policies can profoundly affect regional social dynamics and migration patterns, provoking demographic change and even land conflicts (Padoch et al. 2014, Hecht et al. 2015, Bennett et al. 2018).

Sustainable economic development realizing the full potential of a region's resources and its local people could diminish the unemployment rates and abandonment, create wealth and improve the quality of life, all principal factors for regional development. This requires human skills, knowledge, attitudes, understanding, motivation, leaderships, plans, policies, organizations, funds, resources, physical inputs, collective actions, participation, and new technologies (Woods 1993, Kourlioros et al. 2014).

Sustainable agriculture is expected to satisfy human needs, such as food, fuels, raw materials, freshwater and fiber, to improve environmental quality, to establish a good management of ecosystem services, to preserve natural resources, to endure rural economy and to upgrade the quality of farmers' life and society as a whole (National Research Council 2010). In order to achieve sustainable agriculture, the discussion between the stakeholders and the active participation in decision processes are fundamental (Bitsch 2011).

In order to meet societal expectations and focus on the basis of CAP, if the government desires to develop a sustainable, socially responsible agriculture, it should attempt to reconnect agriculture and society, and overcoming difficulties, such as protests, controversies and conflicts, (deOlde 2019, Mazur-Wierzbicka 2015). The need of social sustainability is necessary to succeed sustainable development of farm management (Brodt et al. 2011). This includes a broader analysis of socio-cultural structure of rural communities, human and labor rights, social justice, health, welfare and fair treatment of all cultures (Bitsch 2010, Beltratti 2005, OECD 1999).

In this context, this chapter aims to record farmers' attitudes and livelihood aspects, in socio-economics and socio-cultural sustainability in the Karla basin in Central Greece. The drained Karla basin has been used for decades as arable land. Nowadays the government tries to reestablish the ecological balance of the area and promote environmental and social sustainability by constructing a reservoir and other technical works. Specifically, this chapter focuses on examining the components that affect agriculture and livestock of the studied area and whether the conditions for growth maximization could be met. In order to reflect the social reality and to reveal the casual mechanisms, it also provides a list of the economic

76 *Modeling for Sustainable Management in Agriculture, Food and the Environment*

and environmental values related to farmers' perceptions and beliefs towards the current and the future state of the area.

Regional Growth

Since, regional development can reduce local disparities by enforcing employment and economic activities and secure social cohesion and political stability, the interest in investments in human capital is renewed. Both elements can improve life quality, connectivity, secure inclusive growth, and promote regions convergence (Kourlioros et al. 2014, Papadopoulou 2014, Iammarino 2017, OECD 2012).

A well-designed regional development takes all region types, rural areas and respective metropoles as well into consideration, by improving their resilience and their national performance. This can be achieved by maintaining competitive advantages, reshaping solid, endurable and fairer regional economies and promoting effective and innovative multi-level governance.

Concerning to human capital, Schultz (1961, 1992) and Adam Smith (1776) noticed that the individuals who invest in education and training achieve a certain level of skills and knowledge, which can bring long-term returns, an advantage for national economies and a boost for economic growth (OECD 1998, 2001, 2007, Spalletti 2014). An improved human capital participates in decision making processes, ameliorates rural policies and management and contributes to possible rural problems solving (Davis et al. 2007). Investment in human capital, will define the future profits from labor markets activities (Mincer and Polachek 1974).

Investments in production, consumption and distribution, especially for smallholders, lead to increased productivity and improved food security (OECD 2007). As long as smallholder farmers cultivate their skills a sustainable intensification is attained, which builds equitable, productive and resilient ecosystems which in turn improve in total the living in rural areas and the rural environment itself. A healthy environment is linked to prosperity and wellbeing (Bennett et al. 2019), delivering socio-economic values through a stream of ecosystem services and an array of goods (Newcome et al. 2005). High quality food production and natural resources for future generations are secured while there is potential for more training and education, access to technologies and information that lead to innovation, increased income and sustainable agriculture (Agriculture for Impact 2013, Penda 2012).

Innovations in the primary sector, such as the adoption of new technologies and practices and the way of using or optimizing them in crop and soil management, in product types, in land use records or in fertilizers and water conservation, demand a skillful human capital (Cohen and Levinthal 1990, Gellynck et al. 2015, Lund Vinding 2006,

Farmers' Perceptions Towards Social-economic Sustainability... **77**

Micheels and Nolan 2016, van Rijn et al. 2012, Aguilar-Gallegos et al. 2015). These technological innovations and infrastructures, such as networks, applications, devices and services, can affect both the regional growth and sustainable development as well as the country's total economy (Kourlioros et al. 2014, FAO 2017). Improving access to valuable information and communication technologies rural population can make the best possible and effective decisions to increase their productivity and income and develop their region (FAO 2017). In addition, information technology in agriculture empowers small-farmers linkage with markets, provides new business opportunities, promotes e-governance, bridges the gap between scientific personnel and farmers and assists with implementing regulatory policies and monitoring progress (FAO 2017). In the future, the primary sector could be driven by information and not only by demand (Milovanović 2014). E-agriculture enhances agri-food systems sustainability while achieves food security by revealing its impacts and increasing efficiency and transparency of the system (Bilali and Allahyari 2018). ICTs contribute to agri-food logistics, stakeholders' relations and precision agriculture, can help decreasing the use of agricultural inputs, ensuring long-term profitability in parallel with land care, as well as reducing environmental externalities (Lehmann et al. 2012).

Sustainable Development of Wetland Protected Areas

Wetland protected areas are a valuable component of agroecosystems and have been consistently used in agriculture, providing an important number of ecosystem services to the socio-economic system. For many decades, wetlands have been considered as unfriendly landscapes without significant roles in the ecosystem and societal health, because of deep water, mud or floods and diseases (Siuta and Nedelciu 2016, Davidson 2014). All over the world lakes, swamps and marshes were drained for farming purposes and malaria eradication. Contrarily, the undrained wetlands were fragmented, salinized, affected by climate change, polluted with chemicals and excess nutrients and leading to biodiversity loss and loss of valuable ecosystem services. (EFT 1995, Siuta and Nedelciu 2016). This implies losses such as human well-being, good water quality and water cycle, habitats, carbon management (Russi et al. 2013, Dise 2009, Ramsar 2015c, Clarkson et al. 2013).

Intentional draining is the most serious unfavorable development often encountered in the effort to preserve wetlands (Harmanctoglu, Alpaslan, Boelee 2001). This land policy negatively affects the environment, the climate, the flora and fauna of the regions (Megevand et al. 2013). Drainage in combination with farmers' ignorance of the sustainable agriculture values in the past, contributed to land degradation. Beyond environmental benefits and nature conservation, the benefits of healthy ecosystems and their restoration also provide socio-economic advantages, such as active involvement of stakeholders to biodiversity conservation (Siuta and Nedelciu 2016).

The second half of the 20th century, in Greece, policy towards wetland protected areas included a period with mandatory land consolidation for all land properties within the Greek state, while from 1995 until the present the question of restoration has dominated (Sivignon 2007, Dodouras and Lyratzaki 2012).

Worldwide, ever since 1971, nations recognize the importance of protecting wetland areas and restoring some of them by promoting sustainable exploitation (Ramsar, Iran 1971, Ramsar, 2016). Aware of threats, abandonment and poor crop management practices, desiring to influence decision makers' attention, the Water Framework Directive (WFD) was formed in each EU country. To stimulate regional economic development the EU subsequently adopted the Biodiversity strategy in parallel with many funding programs. Besides nature protection, this strategy is intended to restore at least 15% of degraded ecosystems by 2020, through mapping and assessing the benefits of ecosystems services, restoring ecosystems and assessing the impact of EU funds on biodiversity (Siuta and Nedelciu 2016).

In order to foster sustainable development of wetland protected areas, main management activities required to be implemented, however, it is crucial to rightly integrate them into the land development plans at local and national level in a first step (Gattenlöhner et al. 2004). According to the World Lake Vision, a number of principles must be met. First of all, the harmony between humans and nature. In addition, decision-making and policy development should be based on every available information and on cooperation between scientists, local population and authorities. This process could be assisted and become more efficient both for farmers and policy makers if it also embodies information and communication technologies (ICT) (Milovanović 2014). The perceptions of locals or other stakeholders and their participation is decisive, while communication and spherical approach facilitate sustainability. At the same time, providing information to local and foreign people encourages their active involvement in the project and builds a transparent, fairer good governance. Managers must consider nature and human needs of present and future generations in order to improve the standards of living while increasing awareness on natural resources conservation, such as water quality, biodiversity and soil quality, and maintaining them with good practices. Furthermore, taking the ecologically valuable areas and the wetland protected areas' significance into account, an efficient administration is needed, which induces socio-economic development creating related activities, for example small scale recreational facilities.

Farmers' Perceptions Towards Social-economic Sustainability... **79**

Lastly, sustainable development educational programs, both for young and old people, should be a priority on a long-term basis in order to guarantee their success (Gattenlöhner et al. 2004).

The importance of information is particularly high for the European Union, where the member-states follow the guidelines of CAP. In order to make an evidence-based policy and right decisions in the European agricultural sector and related sectors the need for up-to-date availability of data and relevant information is essential (Milovanović 2014, European Commission 2015b). For example, the survey on the structure of agricultural holdings evaluates the agricultural situation across the EU and monitoring flows and transitions in holdings, and, by extension, in crop varieties, soil and water management or fertilizers (Eurostat 2010). In case of wetlands management, ICTs contribute to the creation of a centralized repository of geospatial data and meta-data, information and maps of national or global wetlands via geographic information technology and internet (Mathiyalagan et al. 2005). This allows an integration of different soil physical, chemical, biological, meteorological attributes with geologic, land cover and biodiversity data within specific regions boundaries; a comprehensive guide to each study area. ICTs could have an impact across all the environmental monitoring activities and provide such kind of information to the general population in nearly real time, facilitating public participation (Gouveia et al. 2004). All the above enhance the ability of decision-makers to deal with forthcoming environmental, socio-economic and technological challenges.

Background of Greece

During the financial crisis, Greece and other European countries, such as Bulgaria, Romania, Malta, Poland, Lithuania, ran the risk of poverty and social exclusion, severe material deprivation, low employment rates for men but mostly for women especially in rural areas.

Greece's main focal point is to deal with the economy's structural weaknesses that has been exacerbated by the crisis while its regional policy is aligned with the EU regional policy guidelines. Hence, the country participates in 7 sectoral and 13 regional operational European programs. The Greek rural policy derives from the EU Rural Development Program along with other national and EU sources and concerns a variety of rural regions, including islands (OECD 2019). However, the poor institutional quality of the country causes problems to economic development progress, increases lack of trust, corruption and social exclusion, and sets aside low-skilled jobs (Rodriguez Pose and Di Cataldo 2015, Iammarino 2017). An effective and qualitative local governance in Greek rural areas can boost productivity, employment, innovation, and entrepreneurship by reinforcing education and locals' participation (Iammarino 2017). Additionally, the government should be capable to enhance transparency and accountability, design better policies, and fight corruption in order to address territorial distress.

Nevertheless, a centralized country like Greece, with many subnational investments to economic affairs, such as transport, tourism, commercial and labour affairs, industry, agriculture and others like public services and environment protection, falls short of investments in education, healthcare and social welfare (OECD 2017). Unfortunately, due to the financial crisis during the last ten years, public investments in the country have declined significantly.

The agricultural and food sectors constitute important comparative advantages for the country, and it is essential to maintain them while achieving sustainable development. Therefore, the government aims at increasing cooperation and synergies of stakeholders, reducing socio-economic inequalities and enhancing farmers' participation in institutional processes (Hellenic Republic 2018).

In Greece, 43% of the population lives outside of the cities. The life satisfaction indicator is in bottom levels pursuant to the OECD regional database for regional well-being. In the country, the largest regional disparities in well-being outcomes are found with respect to safety, education, health, civic engagement, and community, while job outcomes of all Greek regions are in the bottom 20% of OECD regions (OECD 2018). As reported by the Hellenic Statistical Authority (2018) data, our study area, the region of Thessaly is the sixth largest region of primary sector in Greece. In 2013, 110.555 people got involved in the agricultural sector, but during the crisis in 2016 the number was reduced to 103.233 people. This decrease also led to a reduction of the Utilized Agricultural Area and the entry of a new generation into farming. This causes local farmers concerns about land abandonment, economic recession, social instability and an increase of elderly people in rural areas.

However, according to Eurostat data from 1980 until today, the number of Greek farm losses is one of the smallest among the EU-28, from 953.300 holdings to 685.000. This fact positions the country 5th among the 28 country states, showing the willingness and the persistence of inhabitants to hold onto land and property assets. Between 2003 and 2013, slightly more than 4 million holdings disappeared in the EU, while the total area used for agriculture remained almost stable. This means agricultural concentration increased, with the average area per holding growing by 38%, from 11.7 hectares in 2003 to 16.1 hectares in 2013 (Eurostat 2015). In Greece, over the same period, the utilized agricultural area increased by 22.4% and between 2013 and 2016 it decreased by 6.24%.

The majority of the country's holdings are small and medium sized farms with little capital, which are traditionally slow in adopting ICT

Farmers' Perceptions Towards Social-economic Sustainability... 81

at worldwide level, because of farmers' unfamiliarity with the available technologies or economic outcomes and risks from investing in a new technology (Lehmann et al. 2012, Bewley and Russell 2010). Nevertheless, in an attempt to increase knowledge and awareness and economies of scale in modern farming practices, the government supports a variety of projects, such as selling agricultural products over the internet, awareness raising, information and communication about wetlands restoration and rehabilitation, and digitization of agricultural sector (Michailidis 2010a, GETmap). The goal for rapid and sustainable development of Greek primary sector and farmers' participation in extension programs can be achieved, as the Greek ICTs environment gains ground day by day in the farming community.

The Case Study Area

Agriculture's multi-functionality provides productive reconstruction and redefines a region's development (Karanikolas 2011). Acknowledging the multi-functionality of rural areas and that human behavior affects ecosystem functioning, the former area of the Lake Karla basin was chosen as a case study area, because of its complex characteristics. A region that strives to satisfy organizational linkage among agriculture, livestock industries, and residents who want to benefit from the ecosystem goods and services. This area affected by soil salinity, yield limitations by water and intensive crop farming is an example of application of rural policy and achievement of sustainable agriculture. It is a former degraded wetland and nowadays a rural area consisting of mainly small farms, state-owned land, with a main 3.800 ha constructed reservoir that undergoes changes in productivity, species distribution and integrity of territorial or aquatic resources. The reservoir's construction and the wetland conservation purpose is to supply water, to reinforce and balance the underground aquifer, to reduce energy costs and to create ecological benefits for the area. At the same time, apart from these large-scale projects of water resources upgrade, environmental remediation works on the lowlands are also being implemented.

The Lake Karla Basin covers an area of 1.171 km^2 and is located in the south-east of the prefecture of Larissa and extended to the north of the prefecture of Magnesia, adjacent to Pelion and the Mavrovouni Mountains and it encloses about 50 villages (Fig. 1, 2). Historically, Lake Karla was completely drained in 1962 in order to address flooding problems, to eliminate malaria and to gain land for agriculture. For many generations before the drainage, the inhabitants of the lakeside area were exclusively fishermen, a characteristic that transformed the commerce of other regions of Thessaly, Fthiotis and Epirus, including exports. After the drainage, the Greek state compensated the fishermen and their families in

Figure 1. Location of the Karla basin study area in Thessaly, Greece.

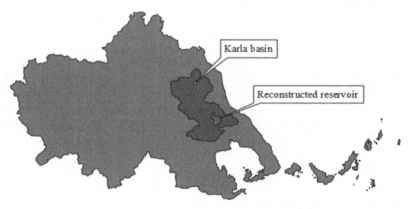

Figure 2. Location of Karla basin and reconstructed reservoir.

the surrounding villages, for losing their livelihood, promising and giving them farmland to survive.

The drainage of Karla watershed paid off with around 9.000 ha of agricultural land, without a specific regulation for land use. Today, the total cultivated area is estimated at 44.200 ha with basic crops consisting of cotton and cereals while agricultural water use accounts for 94, 3% of the total demand in the basin. Official data for the whole basin reported that 65, 1% of population is mainly professional farmers (Vasiliades et al. Project Hydromentor 2015).

Farmers' Perceptions Towards Social-economic Sustainability... **83**

The area has both advantages and constraints. The competitive advantage is the scenic site composed by dense woodland vegetation, pastures, streams, avifauna and culture elements, a reference point between two urban centers. Due to particular natural value and interest it has been integrated into the NATURA 2000 network as a Special Conservation Area with Code 1430007, for birds' breeding, feeding and nesting. Apart from the state weakness to implement strong policies, the limited innovative actions in the area also reduce its competitiveness. In order to preserve and increase its natural wealth while preserving farmers' interests, the adoption of sustainable practices is needed, characterized by innovation (Tornatzky and Klein 1982, Feder and Umali 1993, Wenjert 2002, Rogers 2003, Ghadim et al. 2005 in Lubell et al. 2011). Innovation is important for practices where the economic benefits to the farmer outweigh implementation costs.

Karla basin is suited for mild forms of development that are in harmony with nature and landscape protection and conservation, such as small rural eco-tourism businesses. As several farmers are deprived of the opportunity of choosing crops with a guaranteed production sale and high profits, it would be beneficial for them to involve in alternative activities.

Materials and Methods

The research objective aimed at investigating whether the conditions for growth maximization were met. In order to reflect the social reality and to reveal the causal mechanisms, elements and characteristics of the area were recorded, perceptions and beliefs of its inhabitants were collected.

This research builds on qualitative and quantitative data acquired throughout the project. Collecting, analyzing and mixing both qualitative and quantitative data provides a better understanding of research problems and corroboration (Bian 2012, Johnson et al. 2004, Morse 1991). The study consists of two main parts, the empirical one and the theoretical one. Data were collected from three sources: published documents and statistics, information from questionnaires and field observations. Data analysis was conducting using IBM SPSS 24.0 and land use records were conducting using QGIS 3.2 (IBM Corp., Armonk, NY, QGIS Development Team 2017).

An extensive literature review of economic, social, legal and agricultural documents and directives was conducted to better understand Greece's agricultural policy development and to describe the relevant factors and changes. The review is based also on previous and current Greek rural surveys, economic, social and rural indicators in Greece and Europe, case studies of countries around the world concerning agricultural sustainable management and social responsibility. Articles on farmers behavior and attitudes towards different rural cases, farmers' production schemes and reviews of social research complete the research project.

A structured questionnaire consisting of 22 questions was developed to capture information from farmers. Questionnaires were filled out from 7 June to 7 September 2017. Easy-to-answer questions were presented, semi-open ended and closed-ended, single or multiple-choice questions, 5-Likert scale questions and demographic questions. The questionnaire was distributed in person to men and women alike, aged 18 years and over, inhabitants of 27 communities in the wider area of the former Karla basin. There were three key sections and the main focus of the survey was to explore the components that affect agriculture and pasture of the area. The first one concerned farmers activities related to income, job satisfaction and future generation in farming according to a number of factors. Data for crops varieties and pasture species and subsidies were included. The second section of the survey covered the main topic of this research and it was studying the structure of rural communities, the state-citizen relations and place attachment. The third section was reflecting economic and environmental values of the area related to farmers' perceptions towards the current and the future state of the area. In this final section, was including also the assessment of the value of ICT use in their business and its importance for the future development of the Karla area. In addition, the questionnaire was designed by taking farmers' demographic information into account, such as personal characteristics (i.e. age, gender, education, family members) and area zone. Moreover, the participants checked statements about their communities and the region of the Karla basin, and they were able to comment on the objectives of the RDP 2014–2020. The RDP envisages upgrading of the Greek countryside and the transition of the Greek rural economy to a strong agri-food model. The sample was completely at random and consisted of 218 inhabitants, reflecting the farmers' opinions and attitudes. It was based on related researchs on rural sociology, environmental psychology, planned behavior and economic theories.

In this study, the integration of ICT contributed to the land use recording and interpretation of statistical results. A GIS software was used to produce a serie of vector and raster maps of the area, including variables such as local communities, major roads, water aquifer, crop varieties, soil type, parcels size and numbers. The data were collected by Copernicus land monitoring service and national authorities. To achieve a sustainable growth of rural areas, the agri-system could be controlled via these technologies by monitoring and guiding land use changes and by analysing ecosystem services, environmental policies and factors that shape citizens' prosperity (Cáceres et al. 2017).

Farmers' Perceptions Towards Social-economic Sustainability... 85

The following analysis is based on socio-economic and socio-cultural aspects that emerge in a rural community. The focus was on producing descriptive statistics and corellations, therefore different univariate, bivariate and multivariate analysis methods were performed to explore the relationship between farmers perceptions and region's socio-economic and environmental values. A principal components analysis was performed, which assumes factors to be correlated with each another (Jennrich and Sampson 1966). The sample adequacy and the suitability of the data for factor analysis were examined with the Kaiser-Meyer-Olkin (KMO) coefficient, while the reliability of the data is based on the Cronbach alpha indicator. Reliability analysis was performed to get an overall index of the internal consistency of the scale as a whole and to identify excluded items from the scale.

The purpose of the survey is not for the data to converge on a set of facts or findings but to obtain a comprehensive understanding of general attitudes (Bryman 2004). In addition, questionnaires revealed a relatively consistent set of responses regardless of the region, reflecting the national rural policies and the social and structural similarities among the communities (Forbord et al. 2014).

Natural ecosystems perform fundamental services for life-support and social welfare. These services are linked to a set of human beneficiares and their actions on nature (Newcome et al. 2005). Values of ecosystem services point people's environmental attitude and behaviour, defining the ecological perspectives for society (Newcome et al. 2005, Corraliza and Berenguer 2000). Many people lack knowledge that can benefit from ecosystem services (Fraj and Martinez 2006). Thus, those who mainly are dependent on agricultural sector, need to be aware of the value of ecosystem services, as humans activities have threaten the natural landscape by overharvesting the renewable resources. The loss of services from natural ecosystems, due to environmental externalities, will require costly alternatives. Instead, to keep a balance between the natural system and humans, responsible use and conservation of natural resources and complete implementation of existing regulation for nature are needed (Newcome et al. 2005). In addition, political will for clear environmental policy decisions and changed attitude through information and knowledge about ecosystem fuctions contribute to a sustainable ecosystem (Newcome et al. 2005, Tadaki et al. 2017). In this sense, this research study includes a set of main environmental values presented in Table 1.

Results

In the Karla basin area, long-term inappropriate land use, intensive farming and complex cultivation patterns result in permanent soil

86 *Modeling for Sustainable Management in Agriculture, Food and the Environment*

Table 1. Main environmental values of the research study

Food security
High quality food production
Equal distribution of natural resources
Water purification
Sustainable use of natural resources/ preserve natural resources
Citizen's prosperity
Satisfaction by farming activities
Increase environmental responsibility
Active involvement in social activities
Social, cultural and recreational facilities
Health and safety
Preserve, protect and promote the historical treasure
Education and training
Digital connectivity
Social economy innovation

degradation, low groundwater levels, productivity loss and rural-urban population changes. Therefore, agricultural sustainability has become a major concern for the area, and project designers should recognize that this sustainable change requires collective initiative and responsibility at community level (Woods 1993, Gong 2016).

Before the survey, geoscience data were obtained from public sources for both prefectures Larissa and Magnesia, in order to have an overall view of land use changes of the study area. The knowledge about evolution of the Karla basin, in an environmental, historical and social context, contributes to a fairer sustainable land use. These three figures show the land cover of Karla basin after drainage in 1990, after restoration of Karla's reservoirs in 2012, and area's crop varieties and pastures in 2015 (Figs. 3, 4).

Quantitative Results

To understand the key characteristics of the participants, socio-demographic characteristics are presented in Table 2. Out of 218 participants, 41.3% graduated from high school, and 15.6% had completed their studies or were still studying at a higher education institution at the time of the survey. The 93.6% were farmers that face a number of problems and constraints every day, but the majority of them are in favor of employment. This indicates that they are satisfied with their farming activities in a sense that they like their profession. The 31.7% declared

Farmers' Perceptions Towards Social-economic Sustainability... 87

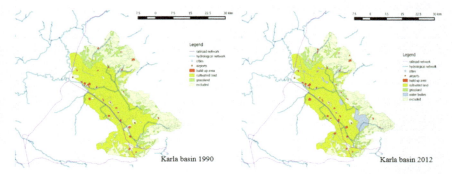

Figure 3. Karla basin after drainage in 1990 & after reservoirs' construction in 2012.

Figure 4. Crop varieties and pastures in Karla basin in 2015.

satisfied with their job, 13.3% as very satisfied and 41.3% as neutral (Fig. 5). However, it is important to make a further research in order to understand better the factors that influence farmers' satisfaction. Considering that could be an effective way of resolving problems of human behaviors in rural areas while improving lowlands and water projects performance.

During the survey, participants were asked to describe their social relationships status with the local authority, the Ministry of Rural Development and Food and the Management operator of the area

88 *Modeling for Sustainable Management in Agriculture, Food and the Environment*

Table 2. Socio-demographic characteristics of participants in the Karla basin area/ (Source: own data)

Characteristic	Mean (Std.deviation)	% of respondents (n = 218)
Gender:	1.93 (0.261)	
1 = Female	-	7.3
2 = Male	-	92.7
Age at the time of survey (years):	3.26 (0.966)	
1 = 18 – 24	-	0.5
2 = 25 – 39	-	23.4
3 = 40 – 54	-	37.2
4 = 55 – 65	-	27.1
5 = 66 <	-	11.9
Highest education level completed:	2.93 (1.195)	
1 = Primary school	-	12.4
2 = Secondary school	-	22
3 = High school	-	41.3
4 = Technical college	-	8.7
5 = University	-	15.6
Household size (persons):	1.57 (0.539)	
1 = 1 – 3	-	44.5
2 = 4 – 6	-	53.2
3 = 7<	-	2.3
Activity:	1.41 (0.876)	
1 = Agriculturist	-	78.4
2 = Pastoralist	-	8.3
3 = Both	-	6.9
4 = Other activity	-	6.4
Agriculture as a main activity:	1.19 (0.395)	
1 = Yes	-	80.7
2 = No	-	19.3

Karla-Mavrovouni-Velestino-Kefalovryso-Pinios estuary. This includes a relative level of respect, equal distribution of resources, hearing the participants' perspectives, two-way communication and information. In general, the results showed that the participants had a fair or good relationship with the local authority, rates of 33.9% and 47.2% respectively, while the relationship with the Ministry was quite different, as 40 persons had any relationship with the government and other 97 had a very poor or poor relationship. Furthermore, 38.5% of participants declared to have no relationship with the Management operator of the area compared to a 20.2% who claimed to have a good such relationship (Fig. 6).

Unaware of local authority's and management operator's possible problems and due to lack of information and communication, the

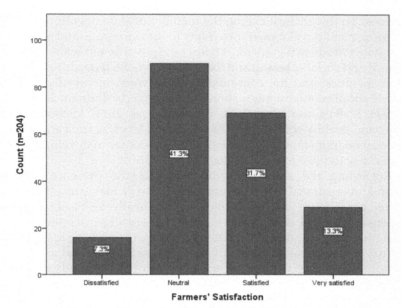

Figure 5. Farmers' satisfaction by their profession.

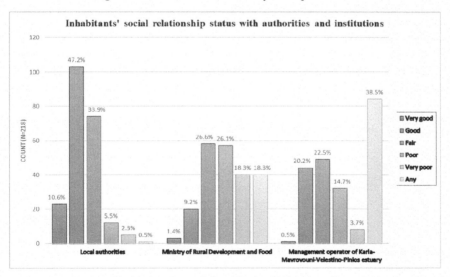

Figure 6. Inhabitants' relationship with local authorities.

inhabitants are not able to sufficiently understand the institutions roles, nor have they fully accepted the protection status of the area. However, a good relationship is useful and crucial to achieve the objective of nature protection and conservation, while improves in general the citizen-state relations. To the greatest extent, the inability of state operators to design and implement development programs for area upgrade and support the inhabitants needs was evident. Whether the government wants to achieve political and social cohesion and local development, it needs to strengthen the cooperation and the communication between involved parties and include social economy innovation into its projects (Putnam 2000; Xavier G. 2008, Halkos and Jones 2011, Proikaki et al. 2014, Alexiou 2014). A strong and healthy social capital requires high levels of trust and vigorous two-way relationships between individuals in order to develop collective beneficial activities (Jones et al. 2009).

Regarding the community lifestyle and the presence of social, cultural, recreational/sport structures in the wider area, the results showed a minimum level of satisfaction. Specifically, 69.7% of participants described the level of social structures as very unsatisfactory, such as social pharmacy, canteens, and seed exchanges. Concerning to the cultural structures, municipal theaters, spiritual centers and cultural associations, the individuals rated them as not at all satisfactory and slightly satisfactory with 35.8% and 27.1% respectively. For recreational and sports structures, such as amusement park, municipal stadiums, observatories and other environmental education sites, the rate of unsatisfied respondents was 40.4% while 6.4% declared the athletic structures as very satisfactory (Fig. 7). For the cultural and recreational development of the region, a certain number of them commented that there is a clear need to exploit and improve the abandoned tourist areas and manage properly the sports facilities. These factors are an important infrastructure capital and a prerequisite for the organization and execution of cultural, social events

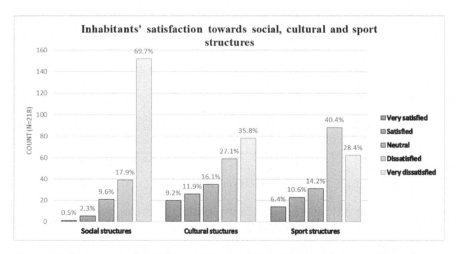

Figure 7. Community lifestyle: participant satisfaction towards social structures.

and activities, as well as for the creation of mass sports poles and economic local development. Consequently, a positive correlation emerged between the above three types of structures and the variable of infrastructure and economic development (Fig. 8).

Nevertheless, on the question of if this way of lifestyle could be better if the participants could change community? The 68.3% of the sample responded negatively implied that, among rural communities, similar situations occur when these belong to the same municipality (Fig. 9). This place attachment could increase environmental responsibility and region sustainable growth. When people support their community, then the community responds greater and more precisely to their needs and improves their quality of life (Williams and Vaske 2003, Lee 2013).

As a result of the lack of social structures, the participants evaluated in 5-Likert scale that their communities have very limited social life. Specifically, more than 55.5% disagreed with this statement, while only 16.5% agreed (Fig. 10). During the financial crisis, low incomes, seasonality of work and reduced state and local economic resources could represent risk of community wealth and social exclusion (European Commission, 2008).

Regarding the political power of the communities in the wider area, the rate of respondents was neutral 40.4% and almost 39% disagreed (Fig. 11). As they stated a lot of communities belong to the same municipality

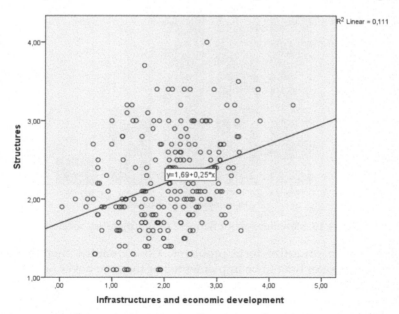

Figure 8. Social structures – Infrastructure capital and economic.

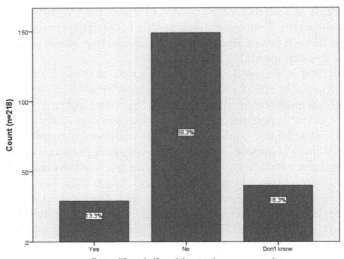

Figure 9. Place attachment to community. development correlation graph.

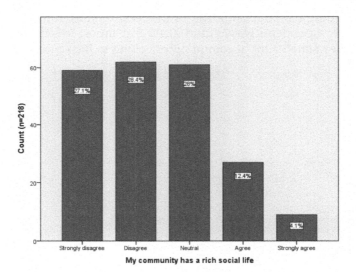

Figure 10. Statement about richness of communities social life.

which fails to prioritize local problems. Consequently, their demands either take a lot of time to be implemented or they are never heard.

However, apart from the political power and the lack of social life, the participants' beliefs towards the preservation of communities' authenticity are positive. A rate of 68.9% of the respondents agreed that despite external influences, such as migration, incorporation of new ideologies,

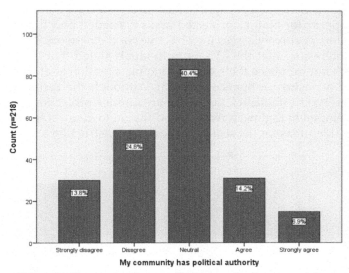

Figure 11. Statement about political power of communities.

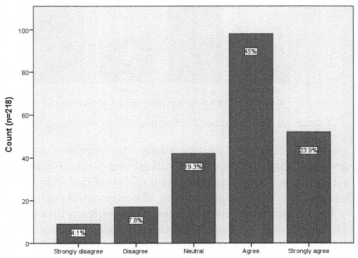

Figure 12. Statement about authenticity of communities.

centralization due to unemployment or shifts of consumers' demands and trends, their communities are able to maintain their authenticity (Fig. 12). This implies that individuals are able to recognize the rich cultural and environmental treasure of their community.

To implement the principle of sustainable development in the Karla basin support for Natura protected areas is needed and the majority of participants positively assess the objectives of the network. Nevertheless, it was interesting that the 45% of individuals stated that the protected-area does not influence their socio-economic situation at all, while 41.7% declared a positive influence (Fig. 13). Although the reconstruction of Karla reservoir establishes the wider area under protection control and eco-development regime, it remains indifferent to many of its inhabitants, creating dilemmas for the real purposes of reconstruction.

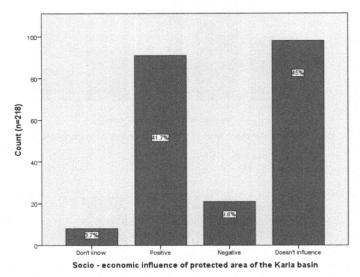

Figure 13. Socio-economic influence of Karla's restoration.

To meet the objectives of sustainable development in the region, participants were asked to assess in 7-Likert and 5-Likert scale 10 specific issues in the area and their importance for its future development. Among these issues, the use of ICTs was involved. The majority of participants had a moderate knowledge about information technologies, although they were aware of Internet and smart mobiles technology despite their age. The ICT use stated as fair or poor with 24.8% and 23.9% rate respectively, while with 18.8% and 13.3% as good and very good. The digital connectivity with other sectors of society was considered as fundamental factor for the future development of the Karla basin area. Responders notably underline the importance of these technologies and their improvement for a sustainable future growth. The rates for important and very important responses were 65.1% and 30.7% respectively (Figs. 14, 15).

Reliability analysis for 22 items of the survey was used to determine the extent to which these questions all reliably measure the same latent

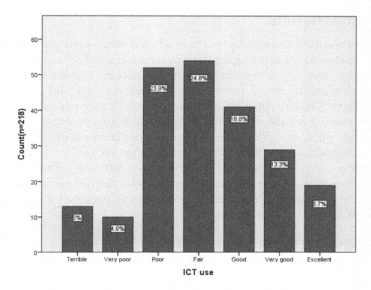

Figure 14. Participants familiarization with ICT use.

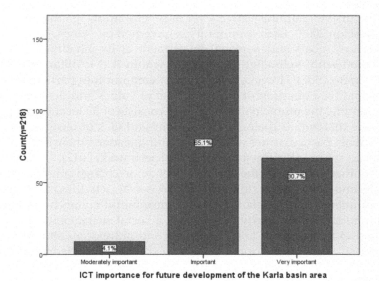

Figure 15. ICT importance for future development of the area.

variable. The value of Cronbach's alpha (a) reliability coefficient was found to be equal to 0.758, thus indicating a reliable result. A reliability coefficient of .70 or higher is considered "acceptable" in most surveys with social background.

Qualitative Results

With open-ended comments and remarks on structured questionnaires, participants were asked to give their perceptions on the closed questions or identify new issues not captured in the survey. It allows individuals to reveal more than the records, to express feelings and experiences, describing what they consider most important. This empty field at the end of the survey gave the opportunity to researcher to compare the reports with other published literature and go further his projects. It could also increase response rates (O'Cathain and Thomas 2004).

In this study 174 out of 218 participants left few comments in the survey, mostly expressing their concerns about the future of agricultural sector and highlighting the farmers' necessity to become better informed and approached by state agencies.

Rural Community and Place Attachment

The majority of the inhabitants declared that they do not desire to change community but certain of them would like to belong to another municipality. This is due to the socio-economic profile of each local community, the heterogeneous characteristics of the communities within a municipality and the uneven administrative level of several municipalities (European Commission 2008). Each community is governed by values, morals, rules, preferences, goals and personal investment of its inhabitants and it is concerned with well-being of all them within it (McMillan and Chavis 1986, Pareto 1907). However, when many communities participate in one municipality, a question of a common set of values and demands arises. For example, the municipality of Kileler consists of 35 local communities. An issue that entails dialogue disruptions and lack of recognition of the individuals particularities and values, and questions their integration in the social system (Kostopoulos 1988, Wojciechowski 2012).

Another issue was the need for behavior change among the local people and their active involvement in social activities, as there is a lack of interest and a relative lack of meaningful connectivity between them and their community. To succeed a social sustainability, a change of mindset is necessary. Local authority and individuals should face the current situation as an opportunity to exchange knowledge and ideas, to learn how to be useful, to create, to experience the positive impact of cooperation, to strengthen bonds, to stimulate interest, and to become active partners. To build a solid, healthy community upon relations of networking increases the trust levels and life quality (Tsobanoglou 2008, Roustang 1987, Wilkinson and Pickett 2009). Besides, a community is characterized by production, distribution and consumption, socialization, social control, social participation and mutual assistance (Stathopoulos 2000).

Social Welfare

Public participation is a principal factor of a healthy society and a main parameter in rural degraded areas (Aitken 2001). Engaging rural population in creative activities can improve the regional development and helps reduce the proportion of people with problem behaviors and safeguards them from risks. This could be achieved by changing attitudes through education, training, social dialogue and new policies. In addition, in many European countries the population is ageing rapidly and provision of care to the elderly and the children is becoming a major issue for governments, as medical infrastructure and staff remain often unavailable in rural communities (Crooks et al. 2011, Robinson et al. 2009, European Commission 2008). The participants' comments also revealed the need to reduce loneliness and help a number of inhabitants to stay attached in their natural and social environment, including raise awareness and implement state programs to support vulnerable groups. When young people are absent, elder people tend to stay at home and may gradually become dependent on others (Triandafyllou and Mestheneos 2001, Eurofamcare 2005 in Delatola-Paganeli 2006).

Government should improve the quality of life of all residents, in particular those in remote or minority communities, given the respect for human dignity, the principle of equal treatment and promotion of social cohesion. Starting with social and health care, maintenance and continuing education, experience and training of welfare staff, the social welfare in rural areas can be improved significantly.

Information and Public Participation

The majority of participants expressed their desire to participate in educational seminars and workshops along with the need for more information from the Ministry of Rural Development and food, agronomists and scientific staff. Even today, many farmers declare that they are informed by other farmers, friends and acquaintances which are not always a valid source, but in some cases it is their only solution. Inhabitants of rural areas demand education and training, they need technical support in all production stages, information about new technologies, taxation, potential new investments and good green practices. Collaboration between them and the scientific staff is needed in order to develop their inventiveness, produce high quality products and specifications that will bring them recognition and the desired income. However, the lack of a help/info desk or specialists in their rural communities may complicate their farming activities but social interactions among them could allow to identify and weigh options and to re-examine their actions (Acosta-Michlik and Rounsevell 2005). In parallel, these interdependences among farmers themselves create new ways of thinking and doing and reinforce their desire for more education and knowledge, while also contribute to the decision-making processes and innovation adoption (Bromley 2008, Del Corso et al. 2015). By establishing local partnerships, local communities could attract attention, promote and protect their collective interests and actions, even incorporate new social responsibilities (Tsobanoglou 2008, Bromley 2008, Wilkinson and Pickett 2009, Del Corso et al. 2015). However, some farmers were negative about cooperating with the University at a research level.

Extreme cases were identified concerning the participants' familiarization with information and communication technologies. In other words, in the area there were inhabitants with expertise in precision agriculture, mobile applications which control irrigation systems, online information and intensive use of e-mails. Nevertheless, there were people with no digital competence and knowledge, except from dial-phone and television. However, the majority expressed the need for farmers' involvement in applied research and more training on technologies, because, often, too much information is provided without knowing what to do with it (Bewley and Russell 2010).

Considering all the comments and remarks, effort is a crucial parameter for rational management and integrated development of rural space in social and cyclical conditions. But firstly, concrete political, social, economic and technological barriers must be eliminated and necessary structures for business development must be created. Moving to a circular economy involves focus shift to reusing, repairing, renewing and recycling existing materials and products while maintaining resources at the highest value level, and it requires the involvement and commitment of many different groups of people (European Commission 2015).

Public participation and voicing views is a way of getting involved in decision-making processes and ensures effective implementation of the adopted or future measures (Jentoft 2005). Stimulating circular economy requires extensive political support at European, national, regional and local level and it is dependent on broader support for society (European Commission 2015).

However, as local population stated, there is a lack of active participation in the decisions. Farmers' involvement in specialized problem-solving and collective decision-making and actions are very important (van de Fliert 2002, 2010). Collective decision-making on social issues carries with it a number of variables that are inextricably linked, such as political, economic, ethical, scientific and ideological values (Wolfle 1980, Gaskell 1982, Thelen 1983 in Aikenhead 1985). Adopting a system of community participation enhances the social capital that affects positively the regional development, community income, natural capital and value chains (Cheong 2004, Isham 2000, Islam and Dickson 2007, WorldFish Center 2007). Social capital is productive and accomplishes goals that would not be achieved in its absence (Feldman et al. 1999, Adam and Borut 2003, Sabatini 2005). The absence of social participation is associated with low levels of empowerment, social influence, and a reduced sense of belonging (Glaser et al. 2000 in Christoforou 2004, Putnam 2000, Iatridis 1990). The population adopts a passive attitude in the decision-making process and its participation is recognized as pseudo-participation as residents receive information and decisions made by members of official leadership (Kerschner 1976 and Christofilopoulos 1987 in Stathopoulos, 2001).

Cultural Site

Several inhabitants highlighted the existing untapped cultural environment. They noted that measures should be taken to preserve, protect and promote the site's historical treasure and physiognomy as important resources for social and social development.

Promotion of historical monuments value and sites of cultural reference are set as factors that shape the historical occurrence of each region. In this context, the role of each citizen is to be more active of knowing the historical environment through participation in scientific meetings, bibliography or oral information. In addition, the European Union's recognition of culture importance as a resource for development and promotion of new forms of business and employment plays a significant role, as the concern for culture is of great economic importance and tourist benefits.

It was also stated that cultural development in Karla basin clearly demonstrates the need to utilize and improve abandoned tourist sites and sports facilities. They are an important infrastructure capital and a prerequisite for organization and execution of cultural, social events and activities and creation of mass poles.

Development of an alternative form of tourism to protect the environment, such as ecotourism in mountainous or lowland areas, reinforces the local community (Dologlou 2008). However, the overall development of tourism, cultural, sporting and leisure activities contributes to community bonds by creating social networks. This way, the government prevents isolation, increases youth employment, helps maintain physical and mental health, creates positive social behaviors, values, skills and abilities of individuals (EU 2014), and offers of recognition to the work of farmers (Froissart and Terret 2014).

Discussion

This research was conducted in the area of Karla basin, in the region of Thessaly, in central Greece and was an attempt to objectively record events, attitudes, perceptions and livelihood aspects of farmers in environmental, economic and socio-cultural issues. These elements improve outcomes, both for environmental conservation and farmers' satisfaction, and help to understand better the structure of agricultural society.

The data analysis and the comments of this survey showed that during the financial crisis the agricultural sector experienced a lot of difficulties but through these years it endeavors to preserve its weight. Apart from environmental and economic problems, farmers confront the risk of social exclusion, lack of accessibility to services and activities, increase of elderly population, land abandonment, and lack of information. Residents' lack of high expectations for settlement of current problems in the area and their pessimist perceptions have negative results in development initiatives and wetland utilization.

Karla basin as an agricultural and protected area has both advantages and constraints. For its management local and state authorities are involved as well as other environmental operators. This composition of agencies complicates the decision-making process and rarely takes farmers opinions into account who ask for more information and favorable policy-making. The inability of government agencies to adequately inform the local population, implement actions, educational programs and workshops and support the broader common interest, creates loose relationships with the region's inhabitants. In addition, because of lack of communication between the stakeholders, several participants in our survey questioned the real reason for Lake Karla reconstruction, as they have not noticed any socio-economic influence in their households.

In general, farmers were satisfied by their job, an important parameter for agriculture conservation, but they were dissatisfied with social actions, which are a remarkable factor for the normalization of economic and social life and the standard of living in the Karla basin area. However, they were fully place attached with their community and in some cases, demanded a municipality change. Building of rural partnerships, preservation and upgrade of the aesthetic and historical landscape, mild development of tourism and improvement of infrastructure capital would contribute positively to the area and the life quality of the inhabitants. Development of local partnerships and public participation of social capital make farmers effective and better managers of their business (Jentoft 2005, Pateman 1970, Simon 1972). Through collective action farmers can reconsider their decisions and options (Bromley 2008). Additionally, community empowerment in combination with information, active participation and organization will contribute to sustainable development of the area and to a two-way citizen-state relationship.

In Greek primary sector, the penetration rate of ICTs remains at low levels. Nevertheless, the majority of farmers were realizing the importance of new technologies in sustainable agriculture, but a few traditional farmers seemed unwilling to be trained in technological systems. The new

ICTs have a positive impact in farmers' life quality, but usually include non-viable costs for individual farmers and could create technological dependence (Gkisakis 2017). ICT is not a panacea, it is a decision support tool that reinforces the decision-makers without restricts their options.

Current environmental governance consists of decision-making structures and processes that foster engagement between governments, private sector and civil society, consisting of scientists, non-governmental organizations, institutions or other social groups (Lemos and Agrawal 2006). However, decisions affecting wetland protected areas are often made without adequate knowledge of farmers' attitudes and practices towards wetlands and their resources (Stevens et al. 1995 in Pyrovetsi and Daoutopoulos 1997). Every region differs and decision-makers must consider the characteristics of the areas, recognize and protect the land tenure and respect farmers' rights, while establishing agreements for local communities and local ownerships (Bennett et al. 2019). It's important to know, who will make the decisions and how they will be implemented; how individuals and regions will benefit or be damaged; and finally, who will take the responsibility for the outcome of these decisions.

The agricultural sector as economic activity produces both of ecosystem services and agricultural disservices that affect negatively or positively other sectors of economy and human activity (Zhang et al. 2007). These services or disservices depend on the technological and institutional environment of agriculture and on connectivity with society (Raggos and Psychoudakis 2006).

A revitalized rural economy provides economic equality, generates sufficient local benefits due to farmers' involvement, creates positive social and cultural impacts and holds local populations in their areas. Therefore, clear policies, guidelines, regulations, good governance and comprehensive legislations are needed in order to achieve strong corporate activities and sustainable rural development. Implementing innovation policies could be the key for broadening the creativity and satisfaction of both decision-makers and recipients, and for encouraging investments in agricultural sector (Iammarino 2017). Furthermore, equitable access of all farmers to markets and value chains promotes more well-functioning markets that facilitate trade and are vital for rural development, poverty reduction and social cohesion (OECD 2011).

Redefinition and modernization of the area as multifunctional with full involvement of its population requires sound management and effective policy making. Even now farmers' opinions and their participation in forming agricultural policies remain underutilized and insufficiently examined. To achieve integrated growth and sustainable competitiveness of the agricultural sector, economic, environmental, and social factors must be taken into account (Lolos 2009).

102 *Modeling for Sustainable Management in Agriculture, Food and the Environment*

The last three decades were characterized by dynamic social, economic change and territorial inequality throughout the European Countries (Bański 2011, Iammarino 2017). However, EU year by year attempts to neutralize the heterogeneities via the CAP. The basic principles of the CAP 2014–2020 are sustainable management of natural resources and food production, promotion of innovation through continuing education and knowledge, increased employment, extraversion of the primary sector and social cohesion (European Commission 2017). Moreover, the European Union, through the Community initiatives LEADER I, LEADER II, LEADER + and the LEADER / CLLD Approach has been working since 1991 to provide an active role in rural areas for further future development and support of the local community, contributing to improving the quality of life of residents through Local Action Groups (LAGs) (European Commission 2006).

A few studies have specifically explored the consequences of land policy on areas which originally were hydrologic basins. This study can be helpful in minimizing the research gap and adding valuable information on the existing notions while the findings will be used to design improved intervention strategies and to reform policies. However, we still have to wait for the project "wetland restoration" to be fully operational in order to get the first results of the re-evaluation of the former Lake Karla basin. Achievement of environmental, technological and socio-economic sustainability of the rural area is a long-term process with many challenges (Hediger et al. 1998, National Research Council 2010).

References

Acosta-Michlik, L. and M. Rounsevell. 2005. From generic indices to adaptive agents: Shifting foci in assessing vulnerability to the combined impacts of globalization and climate change. IHDP Update 1, 14–16.

Adam, F., and R. Borut. 2003. Social Capital: Recent debates and research trends. Social Science Information 42(2), 155–183.

Aguilar-Gallegos, N., M. Muñoz-Rodríguez, H. Santoyo-Cortés, J. Aguilar-Ávila and L. Klerkx. 2015. Information networks that generate economic value: A study on clusters of adopters of new or improved technologies and practices among oil palm growers in Mexico. Agric. Syst. 135, 122–132.

Aikenhead, G.S. 1985. Collective decision making in the social context of science. Science Education 64, 453–475.

Aitken, L. 2001. Social and Community Dimension of Natural Resource Management: A Review of Issues and Related Research. The State of Queensland, Department of Natural Resources and Mines, Brisbane.

Agriculture for Impact. 2013. Sustainable Intensification: A New Paradigm for African Agriculture. A Montpellier Panel Report, London.

Alexiou, Th. 2008. Social Policy, Excluded Groups and Class Action. Published by Papazisis, Athens, pp. 274-277 (in Greek).

Bański, J. 2011. Changes in agricultural land ownership in Poland in the period of the market economy. Agric. Econ. – Czech. 57, 93–101.

Beltratti, A. 2005. The complementarity between corporate governance and corporate social responsibility. Geneva Papers on Risk & Insurance: Issues & Practic. 30, 373–386.

Bennett, A., A. Ravikumar, and P. Gronkleton. 2018. The effects of rural development policy on land rights distribution and land use scenarios: The case of oil palm in the Peruvian Amazon. Land Use Policy 70, 84–93.

Bennett, N.J., A.M. Cisneros-Montemayor, J. Blythe, J.J. Silver, G. Singh, N. Andrews, A. Calo, P. Christie, A. Di Franco, E.M. Finkbeiner, St. Gelcich, P. Guidetti, S. Harper, N. Hotte, J.N. Kittinger, Ph. Le Billon, J. Lister, R. Lopez de la Lama, E. McKinley, J. Scholtens, A.M. Solas, M. Sowman, N. Talloni-Alvarez, L.C.L. Teh, M. Voyer and U.R.. Sumaila. 2019. Towards a sustainable and equitable blue economy. Nat. Sustain. 2, 991–993..

Bewley, J.M. and R.A. Russell. 2010. Reasons for slow adoption rates of precision dairy farming technologies: evidence from a producer survey. *In*: Proceedings of the First North American Conference on Precision Dairy Management.

Bian, H. 2012. Mixed Methods Research. Office for Faculty Excellence. East-Carolina University.

Bilali. El.H. and M.S. Allahyari. 2018. Transition towards sustainability in agriculture and food systems: Role of information and communication technologies. Information Processing in Agriculture 5, 456–464.

Bitsch, V. 2011. Sustainability Agriculture, Social Responsibility and Dairy Farming. Michigan Dairy Review, 16(1), 1-4.

Bitsch, V. 2010. Labor Aspects of Sustainability. Annual World Forum and Symposium of the International Food and Agribusiness Management Association. Boston/MA. Available at http://www.ifama.org/.

Brodt, S., J. Feenstra, G. Ingels and C.D. Campbell. 2011. Sustainable Agriculture. Nature Education Knowledge 3(10), 1.

Bromley, D.W. 2008. Volitional pragmatism. Ecological Economics 68(1-2), 1–13.

Bryman, A. 2004. Social Research Methods. Second ed. Oxford University Press, Oxford.

Cáceres, A., E. Pol, L. Narváez, A. Puertaa and O. Marfà. 2017. Web app for real-time monitoring of the performance of constructed wetlands treating horticultural leachates. Agricultural Water Management Journal 183, 177–185.

Cheong, S.M. 2004. Managing fishing at the local level: The role of fishing village cooperatives in Korea. Coastal Management 32, 191–202.

Christoforou, A. 2004. In the determinants of social capital in countries of the European Union. European Social Policy: Meeting the Needs of a New Europe. University of Oxford. pp. 2–37.

Clarkson, B.R., A.E. Ausseil and P. Gerbeaux. 2013. Wetland ecosystem services. *In*: Dymond, J.R. (ed.). Ecosystem Services in New Zealand – Conditions and Trends. Manaaki Whenua Press, Lincoln, New Zealand.

Cohen, W. and D. Levinthal. 1990. Absorptive capacity: A new perspective on learning and innovation. Administrative Science Quarterly 35, 128–152.

104 *Modeling for Sustainable Management in Agriculture, Food and the Environment*

Corraliza, J.A. and J. Berenguer. 2000. Environmental values, beliefs and actions: A situational approach. Environment and Behavior 32(6), 832–848.

Crooks, V.A., N. Schuurman, J. Cinnamon, H. Castleden and R. Johnston. 2011. Refining a location analysis model using a mixed methods approach: Community readiness as a key factor in siting rural palliative care services. Journal of Mixed Methods Research 5(1), 77–95.

Davidson, N. 2014. How much wetland has the world lost? Long-term and recent trends in global wetland area. Marine and Freshwater Research 65.

Davis, K., J. Ekboir, W. Mekasha, C.M. Ochieng, D.J. Spielman and E. Zerfu. 2007. Strengthening agricultural education and training in Sub-Saharan Africa from an innovation systems perspective: Case studies of Ethiopia and Mozambique. The Journal of Agricultural Education and Extension 14(1), 35–51.

Davis, T.J. and I.A. Schirmer. 1987. Sustainability issues in agricultural development: Proceedings of the seventh agriculture sector symposium (English). Washington, DC: The World Bank.

de Olde, E.M. and V. Valentinov. 2019. The moral complexity of agriculture: A challenge for corporate social responsibility. Journal Agric Environ Ethics 32, 413–430.

Delatola-Paganeli, M. 2010. Voluntary and municipal social structures for the elderly in greek rural areas: A Tinos island study. Greek Journal of Nursing Science, 4(2), 86–93 (in Greek).

Del Corso, J.P., C. Kephaliacos and G. Plumecocq. 2015. Legitimizing farmers' new knowledge, learning and practices through communicative: Application of an agro-environmental policy. Ecological Economics 117, 86–96.

Dise, N.B. 2009. Peatland response to global change. Science 326, 810–811.

Dodouras, St. and I. Lyratzaki. 2012. Culture and wetlands in the Mediterranean: The case of Lake Karla, Greece. pp. 249–256. *In*: Oral presentations: Ecosystem Goods and Services; Social and Cultural Values. Proceedings of International Conference MarCoastEcos. Tirana, Albania.

Dologlou, N. 2008. Mountain Tourism: Problems and needs. Journal Avlaia, special edition for philoxenia 2009 exposition, Thessaloniki (in Greek).

Edel, K., M. Ryan, J. Finn and T. Hennessy Teagasc. 2015. Farm-level indicators for evaluating sustainability and emerging new policy topics. Funding of European Commision.

EFT (Environmental Foundation of Turkey). 1995. Environmental Profile of Turkey. Turkey: Onder Matbaa.

European Commission. 2006. Fact sheet—The LEADER Approach. Luxembourg: Office for Official Publications of the European Communities.

European Commission. 2008. Poverty and social exclusion in rural areas – Final study report. In Directorate-General for Employment, Social Affairs and Equal Opportunities Unit E2. Luxembourg: Office for Official Publications of the European Communities.

European Commission. 2015a. Annual Activity Report – Directorate General for Agriculture and Rural Development. Luxembourg: Office for Official Publications of the European Communities.

European Commission. 2015b. Monitoring the Digital Economy & Society 2016–2016. Luxembourg: Publications Office of the European Union.

European Commission. 2016. Cohesion policy support for the circular economy. Luxembourg: Office for Official Publications of the European Communities.

European Commission. 2017. CAP explained, Direct Payments for Farmers 2015–2020. Luxembourg: Office for Official Publications of the European Communities.

European Commission. 2017b. The future of food and farming – for a flexible, fair and sustainable Common Agricultural Policy. Press release. Brussels.

European Commission. 2018. Monitoring Agri-trade Policy. MAP 2018-1. p. 26. Brussels, Belgium: European Commission, Agriculture and Rural Development.

Eurostat. 2010. Europe in figures. Eurostat yearbook. Edition 2010. Luxembourg: Publications Office of the European Union.

Eurostat. 2015. Agriculture statistics at regional level. Luxembourg: Publications Office of the European Union.

Eurostat. 2017. Agriculture, forestry and fishery statistics. Statistical books. Edition 2017. Luxembourg: Publications Office of the European Union.

Eurostat. 2017. Eurostat Regional yearbook. Statistical books. Edition 2017. Luxembourg: Publications Office of the European Union.

Falconer, K. 2000. Farm-level constraints on agri-environmental scheme participation: A transactional perspective. Journal of Rural Studies 16, 379–394.

FAO (Food and Agriculture Organization of the United Nations). 2017. Information and Communication Technology (ICT) in Agriculture: A Report to the G20 Agricultural Deputies. Rome.

Feldman, P.J., S. Cohen, S.J. Lepore, K.A. Matthews, T.W. Kamarck and A.L. Marsland. 1999. Negative emotions and acute physiological responses to stress. Department of Psychology. Paper 254.

Forbord, M., H. Bjørkhaug and R.J.F. Burton. 2014. Drivers of change in Norwegian agricultural land control and the emergence of rental farming. Journal of Rural Studies 33, 9–19.

Fraj, E. and E. Martinez. 2006. Environmental values and lifestyles as determining factors of ecological consumer behaviour: An empirical analysis. Journal of Consumer Marketing 23(3), 133–144.

Froissart, T. and T. Terret. 2014. Peasant vulnerability, rural masculinity and physical education in France, from the Early Twentieth Century to the Liberation. Rural History 25(1), 61–77. Cambridge University Press.

Gaskel, P.J. 1982. Science, technology and society: Issues for science teachers. Stud. Sci. Educ., 9:, 33–46.

Gattenlöhner, U., M. Hammerl-Resch and S. Jantschke (Eds.). 2004. Reviving Wetlands – Sustainable Management of Wetlands and Shallow Lakes. Publisher n place

Gellynck, X., J. Cárdenas, Z. Pieniak and W. Verbeke. 2015. Association between innovative entrepreneurial orientation, absorptive capacity, and farm business performance. Agribusiness 31, 91–106.

106 *Modeling for Sustainable Management in Agriculture, Food and the Environment*

Ghadim, A.A., D.J. Pannell and M. Burton. 2005. Risk, uncertainty, and learning in adoption of a crop innovation. Agrictultural Economics 33(1), 1–9.

Gong, Lu, Guixiang He and Weiguo Liu. 2016. Long-term cropping effects on agricultural sustainability in Alar Oasis of Xinjiang, China. Sustainability 6(1), 1–11.

Gouveiaa, Ch., A. Fonsecaa, C. Antonio and F. Ferreira. 2004. Promoting the use of environmental data collected by concerned citizens through information and communication technologies. Journal of Environmental Management 71, 135–154.

Gkisakis, V. 2017. Is the Digital Revolution in Agriculture Compatible with Sustainability and Agroecology? In first Agroecology Europe forum. Workshop. Lyon.

Halkos, G. and N. Jones. 2011. Social factors influencing the decision to pay for the protection of biodiversity: A case study in two national parks of Northern Greece, MPRA Paper. University Library of Munich, Germany 34581.

Harmanctoglu, N., N. Alpaslan and E. Boelee. 2001. Irrigation, health and environment: A review of literature from Turkey. Colombo, Sri Lanka: International Water Management Institute (IWMI) (IWMI working paper 6). 21 p.

Hecht, S.B., A.L. Yang, B. Sijapati Basnett, C. Padoch and N.L. Peluso. 2015. People in motion, forests in transition: Trends in migration urbanization and remittances and their effects on tropical forests. Occasional Paper 142. Bogor, Indonesia: CIFOR.

Hediger, W., A.D. Theler and B. Lehmann. 1998. Sustainable Development of Rural Areas – Methodological Issues. In 38th Congress of the European Regional Science Association. Vienna.

Hellenic Statistical Authority ELSTAT. 2018. Farm structure survey for 2016. Press release. Hellenic Republic.

Hellenic Republic. 2018. Greece: A growth strategy for the future.

https://ec.europa.eu/regional_policy/sources/docgener/work/201707_regional_development_matters.pdf

https://ec.europa.eu/eurostat/web/agriculture/overview

http://www.europeangeoparks.org/

http://www.oecd.org/regional/regionaldevelopment.htm

https://ag4impact.org/database/

https://www.getmap.eu/project/awareness-raising-information-and-communication-as-part-of-the-action-knowledge-and-awareness-increase-about-the-restoration-and-rehabilitation-of-wetlands-in-attica/?lang=en

Iammarino, S., A. Rodríguez-Pose and M. Storper. 2017. Why Regional Development Matters for Europe's Economic Future. Working Paper 07/2017, Publications Office of the European Union, Luxembourg. http://ec.europe.eu/regional_policy/sources/docgener/work/201707_regional_development_matters.pdf.

Iatridis, S.M. 1990. Social Policy Planning: Theory and Practice of Social Planning. Athens: Gutenberg (In Greek).

Isham, J. 2000. Can investments in social capital improve well-being in fishing communities? A theoretical perspective for assessing the policy options in

10th Biennial Meeting of the International Institute of Fisheries Economics and Trade. Corvallis, Oregon, USA: IIFET.

Islam, G. and M. Dickson. 2007. Turning Social Capital into Natural Capital: Changing Livelihoods of Fishers through Community Based Fisheries Management. Dhaka: WorldFish Center.

Jennrich, R. I. and P.F. Sampson. 1966. Rotation for simple loadings. Psychometrika 31, 313–323.

Jentoft, S. 2005. Fisheries co-management as empowerment. Marine Policy 29, 1–7.

Johnson, R.B. and A.J. Onwuegbuzie. 2004. Mixed methods research: A research paradigm whose time has come. Educational Researcher 33(7), 14–26.

Jones, N., H. Jones, L. Steer and A. Datta. 2009. Improving impact evaluation production and use. Working Paper 300. Overseas Development Institute, London.

Karanikolas, P., M. Vassalos, N. Martinos and K. Tsimpoukas. 2011. Economic viability and multifunctionality of agriculture: The case of North Amorgos. In: Proceedings of the 5th Interdisciplinary Conference of Metsovio Center Interdisciplinary Research of EMP, B': 401–421, Editions EMP. Athens.

Kostopoulos, Tr. 1988. Regional Development and People's Participation: The Case of Prefecture Councils in Greece. Doctoral Thesis. Panteion University. (In Greek)

Kourlioros, H., G.M. Korres, G.O. Tsobanoglou and A. Kokkinou. 2014b. Socio-Economic Sustainability, Regional Development and Spatial Planning. European and International Dimensions and Perspectives.

Lee, T.H. 2013. Influence analysis of community resident support for sustainable tourism development. Journal of Tourism Management 34(33), 37–46.

Lehmann, R.J., R. Reiche and G. Schiefer. 2012. Future internet and the agri-food sector: State-of-the-art in literature and research. Computers and Electronics in Agriculture 89, 158–174.

Lemos, M.C. and A. Agrawal. 2006. Environmental governance. Annu. Rev. Environ. Resour. 31, 297–325.

Lolos, S.E.G. 2009. The effect of EU structural funds on regional growth: Assessing the evidence from Greece, 1990–2005. Econ Change Restruct. 42, 211–228.

Lubell, M., V. Hillis and M. Hoffman. 2011. Innovation, cooperation, and the perceived benefits and costs of sustainable agriculture practices. Ecology and Society 16(4), 22–34.

Luhmann, H. and L. Theuvsen. 2017. Corporate social responsibility: Exploring a framework for the agribusiness sector. Journal of Agricultural and Environmental Ethics 30(2), 241–253.

Lund Vinding, A. 2006. Absorptive capacity and innovative performance: A human capital approach. Econ. Innovation New Tech. 15, 507–517.

Mathiyalagana, V., S. Grunwaldb, K.R. Reddyb and S.A. Bloomb. 2005. Application note A WebGIS and geodatabase for Florida's wetlands. Computers and Electronics in Agriculture 47, 69–75.

Mazur-Wierzbicka. E. 2015. The application of corporate social responsibility in European Agriculture Miscellanea Geographica – Regional Studies on Development 19(1), 19–23.

McMillan, D. and D. Chavis. 1986. Sense of Community: A definition and theory. Journal of Community Psychology. 14, 6–23.

Megevand, C. 2013. Dynamiques de déforestation dans le bassin du Congo: Réconcilier la croissance économique et la protection de la forêt. Washington, DC: World Bank.

Michailidis, A., A. Koutsouris and K. Mattas. 2010a. Information and communication technologies as agricultural extension tools: A survey among farmers in west Macedonia, Greece. Journal of Agricultural Education and Extension 16(3), 249–263.

Michailidis, A. 2010. Chapter 3 – Greece. pp. 83–114. In: R. Saravanan [eds.]. ICTs for Agricultural Extension: Global Experiments, Innovations and Experiences. New India Publishing Agency, India.

Micheels, E.T. and J.F. Nolan. 2016. Examining the effects of absorptive capacity and social capital on the adoption of agricultural innovations: A Canadian prairie case study. Agric. Syst. 145, 127–138.

Milovanović, S. 2014. The role and potential of information technology in agricultural improvement. Economics of Agriculture 2. Review Article.

Mincer, J. and S. Polachek. 1974. Family investments in human capital. Journal of Political Economy. 82, 76–108.

Morse, J.M. 1991. Approaches to qualitative-quantitative methodological triangulation. Nursing Research 40, 120–123.

National Research Council. 2010. Toward Sustainable Agricultural Systems in the 21st Century. Washington, DC: The National Academies Press.

Newcome, J., A. Provins, H. Johns, E. Ozdemiroglu, J. Ghazoul, D. Burgess and K. Turner. 2005. The Economic, Social and Ecological Value of Ecosystem Services: A Literature Review. Final report for the Department for Environment, Food and Rural Affairs. Available from: https://silo.tips/download/the-economic-social-and-ecological-value-of-ecosystem-services-a-literature-revi#

O'Cathain, A. and K.J. Thomas. 2004. Any other comments? Open questions on questionnaires – A bane or a bonus to research? BMC Med Res Methodol 4, 25.

OECD. 1998. Human Capital Investment: An International Comparison, OECD, Paris.

OECD. 1999. Environmental Indicators for Agriculture. Volume 1. Concepts and Framework. OECD Publishing.

OECD. 2001. The Well-being of Nations. The Role of Human and Social Capital, OECD, Paris.

OECD. 2007. Beyond GDP – Measuring Progress, True Wealth and the Wellbeing of Nations, OECD, Paris.

OECD. 2011. *What is Social Capital?* Available from: https://www.oecd.org/insights/37966934.pdf

OECD. 2012. Structural reforms in time of crisis. pp. 17–50 In: Economic Policy Reforms 2012: Going for Growth, OECD Publishing.

OECD. 2017. The governance of land-use: Country fact sheet Greece. In: Land-use Planning Systems in the OECD: Country Fact Sheets. OECD Publishing.

OECD. 2018. Regions and cities at a glance – Greece. OECD Publishing. http://www.oecd.org/regional

OECD. year Regional Database. Visualisation: https://www. oecdregionalwellbeing.org

OECD. year Human Capital *Glossary of Statistical Terms*. Available at: http://stats. oecd.org/glossary/detail.asp?ID=1264

Padoch, C., A. Stewart, M. Pinedo-Vasquez, L. Putzel and M.M. Ruiz. 2014. Urban residence, rural employment, and the future of Amazonian forests. pp. 322–335. In: Hecht, S.B., Morison, K.D. and Padoch, C. (Eds.). The Social Lives of Forests. Chicago University Press, Chicago.

Papadopoulou, O. 2014. Investing in human capital: An implication of mincer equation. pp. 25–31. In: Socio-Economic Sustainability, Regional Development and Spatial Planning: European and International Dimensions and Perspectives. Publisher: University of Aegean.

Pareto, V. 1907. [1980]. L'économie et la sociologie du point de vue scientifique. Rivista di Scientia. Œuvres Complètes. 22. Droz, Genève.

Pateman, C. 1970. Participation and Democratic Theory. Cambridge: Cambridge University Press.

Penda, S.T. 2012. Human capital development for agricultural business in Nigeria. *International Food and Agribusiness Management Review* 15(A), 89–91.

Proikaki, M., N. Jones, N. Nagopoulos, M. Chatziantwniou and K. Evangelinos. 2014. Incorporating social indicators of sustainability in public policies for environmentally degraded areas: The case of the Asopos River. pp. 85-90. In: Socio-Economic Sustainability, Regional Development and Spatial Planning: European and International Dimensions and Perspectives. University of Thessaly.

Putnam, R. 2000. Bowling Alone: The Collapse and Revival of American Community. New York: Simon and Schuster.

Pyrovetsi, M. and G. Daoutopoulos. 1997. Contrasts in conservation attitudes and agricultural practices between farmers operating in wetlands and a plain in Macedonia, Greece. Environmental Conservation 24(1), 76–82.

QGIS Development Team. 2017, 2018. QGIS Geographic Information System. Open Source Geospatial Foundation Project. http://qgis.osgeo.org

Raggos, A. and A. Psychoudakis. 2006. The effect of production structure on the multifunctional characteristics of agriculture. In: 9th Congress ETAGRO, Athens (in Greek).

Ramsar, Iran, 2.2.1971 as amended by the Protocol of 3.12.1982 and the Amendments of 28.5.1987.

Ramsar. 2015a. Facsheet 1. Wetlands: Why should I care? Accessed http:// www.ramsar.org/sites/default/files/documents/library/factsheet1_why_should_i_ca re_0.pdf

Ramsar. 2015c. Factsheet 3. Wetlands: A global disappearing act. Accessed http:// www.ramsar.org/sites/default/files/documents/library/factsheet3_global_disappearing_act_0.pdf

Ramsar. 2016. An Introduction to the Ramsar Convention on Wetlands, 7th ed. (previously The Ramsar Convention Manual). Ramsar Convention Secretariat, Gland, Switzerland.

Robinson, C.A., B. Pesut, J.L. Bottorff, A. Mowry, S. Broughton and G. Fyles. 2009. Rural palliative care: A comprehensive review. Journal of Palliative Medicine 12, 253–258.

Rodríguez-Pose, A. and M. Di Cataldo. 2015. Quality of government and innovative performance in the regions of Europe. *Journal of Economic Geography* 15(4), 673–706.

Rogers, E. 2003. Diffusion of Innovations. 5th Edition. The Free Press.

Roustang, G. 1987. Employment: A Societal Choice. Paris: Syros.

Russi, D., P. ten Brink, A. Farmer, T. Badura, D. Coates, J. Förster, R. Kumar and N. Davidson. 2013. The Economics of Ecosystems and Biodiversity for Water and Wetlands. London and Brussels: Institute for European Environmental Policy, Ramsar Secretariat, Gland, Switzerland.

Sabatini, F. 2005. Social capital as social networks: A new framework for measurement. University of Rome. www.socialcapitalgateway.org

Simon, H.A. 1972. Theories of bounded rationality. pp. 161–176. In: Decision and Organization: A Volume in Honor of Jacob Marschak. Vol. 1. North-Holland Publishing Company. Amsterdam, The Netherlands.

Siuta, M. and C.E. Nedelciu. 2016. Report on Socio-Economic Benefits of Wetland Restoration in Central and Eastern Europe. A Publication by CEEweb for Biodiversity, Budapest, Hungary.

Sivignon, M. 2007. The Greek wetlands: From degradation to rehabilitation. Edições Universitarias Lusoãfonas. Lisbon, 243–248.

Stathopoulos, P.A. 2000. Community Work, Processing, Methods and Intervention Techiques. Athens: Hellene (In Greek).

Stathopoulos, P.A. 2001. Community Work, Theory and Practice. Athens: Hellene (In Greek).

Spalletti, St. 2014. The Economics of Education in Adam Smith's "Wealth of Nations". Journal of World Economic Research 3(5), 60–64.

Schultz, T.W. 1961. Investment in Human Capital. American Economic Review 51(1), 1–17.

Schultz, T.W. 1992. Adam Smith and Human Capital. pp. 133–143. In: Fry, M. (ed.), Adam Smith's Legacy: His Place in the Development of Modern Economics. London: Routledge.

Smith, A. 1776. An Inquiry into the Nature and Causes of the Wealth of Nations, in Metalibri Digital Library, Edited by S.M. Soares, 2007.

Tadaki, M., J. Sinner and K.M.A. Chan. 2017. Making sense of environmental values: A typology of concepts. Ecology and Society 22(1), 7.

Tornatzky, L.G. and K.J. Klein. 1982. Innovation characteristics and innovation adoption-implementation: A meta-analysis of findings. IEEE Transactions on Engineering Management 29, 28–45.

Triantafillou, J. and E. Mestheneos. 2001. Ch. 4, Greece. In: Philp, I. (ed.), Family Care of Older People in Europe – COPE. Biomedical and Health Research, Vol. 46. IOS Press, The Netherlands.

Tsobanoglou, G. 2008. The Rise of the Social Economy. Athens: Papazisi Publications.

Van de Fliert, E., and A.R. Braun. 2002. Conceptualizing integrative, farmer participatory research for sustainable agriculture: From opportunities to impact. Agriculture and Human Values 19, 25–38.

Farmers' Perceptions Towards Social-economic Sustainability... **111**

Van de Fliert, E. 2010. Participatory communication in rural development: What does it take for the established order? Extension Farming Systems Journal 6(1), 95–99.

Van Rijn, F., E. Bulte and A. Adekunle. 2012. Social capital and agricultural innovation in Sub-Saharan Africa. Agric. Syst. 108, 112–122.

Vasiliades, L., P. Sidiropoulos, J. Tzabiras, K. Kokkinos, M. Spiliotopoulos, G. Papaioannou, Chr. Fafoutis, K. Michailidou, G. Tziatzios, A. Loukas and N. Mylopoulos. 2015. Hydromentor: An integrated water resources monitoring and management system at modified semi-arid watersheds. Geophysical Research Abstract, 17, EGU2015.

Vlachopoulou, E.I. and G. Tsobanoglou. 2014. International dimensions of fisheries co-management. pp. 132–137. In: Socio-Economic Sustainability, Regional Development and Spatial Planning: European and International Dimensions and Perspectives. Publisher: University of Aegean.

Wejnert, B. 2002. Integrating models of diffusion of innovations: A conceptual framework. Annual Review of Sociology 28(1), 297–326.

Wilkinson, R. and K. Pickett. 2009. The Spirit Level: Why Equality is Better for Everyone. 2nd ed. London: Penguin Group.

Williams, D.R. and J.J. Vaske. 2003. The measurement of place attachment: Validity and generalizability of a psychometric approach. forest science, 49(6):830–840.

Wojciechowski, B. 2012. Human Rights as the Basis of a Multicultural Society. Available at: https://www.intellectum.org/en/2012/12/23/human-rights-as-the-basis-of-a-multicultural-society/

Wolfle, D. 1980. Public policy decision making and scientific literacy. In: D. Wolfle et al. (eds.), Public Policy Decision Making and Scientific Literacy: Information Needs for Science and Technology (Report No. NSF-80-2 1-A6). Washington DC: National Science Foundation.

Woods, B. 1993. FAO. Communication, Technology and the Development of People. Routledge. London. UK.

WorldFish Center. 2007. Social Capital: Community Based Fisheries Management. Dhaka: WorldFish Center.

Xavier, G. 2008. Gated and guarded communities – Security concerns or Elitist practice? In: 5th Asian Law Institute Conference, 22-23 May 2008, Singapore.

Zhang, W., T.H. Ricketts, C. Kremen, K. Carney and S.M. Swinton. 2007. Ecosystem services and dis-services to agriculture. Ecological Economics 64(2), 253–260.

CHAPTER

5

Advanced Crop Protection Techniques and Technologies

Athanasios T. Balafoutis[1]*, Charikleia K. Kavroumatzi[2], Michail Moraitis[1], Konstantinos Vaiopoulos[1], Nikos Mylonas[2], I. Tsitsigiannis[2], Yiannis Ampatzidis[3], Dimitrios, Spyros Fountas[2], Dionysis Bochtis[1]

[1] Institute for Bio-Economy & Agro-Technology, Centre of Research & Technology Hellas, Dimarchou Georgiadou 118, 38333, Volos, Greece
[2] Agricultural University of Athens, Iera Odos 75, 11855, Athens, Greece
[3] Department of Agricultural and Biological Engineering, University of Florida, Southwest Florida Research and Education Center (SWFREC), 2685 FL-29, Immokalee, FL 34142, USA

Introduction

Global agriculture relies on synthetic Plant Protection Products (PPP) for pest control to support sustainable yield productivity. PPPs prevent, destroy or control a harmful organism or disease to protect crops or desirable or useful plants. PPPs are primarily used in the agricultural sector but also in forestry, horticulture, amenity areas and in home gardens. They contain at least one active substance and they have at least one of the following functions: (i) protect plants and their products against pests/diseases, prior or post to harvest, (ii) influence the life processes of plants (such as substances influencing their growth, excluding nutrients), (iii) preserve plant products and/or (iv) destroy or prevent growth of undesired plants or parts of plants. PPPs are divided, according to their use, into three main categories: (a) herbicides, which destroy weeds that grow near crops at the expense of cultivated plants, (b) insecticides, which kill insects that act against the plants and (c) fungicides, which are used

*Corresponding author: a.balafoutis@certh.gr

Advanced Crop Protection Techniques and Technologies

to kill parasitic fungi or their spores and the corresponding diseases they develop (EC 2020a). Another classification can be made according to their mode of action, systemic PPPs are absorbed by the plant usually through the roots and then translocate through it while contact PPPs do not. Foliar applied PPPs may be either contact or systemic (NIPHM 2018).

Farmers and crop advisors follow conventional crop protection strategies that were established after the Green Revolution (1950–1960), maintaining significant use of PPPs despite the negative impacts on the environment and human health. This happens as pests diminish global potential crop yield up to 40%, a figure that would be twice as large if no synthetic PPPs were used (Oerke 2006). This clearly indicates that more sustainable PPPs should be used under common rules for safer and more efficient application. Reducing the negative impacts of PPPs is a major global societal challenge, as 72% of EU citizens are worried about PPP residues and seeing it as the most important food-related concern, according to Eurobarometer on "Food-related risks" (EC 2020b). The European Food Safety Authority announced that 98.9% of food products contain synthetic PPPs residues (with 1.5% of them in excess of the legal limits), while 27.3% of food samples have traces of more than one synthetic PPP (EFSA 2013). Sustainable use of PPPs to reduce their risks and impacts on people's health and the environment and the issue of plants resistance to PPPs are becoming a significant problem for the farming community.

For reducing the negative impacts, PPP industry and research entities have been developing more sustainable novel PPPs either biological or synthetic that show high efficacy in lab environment, but presenting a significant reduction of their efficiency under field conditions. Spraying technologies, on the other hand, have shown an important improvement in terms of efficiency and safety by adopting the latest advances in electronics, data management and safety aspects. As a result, new sprayers have revolutionary improvements including alternative methods for dose/volume selection adapted to canopy structure, recommendations/ technologies to reduce drift, resident exposure and point sources' contamination. Finally, for reducing PPP's usage, Decision Support Systems (DSS) for prediction of disease outbreaks have been developed for certain crops and diseases in many cases within a Farm Management Information System (FMIS), while precise early detection systems have been developed only at research level for certain crops, working mainly under experimental conditions.

The information on recent advances in crop protection techniques and technologies is scattered and therefore this chapter delves upon the latest developments in new types of PPPs (synthetic and biological), integrated pest management, disease prediction models, DSS, FMIS and application technology (including spraying machinery and machine embedded ICT

114 *Modeling for Sustainable Management in Agriculture, Food and the Environment*

tools). This chapter is a ready reference for students, policy-makers, scientists, researchers and extension workers.

New Chemical PPP Formulations and Bio-PPPs

PPPs are formulations aiming to protect crops or their products from pests (i.e. insects, microorganisms, weeds) during production, storage and transport. Research has shown that sufficient and constant food supply cannot be preserved omitting the use of PPPs. The range of PPPs has risen significantly, supplying farmers with a more comprehensive and efficient pest management inventory. Nevertheless, fewer novel active substances have been developed over the last decade. On the other hand, there has been an especially fast increase in the development of biological PPPs. Partially due to strict guidelines, the research and production costs of PPPs have been raised, while at the same time the estimated time for PPPs to be placed on the market after their first synthesis has been elongated[1].

In this context, current practices face major challenges resulting in the demand of new and innovative PPPs. The intensive use of the same PPPs, active ingredients and modes of action has been pressing constantly to a natural selection promoting resistance development. Furthermore, having an exponentially growing population combined with the concurrent environmental and toxicological risks of PPPs, the need for sustainable agriculture with integrated pest management at its core gets imperative. Against this background, PPPs must meet certain objectives (Keith et al. 2008). They should:

- show stability and persistence for notable time under environmental pressure (UV light, heat, precipitation)
- be target specific
- gain access in the target organism (disease pathogens, pests and weeds)
- resist the metabolism of the organism
- transport to the target (protein) and effectively inhibit it
- be environmentally friendly
- provide no negative health consequences
- be cost-efficient in formulating and manufacturing
- ideally provide a new mechanism of action and
- have positive impact on societal level and being profitable

Hence, new categories of products were discovered and the latest technologies were implemented for the enhancement of the existing PPPs. These novel formulations will be introduced in the following

---

[1] https://ec.europa.eu/food/plant/pesticides_en

Advanced Crop Protection Techniques and Technologies **115**

sections. According to Phillips McDougall (2018), during the last decade, the total number of synthetic PPPs which met the marketplace or are in development stage is at least 105, and most of them are harmless to humans and eco-friendly: 43 fungicides, 34 insecticides/acaricides, 6 nematicides, 21 herbicides, and 1 herbicide safener.

New Active Ingredients/New Modes of Action

In order to conform to the current safety regulations, several PPPs have been pulled out from the market in the past few years, either because they have been prohibited or because they have not been accepted during the re-registration phase. For instance, the US Environmental Protection Agency (EPA) has a list of over 60 active ingredients that are no longer accessible in the US, while a decline in new chemical entities entering the market place has been reported (Phillips McDougall 2018). The emerging pest resistance to entire families of fungicides and insecticides is undoubtedly a solid situation all over the world. On that premise, crop protection is relying on the development of new molecules, among other approaches. Another strategy is the use of analogue chemistry which is aiming to provide analogue active ingredients that possess superior or distinct properties with respect to the original lead compound, including those that cover very different biological targets. Analogues usually share the same mode of action as the original lead, with a potential disadvantage in pest and weed resistance growth.

In fungicide development, three major fungicide classes are in the spotlight. The most widespread class is the SDHIs (succinate dehydrogenase inhibitors) or those considered to be SDHIs because of their chemical structures. They act on complex II of the mitochondrial electron transport chains. Because of some fungal resistance that has been reported on the existing molecules of this group, post-SDHI fungicides are now recommended. During the past decade, 17 SDHI fungicides were introduced. Penthiopyrad, isofetamid, and pyraziflumid have already been marketed, while pyrapropoyne is under development. Isofetamid has broad-spectrum antifungal activity against Ascomycota and Deuteromycota fungi and is effective against existing SDHI-resistant pathogens (Umetsu and Shirai 2020). At last, inpyrfluxam exhibits high efficacy against major plant diseases in the European region (Sumitomo Chemical 2019). Another interesting group of fungicides with known developed pathogen resistance is DMIs (demethylation inhibitors). Three new active ingredients are in development stage of which mefentrifluconazole and pyrisoxazole should be underlined. In fact, mefentrifluconazole is the first isopropanol azole discovered and ever developed with authorisation for use on wheat and barley against dominant diseases (Tesh et al. 2019). The third group is inhibitors of the mitochondrial electron transport chain complex III, i.e., QoI (quinone outside inhibitors) and QiI (quinone inside inhibitors). 12 compounds have been introduced or are under development as inhibitors of the mitochondrial electron transport chain complex III since 2010 (Umetsu and Shirai 2020). Only two of them act as QiI fungicide, while the rest refers to QoI fungicides. It is significant to highlight metyltetraprole, a new fungicide with a unique tetrazolinone moiety that is highly efficient against resistant to existing pesticides pathogens.

In the field of novel modes of action and unique chemical structures, eight fungicides launched or going to be launched with either known or unknown mode of action (Umetsu and Shirai 2020). Some of them are oxathiapiprolin, a new class of piperidinyl thiazole isoxazoline fungicides (Pasteris et al. 2016) and quinofumelin with new action characteristics. Some other fungicides are under development such as dichlobentiazox, a novel compound discovered in search of saccharin derivatives that seems to be a plant defense activator.

In insecticide development, there's a shift from organophosphates, carbamates, and synthetic pyrethroids to nicotinic and diamide insecticides. Nicotinic insecticides are divided into three generations and some of the second generation insecticides have been deemed as toxic to non-target organisms, especially to honeybees. As a result, three agents of this generation are prohibited for field use at present in EU (Umetsu and Shirai 2020). Four nicotinic insecticides, such as flupyrimin and triflumezopyrim, are on the market and another five of the diamide group are launched or being developed, such as cyantraniliprole and tetraniliprole. Moreover, during the past decade, 11 insecticides compounds where introduced, that are not classified in any of the above categories, and seem to have several novel modes of action, showing up as potent resistance management candidates (Umetsu and Shirai 2020). For example, broflanilide, having a unique chemical structure, is categorized as a meta-diamide and displays high efficiency against various pests, including lepidopteran, coleopteran, and thysanopteran pests (Katsuta et al. 2019) and spiropidion is a new tetramic acid family member insecticide and acaricide in the developmental stage (Umetsu and Shirai 2020).

The new trends in herbicide development are focused on ALS-inhibiting herbicides targeting the enzyme acetolactate synthase. They are some of the most broadly used herbicides with several weed resistance reported. The most actively studied are the HPPD-inhibiting herbicides. PPO-inhibiting herbicides which act on protoporphyrinogen-IX oxidase (PPO) is another group of herbicides that attracted researchers' interest, even though it seems the number of related patents has been decreased during the past few years. Very-long-chain fatty acid elongase (VLCFAE)-inhibiting herbicides, auxin-like herbicides and herbicide safeners (a group of chemically diverse compounds with the unique ability to protect

Advanced Crop Protection Techniques and Technologies **117**

grass crops from herbicide injury without reducing herbicide activity in target weed species) are also some domains with research activity. What is the most significant achievement though, is the discovery of three new modes of actions in herbicide development for the first time after almost 30 years (cyclopyrimorate, tetflupyrolimet, cinmethylin) (Umetsu and Shirai 2020).

Nanotechnology: Nanoparticles

Nanotechnology has a wide range of applications, providing a plethora of prospects in a variety of fields such as medicine, pharmaceuticals, industry and agriculture. New properties and mode of actions are being introduced with the conversion of material into nano-scale (1–100 nm). Some new features include potential anti-microbial or insecticidal activity (Rai and Ingle 2012). Thus, nano-pesticides, nano-fungicides and nano-herbicides are already being used in agriculture (Owolade et al. 2008). Basically, nanoparticles may contribute in plant protection with two distinct ways; acting similarly with PPPs against pathogens and pests as well as carriers for other existing molecules e.g. active ingredients, genes, double-stranded RNA (dsRNA) (Bhattacharyya and Jha 2012). They can be applied easily by spraying or soaking onto leaves and roots. An important benefit they introduce is a combination of efficacy and stability in the environment (sun, rain, heat) that could elongate the period between applications, eventually their number as well as the total cost. As carriers, nanoparticles can act beneficially, by enhancing the life span of PPPs, improving solubility of poorly water-soluble PPPs, minimizing toxicity, and endorsing site-specific uptake into the target organism (Hayles et al. 2017). Furthermore, nano-delivery systems allow the controlled release of agrochemicals and target-specific delivery of biomolecules, e.g. nucleotides, proteins etc. (Wang et al. 2016).

Metal nanoparticles containing copper (Cu-NPs, CuO-NPs), silver (Ag-NPs) and zinc (ZnO-NPs) have been proven efficient against a variety of fungal and bacterial pathogens (Ouda 2014, Kairyte et al. 2013). Nano-silica has already been employed on pest control. Nano-encapsulation is one of the PPPs improvement approaches with the example of clay nanotubes, halloysite, that have been designed as carriers of PPPs. Pyrethroid-based active compounds seem to be especially responsive to behaviour adjustments resulting from nano-formulation. Two representatives, already accessible on the market, are γ-cyhalothrin and λ-cyhalothrin (Meredith et al. 2016, Slattery et al. 2019). The latter is also marketed as a quick release microencapsulation and the active ingredient is unleashed on contact with the leaves. Whereas in the product "gutbaster", a stomach poisoned insecticide is nano encapsulated that is solely released after contact alkaline environments, such as the stomach of certain insects (Prasad et al. 2014, Ali et al. 2014).

Clay nanotubes, halloysite, have been designed as carriers of PPPs. Chitosan-based nano-carriers are also a vehicle for the delivery of a compound to plant cells because of their positive charge. Designing chitosan-complexed single-walled carbon nanotubes, the delivery of plasmid DNA to chloroplasts of different plant species is feasible without external aid. Successful transformation of chloroplasts using this technology was achieved in mature *Eruca sativa*, *Nasturtium officinale*, *Nicotiana tabacum*, and *Spinacia oleracea* plants and in isolated *Arabidopsis thaliana* mesophyll protoplasts (Kwak et al. 2019).

Plant Growth Promoting Fungi (PGPF) and Rhizobacteria (PGPR)

Microorganisms have several mechanisms they deploy in order to prevail in their environment. Some are able to produce antimicrobial agents (Phongpaichit et al. 2006, Verma et al. 2009) and secondary metabolites (Wang et al. 2007) or simply antagonize a plant pathogen for space and nutrients. Others can also induce plant defense systems. These organisms are known as biological control agents (BCAs) and have raised researcher's interest as potential alternatives of agrochemicals (Waghunde et al. 2016). Research has shown that some endophytic microorganisms are able to interfere in host's tolerance to biotic or abiotic stress, nutrient distribution as well as in plant's growth and yield as they are a valuable source of several key components, such as phytohormones (auxins and gibberellins) (Jaber and Araj 2017, Bamisile et al. 2018). Plant growth-promoting fungi (PGPF) and rhizobacteria (PGPR) interacting with pathogens seems to activate plant's defense mechanisms such as induced systemic or systemic acquired resistance (ISR or SAR respectively) mechanisms. Not only do they benefit the plants by confronting pathogens and releasing signals, but they also assist in organic matter decomposing, nutrient availability and many other ways (Sivasakthi et al. 2014). During the last years, their use has been significantly increased worldwide as a cost-effective replacement or supplement to synthetic PPPs (Borah et al. 2018). There are numerous bio-PPPs, some of them well established in the crop protection market having commercialized such organisms as *Trichoderma* spp., *Bacillus* spp., *Aureobasidium* spp. and many others.

Biocontrol Products (Elicitors, Semiochemicals) and Essential Oils

Green technologies resulted to intensive research on biostimulants and biocontrol implementation (Boller and Felix 2009, Bhattacharyya and Jha 2012). It is well known that plants are equipped with defense mechanisms that can be induced by plant-pathogen interactions and could offer protection against a wide range of pathogens (Schwessinger and Ronald

Advanced Crop Protection Techniques and Technologies **119**

2012). The stimulation of plant's own immune system has been proven to be a useful strategy in disease control, as it provides potential long-lasting, wide-ranging disease control (Walters et al. 2014). Plant defense is activated once "foreign" molecules are detected during an infection, identified as elicitors. In general, as elicitors are perceived all the signal molecules that interpret with plant defense responses (Vallad and Goodman 2004). Commercially, elicitors have a broad usage mostly as additional methods in order to reduce chemical inputs, especially in integrated pest management approaches. They may be utilized separately or combined with other PPPs, one or multiple times during the season (Walters et al. 2013). An example in this case is BTH (benzo-(1, 2, 3)-thiadiazole-7-carbothioic acid S-methyl ester). It is a molecule with resemblance to the plant hormone salicylic acid and it is capable of causing the expression of several defense genes against pathogens (Morris et al. 1998, von Rad et al. 2005). An example of a physical elicitor is laminarin, a storage polysaccharide (a b-1,3-glucan with some b-1,6-linked branches) of the brown alga *Laminaria digitate,* registered in many European countries against different diseases (European Commission EGTOP 2011). Another novel elicitor is COS-OGA that consists of a complex of chitosan fragments (chitooligosaccharides, COS), that are compounds found in fungal cell walls and crustacean exoskeletons (Cabrera et al. 2010).

Semiochemicals are substances involved in biological communication, subdivided in allelochemicals and pheromones referred to interspecific and intraspecific individuals (Vet and Dicke 1992). Due to their low or non-toxicity and high specificity, semiochemicals are a safe alternative or supplement to agrochemicals. Exploitation of these compounds include insect pheromones for use in pest monitoring, mating disruption, trapping and push-pull strategies. Mating disruption technique is well-known globally against moths in orchards, vegetables etc. (Cardé 2007). Few years ago, methyl salicylate (MeSA) raised the interest due to its increased capability to lure natural enemies such as coccinellids, syrphids, lacewings, predatory bugs and some parasitic Hymenoptera (Rodriguez-Saona et al. 2011). This molecule can be found in certain plants after a pest infestation (Pichersky et al. 2002). Another promising approach is the "push-pull strategies" in which repellents are being used to keep pests away from the cultivated field, while some other attractants pull them to traps (Cook et al. 2007).

Essential oils (EOs) are plant metabolic compounds with antimicrobial, antioxidant (Obolskiy et al. 2011; El Asbahani et al. 2015) and potential herbicidal properties. They mostly contain terpenes along with other chemical compositions. However, their efficiency is easily affected by the oil extraction method and even the climate as they act quickly and it is possible to get volatile rapidly. This is a setback that can be settled by alternative formulations. For example, microencapsulation could limit the

120 *Modeling for Sustainable Management in Agriculture, Food and the Environment*

applied dosage, reduce their volatility, thus increasing the persistence and decelerate its degradation once in the field (Scarfato et al. 2007).

RNAi Based Pesticides

RNA interference (RNAi) is a natural process that can cease the expression of targeted genes. An RNAi type of phenomenon was firstly reported in plants, associated with the purple or white colour in petunia flowers, known as 'co-suppression or post transcriptional gene silencing' and in fungi as 'quelling' (Cogoni et al. 1996, Napoli et al. 1990, Romano and Macino 1992). In bacteria also, such a phenomenon has been reported, known as clustered regularly interspaced short palindromic repeats (CRISPR) (Wilson and Doudna 2013). RNAi has many potential applications, both in medical field against diseases, and in crop protection for disease and pest control. To date, RNAi strategies have been focused on the use of transgenic plants that express double-stranded RNAs (dsRNAs) against selected targets (Dalakouras et al. 2020). The use of transgenes and genetically modified organisms (GMOs) has, however, raised substantial scientific and public concerns. The need has therefore emerged for alternative strategies to avoid the use of transgenes and instead resort to direct exogenous application of RNA molecules that could potentially trigger RNAi. In plants, exogenous application of RNA molecules, dsRNAs or short interfering RNAs (siRNAs) can trigger RNAi in a GMO-free manner. There are already applications of RNA in plants that successfully triggered RNAi of plant genes, viruses, viroids, fungi, insects and mites.

Nevertheless, the application of this technology in greenhouses and fields depends on dsRNA quality, its stable delivery, and the extended duration of protection as well as its large-scale production. Conjugating RNA molecules to nanoparticles and carrier peptides significantly increases their nuclease resistance and delivery capacity. Exogenously administered 22 nucleotide siRNAs are the most active inducers of local and systemic RNAi in plants. High pressure spraying allows for the symplastic delivery of exogenous RNA, while petiole absorption and/or trunk injection results in the apoplastic delivery of exogenous RNA. As a result, the production of RNA-based biopesticides is gaining popularity as a co-opted to chemical control strategy, with pests and pathogens targeted with precision and specificity. Beside the research, development of regulatory frameworks, risk assessments and prevention and mitigation strategies are essential to the widespread implementation of topical RNAi technologies. Once settled, these steps would provide the crop protection industry with the requisite confidence to invest on the production of innovative dsRNA-based products. Readily apparent threats to human health seem low, with numerous barriers to absorption and a long history of dsRNA intake from

Advanced Crop Protection Techniques and Technologies **121**

plant material (Fletcher et al. 2020). While pesticide development studies have been extensively performed over the past decade based on genomic knowledge, structural activity and chemical biology studies, practically no commercial RNAi based pesticides have been yet developed. Several plant protection companies invest a significant part of their R&D program into this technology in order to enrich their PPPs portfolio with RNAi based products in a few years.

Conclusions

It is indisputable that the pesticides developed during the last decade have been crucial in crop protection and is anticipated to play a major role in the future. Despite that, in recent years, global pesticide production has been slowly oriented from synthetic PPPs to bio PPPs, RNAi pesticides and last but not least to abiotic stress control agents. As lower-environmental-impact alternative to traditional synthetic PPPs, biopesticides are becoming more popular nowadays. All the above, would result in a holistic and sustainable approach on tomorrow's agriculture.

Farm Management Information and Decision Support Systems

Farm Management Information Systems Concepts and Applications

The recent technological advancements in the past years have enabled a rapid change in the working environment in agriculture. Agriculture has entered a new era in which the key to success is access to timely information and elaborated decision making. The farmer and the agronomists should be up-to-date using the latest technologies and applications available (Fountas et al. 2015a). The software tools to be used by the farmers are referred as Farm Management Information Systems (FMIS), as an answer to the need for communication and data transfer between databases, and to meet the requirements of different stakeholders. Sørensen et al. (2010) defined an FMIS as a planned system for collecting, processing, storing, and disseminating data in the form needed to carry out a farm's operations and functions. Essential FMIS components include specific farmer-oriented designs, dedicated user interfaces, automated data processing functions, expert knowledge and user preferences, standardized data communication and scalability; all provided at affordable price to farmers (Murakami et al. 2007).

A key question has been, whether commercial FMIS have been able to capture the functionalities needed to match farmers needs and such systems can deal with the increasing amount of data to be collected and analysed. An analysis and comparison of existing FMIS was conducted between commercial and academic ones (Fountas et al. 2015a). This study revealed that commercial applications are mostly dealt with everyday farming activities data processing, while academic still explore new horizons in research with high sophistication and complexity, capturing new trends involving spatial and temporal management, distributed system involving interoperability of sensing devices, future internet components and web services. Commercial applications tend to focus on solving daily farm tasks with the aim to generate income for the farmers through better resource management and field operations planning. The advances that are needed in the development of FMIS include improvements in technology, adaptation motives, specific new functionalities and, greater emphasis on software design governed by usability and human–computer interaction. The diffusion of information management as business innovation in the farming community could benefit from the comprehensive research developed in the last decades on the adoption of advanced technologies, such as Artificial Intelligence and Big Data analytics. When the FMIS are also interlinked with the available farm machinery, then the system is more complex and needs further attention. However, such a holistic approach should be taken in order to enable interoperability and interaction between all different actors within the agricultural domain (Fig. 1; Fountas et al. 2015b).

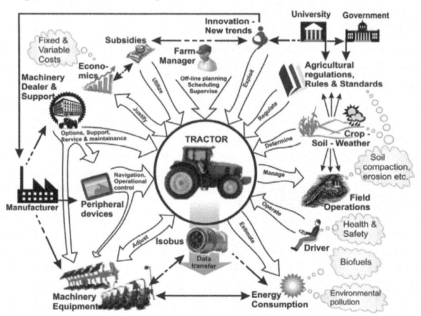

Figure 1. Farm machinery management information system (Fountas et al. 2015b).

Advanced Crop Protection Techniques and Technologies

However, it has to be noticed that farmers often lack the technical knowledge and skills necessary to use FMIS. This technical knowledge relates to the practical use of agricultural software, as well as farmers' awareness on the ways their data is being processed. Many FMIS are offered by major agricultural companies (i.e. FieldView, Trimble Ag Software, John Deere Operations Center), or by companies with FMIS as the main product (i.e. 365Farmnet, Isagri, FarmLogs). There is often no easy way to transfer data from one FMIS or software to another, or combine data from two or more FMIS, and even though there are available interfaces (Application Programmer's Interfaces (API)) to build around the data model of their system, this still leaves the difficult task of translating from the source data model to the target data model to the user.

Decision Support Systems for Spraying Pesticide Applications

The spread of diseases and insects and the severity of these pests result in different levels of spatial and temporal impact on the crop under consideration. Rational and cost-effective pest management requires the consideration of many factors. The number and complexity of the factors affecting the pest spreading makes it difficult to reach a sound and rational decision for pest management. The process of decision making that the farmers and advisors should follow is a complex process, and requires systematic collection and analysis of the gathered information (Fountas et al. 2006). To do so using information and computing technology, we use Decision Support Systems (DSS), which are interactive computer-based systems that consider strategic decisions for pest control even under complex and uncertain conditions (Shtienberg 2013) that help eliminate unnecessary use of synthetic PPPs by providing precise knowledge of the risk of an epidemic at field level. DSS include Pest and Disease Models which are coupled with Crop Growth Models. These models are based mostly on hourly or daily data such as air temperature, precipitation, relative humidity, leaf area index, canopy, and leaf wetness to produce quantitative results and alerts (Donatelli et al. 2017). These data are provided from nearby weather station networks or from on-site weather stations. The latter have proven to be more reassuring to many growers due to the physical presence of weather-monitoring hardware in their fields, and due to the latest reduction of the cost for local weather stations, this will show a rapid increase in the near future. Using field-level meteorological data as source for crop disease models or insect population growth models can provide added value to pest dispersal rate function of DSS on spatial and temporal scale with the use of Geographical Information Systems (GIS). An example could be the precipitation that has very strong local severity that can be significantly different between fields of the same region.

There is quite a controversial attitude towards the acceptance of DSS for farmers, but in the recent years with the more accurate weather information, they seem to receive high acceptance, as part of a holistic Integrated Pest Management (IPM) system, with direct and concrete application in terms of pest control and a reduction in reliance on conventional pesticide applications (Rossi et al. 2012). The effective implementation of DSS requires efficient pest monitoring systems to assess the actual pest profile and pressure at different spatial and temporal scales. There are a number of such DSS in agriculture to control both diseases and insects. One example of such a DSS based on Geographical Information Systems has been developed as part of the OPTIMA EU-funded project for three diseases; downy mildew in vineyards, apple scab in apple trees, and Alternaria leaf blight in carrots (www.optima-h2020.eu). An early version of the DSS can be seen in Fig. 2.

Figure 2. Spatio-temporal DSS for three crops (www.optima-h2020.eu)

Advanced Crop Protection Techniques and Technologies   **125**

Another example is the work of Pérez et al. (2020) that have developed a simple to use hand-held decision support tool for potato late blight to be used in South America. It was based on a disk with three concentric circles, representing the disease epidemics and providing a spray recommendation. In the case of olive orchards, one of the most significant pests is olive fruit fly and there are a number of systems developed for this, using digital traps, georeferenced tree locations and proposing precision treatment per specific tree locations (Miranda et al. 2019, Sciarretta et al. 2019). In addition, for olive orchards a software was developed, named X-FIDO (Cruz et al. 2017), for detecting symptoms of olive quick decline syndrome (OQDC) on leaves of Olea europaea L. infected by Xylella fastidiosa. These DSS can reduce diagnosis time and cost, and could be used to provide precision management information to control the spread of these diseases. Partel et al. (2019) developed an automated vision-based technology for monitoring insects in orchards (e.g., Asian citrus psyllid) utilizing artificial intelligence. This technology creates a map of the detected number of insects for each scouted tree that can be used for precision and variable rate spraying applications. Ampatzidis and Partel (2019) and Ampatzidis et al. (2020) developed a cloud-based application, named Agroview (Fig. 3), for precise and effective crop management in orchards. This user-friendly application has a great potential to provide individual plant analysis over large areas, detect diseased/stressed plants, and compare phenotypic characteristics on different sets of plants (Ampatzidis et al. 2019). It could be used to generate a prescription map compatible with precision equipment for variable rate applications.

In vineyards, there are also a number of DSS to control diseases and pests and include spraying recommendations. One of this has been proposed for the control of powdery mildew in Chilean vineyards including periodic fungicide spraying, which was proved to reduce the severity and the disease having both economic and environmental benefits for the farmers (Valdés-Gómez et al. 2017). In another example, Cruz et al. (2019) developed a vision-based program and a smartphone application for detecting grapevine yellow symptoms in vineyards. Finally, in cereals there have been a number of DSS for various diseases and pests. For example a DSS called I-Taimekaitse has been developed in Estonia and after testing for a number of years, a reduction of application doses was found for the control of the main fungal disease in spring named Pyrenophora teres (Drechsler, am Drechlera teres Sacc. Shoem) reaching 30 to 60% in comparison to conventional practices (Sooväli et al. 2017).

Conclusions

The combination of FMIS and DSS seems to be a solution that will provide farmers with a tool that can combine conventional farm diary information

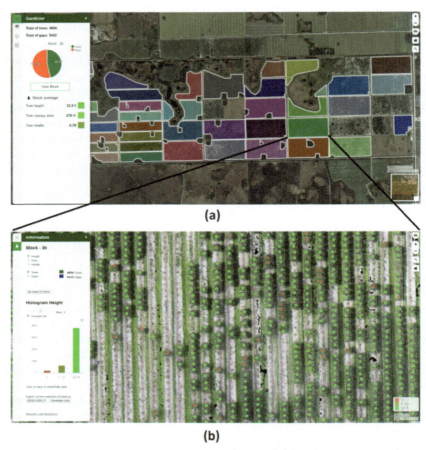

Figure 3. Agroview user interface to visualize data collected from aerial platforms (e.g., UAVs and satellites): (a) multiple citrus blocks (average field statistics for each block), and (b) individual field and tree information (e.g., tree categories based on height or canopy size) (Ampatzidis et al. 2020).

(dates of agricultural practices, quantities of inputs, machinery and facilities maintenance, seasonal costs, sales, profit calculation, mapping of crop status based on proximal or sensor based information, etc.) with agronomic advisory based on models and algorithms that use optimized meteorological, pedological and crop data. Since information and computing technology increases continuously its accuracy and field data gathering all across the globe is also significantly grown, the combined FMIS/DSS tools is expected to become the most useful assistance for the farmer in order to control the farm's status in a detailed manner with reduced personal scouting in comparison to current practice.

Advanced Crop Protection Techniques and Technologies

Detection Systems based on Artificial Intelligence

Introduction to Artificial Intelligence

Intuition to Machine Learning

Machine Learning is an application of Artificial Intelligence that provides computers with the ability to learn without being explicitly programmed. It comprises of various mathematical algorithms which makes learning possible. These algorithms are quite old and came into the spotlight, only when building systems got powerful enough to run these algorithms. Machine learning has proven to be beneficial in lots of fields such as businesses, health care, finance, automobiles and agriculture.

Types of Machine Learning Problems

Supervised Learning: The inputs and outputs of the data being fed are known to the user. The user also has an idea about the kind of predicted output achieved for any input. It is further divided into two sub parts:

Regression: The output data can be in continuous form (i.e. range from 0 to 5000) or percentage-wise. Let's take the example of predicting the presence of downy mildew disease in vineyards and approaching this as a simple regression problem. Based on the agronomic knowledge, humidity is a parameter that escalates the downy mildew presences and expansion. So, using a regression analysis the severity of disease presence can be correlated to the air humidity measurements. Data collected from previous years, will provide humidity measurements (x) and disease presence (y). So, a function $y = f(x)$ will be established considering a specific regression order that shows how accurately the regression fit on the reference x, y data. Based on the relevance of the new input humidity measurements (x_i) and the order of the regression, the disease severity (y_i) is able to be predicted. In the function below, a linear regression (first order) is considered, with xx being the independent or predictor variable, yy the response variable, β_0 the intercept and β_1 the slope.

$$y_i = \beta_0 + \beta_1 x_i$$

Classification: The output data is in discrete form (i.e. 0, 1, 2, ...), but it should not be a fraction. Using the example of apple scab disease, images of healthy leaves are assigned in class 0 and images of infested leaves in class 1, when using cameras to detect the problematic areas and the classifier in this example is the k-Nearest Neighbor (k-NN) (Fig. 4).

Therefore, the classification procedure is as follows. Each image is accompanied by a set of features, in most cases: i) color features, ii) shape features and iii) texture features. Considering that apple scab appears as visible color anomalies on the leaves, it is expected that the major differences will be in color features during the classification process.

Consequently, in the training phase the set of features associated with healthy apple leaves (class 0) and apple scab leaves (class 1) have been defined. So, in every new apple image of unknown class, the features will be calculated and this observation will be placed on the features map. For this example, a 2-D feature plane with y-axis for color features and x-axis for shape features was considered. Depending on the k nearest set of features (k=1 in the example), any new observation will be assigned either in class 0 or class 1, based on the proximity to the already known classes (dmin).

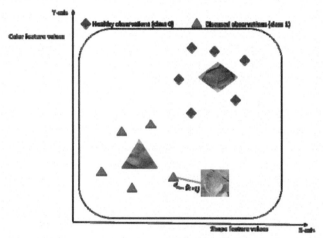

Figure 4. k-Nearest neighbor classification example.

Unsupervised Learning: Here, data of which input is known, but output is unknown are provided. Techniques such as clustering these groups of data into separate classes are very popular in this kind of analysis. Applications using unsupervised learning are detecting anomalies that do not fit to any group or segmenting datasets by some shared attributes. For example, DBSCAN is a clustering method that employs density and topology information to segment vegetation pixels from bare soil pixels in many vision applications in the agricultural domain.

Reinforcement Learning: This is a special type of machine learning which focuses on learning through penalty and rewards. This is mostly implemented in Video Games and Robotics. Exposing the fundamental concept of this method used in farming applications, many agricultural robots learn from mistakes like colliding with obstacles or failing to pick a fruit through penalty scores. At the same time, they figure out the shortest path to bypass obstacles or grab a fruit with the minimum number of motions, through rewarding optimum practices.

Artificial Intelligence (AI) has shown a drastic increase of applications in agricultural production.

Deep Learning (part of AI universe) constitutes the state-of-the-art method for image processing, with promising results for addressing farming problems such as plant disease diagnosis and pesticide recommendations. Deep learning notation refers to the computer software technique that mimics the network of neurons in a brain. This technique offers great performance in terms of feature extraction and prediction accuracy.

Deep learning methods, and specifically convolutional neural networks (CNNs), are gaining fast growth for the automation of crop classification and disease identification. The main reason is that, contrary to conventional machine-learning techniques, CNN training allows to learn automatically representations of data with multiple levels of abstraction. Although CNNs are very data-demanding, a technique called transfer learning is used to overcome this requirement by reusing patterns learned by state-of-the-art CNNs in related tasks. A schematic representation of a CNN architecture for image classification of apple and tomato leaves that are either healthy or diseased is depicted in Fig. 5.

Techniques stemmed from deep learning are also playing an important role in disease detection applications and will lead the future decision making by taking into account several factors like environmental conditions, harvesting practices, financial needs, soil characteristics or water availability.

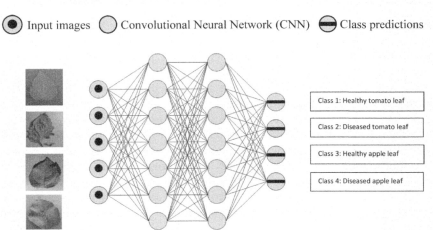

Figure 5. Convolutional Neural Network (CNN) architecture for leaves classification.

130 *Modeling for Sustainable Management in Agriculture, Food and the Environment*

Transfer Learning: Transfer learning is a popular training technique used in deep learning, where models that have been trained for a task are reused as starting point for another model. Usually, the challenge of training an Image Classifier for distinguishing healthy and infected plant leaves would require massive amount of data, large computing power, and lots of human effort. Instead, researchers build models, trained on large image datasets like ImageNet, COCO, Open Images, and share these models to the general public for reuse. Transfer learning is quite effective for image classification problems (Espejo-Garcia et al. 2020), because Neural Networks learn in an increasingly complex way (i.e. the deeper you go down the network the more image specific features are learnt).

Other Artificial Intelligence Advances: Another technique will be relevant in the near future: Generative Adversarial Networks (GANs). In fact, some recent works, such as Arsenovic et al. (2019), have evaluated their performance. GANs are a type of neural network architecture that allows neural networks to generate synthetic data similar to the original one. This type of networks (besides their extensions such as Wasserstein GANs) could address the problem of data scarcity within agricultural computer vision when transfer learning and traditional data augmentation are not enough. The main advantage of GANs is that they can create pictures with synthetic "real" crops instead of just rotating or adding noise to existing ones. This synthetic data could be used to improve the generalization ability of a CNN that obtains poor results at disease detection tasks, due to the constraints in the size of the original dataset and the limitations of traditional techniques.

Disease Detection Studies Using Artificial Intelligence

Pest and plant disease diagnosis through optical observation of the symptoms, encompasses a considerably high degree of complexity. In addition, the large number of cultivated plants, phytopathological problems and unique disease visible symptoms that might differ in each case, due to several biological mechanism, prevent even experienced agronomists and plant pathologists from successfully diagnosing specific diseases, and consequently lead to mistaken conclusions and treatments.

Therefore, AI has found fertile ground in many applications related with the accurate detection of diseased leaves and fruits. Color cameras provide useful color, shape and textural information that allow the AI classifiers decide if the content of each image belongs to the healthy or diseased class. In supervised learning, these classifiers produce the corresponding predictions based on features that have been manually engineered by experts. As an example, in Li et al. (2011), fifty shape, color, and texture features were extracted from images of several diseases, and the SVM classifier, a machine learning method was used to perform

Advanced Crop Protection Techniques and Technologies **131**

the disease recognition. Their experimental results (testing phase) gave recognition rates of grape downy mildew and grape powdery mildew of 90% and 93.33%, respectively. Another study (Dubey and Jalal 2012) leveraged state-of-the-art features for accurate classification, K-Means clustering for leaf segmentation and Multi-Class SVM for classification, yielding accuracy up to 93% for apple scab, apple blotch, and apple rot. In wheat leaves disease was detected with an accuracy of 95%, using feature selection and fuzzy c-means technique (Mondal and Kole 2016). Cruz et al. (2017 and 2019) and Ampatzidis et al. (2018) utilized CNN and transfer learning, which enables the application of deep learning to overcome the lack of sufficient training examples, to develop AI models to detect diseases on grapes (grapevine yellows) and olives (olive quick decline syndrome) based on symptoms development on leaves. They developed innovative methods for framing a CNN to improve performance when carrying out transfer learning, and combined the data with context at different levels to improve convergence of learning when re-applying an already trained deep learner to a new problem. But what happens when the visible spectrum cannot unveil disease evidences (since several diseases and disorders produce similar symptoms or no visual symptoms, especially in the asymptomatic—early disease development—stages)?

Multispectral, hyperspectral and thermal cameras provide more sophisticated information of the crop reflectance, allowing the effective detection of diseases even during the asymptomatic stage, when the disease stress is not visible to the naked eyes. Such research concepts are tested in diseased crops including avocado (Abdulridha et al. 2019a, Abdulridha et al. 2018, Harihara et al. 2019), citrus (Abdulridha et al. 2019b, Sankaran and Ehsani 2013), banana, lemon and mango (Arivazhagan et al. 2013), tomato (Abdulridha et al. 2019c) as well as downy mildew and black rot diseases in grapevines (Waghmare et al. 2016), among others. However, field deployment of such computer vision techniques are challenged by the unstructured field environment. Fruit occlusion and poor lighting conditions are the major problems that vision-based systems are suffering. Therefore, in several cases experts use artificial lighting such as halogen lamps or shading frames, in order to overcome the illumination uncertainties. A major challenge of using deep learning techniques in classification tasks, is the big volumes of training data that are required to achieve high accuracy prediction results (Barbedo 2018).

Conclusions

The development of AI and deep learning specifically has been significant in the recent years due to the increased computation ability of modern workstations and therefore research on disease and pest detection systems based on these techniques have found thorough application. However,

132 *Modeling for Sustainable Management in Agriculture, Food and the Environment*

such systems still lack accuracy due to short databases of diseased and healthy canopy images and the fact that crop canopy cannot be scouted in its whole volume rather its external surface. Even though, the combination of the work done globally for each specific disease into a unified database could increase accuracy, while new techniques and algorithms for predicting disease dispersal in the core of the canopy should be developed.

Spraying Technology

Introduction

The application of PPPs is executed by various techniques such as through irrigation water, dispersal of granular products, sprinkling and spraying. In the field, the majority of PPPs is applied by spraying. The spraying application is carried out by dissolving the product in water (spray solution) and its effectiveness depends on the PPP used, the method of application, the weather conditions, the plants' stage of growth as well as the stage of development of the parasite. Spraying is based on the creation of droplets of spray solution to cover the required plant or soil surface and its aim is summarized into covering to the fullest extent possible the desired surface with the spray liquid and consequently, with the active substance contained in it. The creation of droplets occurs when the spray liquid is forced through a narrow passage with relatively high pressure, due to the turbulence created as it passes through the stationary air layer. Alternatively, the spray liquid is fed into a strong stream of air which causes the droplets to split. Droplets can also be created with the help of centrifugal force, if the spraying solution is led to spinning discs (Bourodimos 2014).

There are various types of spraying machines, the most common in field operations are boom sprayers for open fields and airblast sprayers for 3D crops such as orchards and vineyards.

Types of Sprayers

According to Bourodimos (2014), there are many different types of spraying machinery, ranging from common, hand-operated devices to complex machines that weigh several tones. The factors that determine the choice of the right sprayer for each application are the PPP type and composition, the application rate, the product label recommendations, the crop type, the size and localization of target area, the distance from any sensitive area and the spraying application target.

Sprayers can be classified to various categories depending on the classification criteria used. According to the source of the driving force, for example, sprayers can be divided in two main categories, the manual

Advanced Crop Protection Techniques and Technologies **133**

and the motorized type. In the first case, the required power is provided by the operator himself/herself while in the motorized ones the power is provided either by the tractor via the power take-off (PTO) or by a separate motor. Another common method of sprayer classification is according to the way they operate. Sprayers can operate with hydraulic pressure, compressed air or with air sprinklers.

According to the way sprayers are transported they can be classified into (i) handheld sprayers that are being transported and operated by hand, (ii) knapsack sprayers that are carried via shoulder straps, (iii) mounted sprayers on the tractor and are operated via the hydraulic couplers, (iv) trailed sprayers hitched on the tractor's hook and (v) self-propelled sprayers, which are special vehicles with built-in spraying systems

Finally, based on the intended use, there are sprayers are for small-scale applications, open-field crops (boom sprayers), 3D crops (airblast sprayers), special uses and aerial use. A brief description of the different sprayer types based on the above categorization is presented below.

Small-scale sprayers: This category includes general-use small-scale sprayers, knapsack and handheld sprayers. General-use small-scale sprayers are mainly intended for spraying nurseries, small orchards and gardens and are suitable for small remote areas. They are powered by gas engines and their spray liquid tank has a capacity of 100 to 150 L, while the larger ones up to 500 L. There are also general-use sprayers that do not have a tank and draw the spray solution from a separate container. The solution is prepared and applied by the operator and their main disadvantage is that the application dose can hardly be adjusted. Finally, these sprayers may or may not have wheels.

Another common type of small-scale sprayers is the knapsack (backpack) sprayers. They are used among else in small farms, greenhouses, vegetable gardens and individual trees. They consist of the spray liquid tank, a pump, a compression chamber, a lance and a flexible plastic tube which connects the pump to the lance. The lance includes a metal or plastic tube at one end of which there is a valve that allows or interrupts the spraying and at the other end the nozzle. The spray liquid tank is usually plastic, with a capacity of up to 25 L. For spraying herbicides, a short boom with more than one nozzle may be fitted to the end of the lance. Although most knapsack sprayers are operated manually, they can also be motorized through a small gas engine or an electric motor with a rechargeable battery.

Handheld sprayers are small containers that are carried by hand or on the operator's shoulder. Liquid pressure is generated by small manual pumps or compressed air. The size and density of the droplets vary and depends on the pressure of the container and the type of the nozzle used. They are mostly intended for home use in small areas such as small

134 *Modeling for Sustainable Management in Agriculture, Food and the Environment*

flower gardens and correspondingly low quantities of pesticides. They are economical and simple to use, operate and maintain (Johanningsmeier and Randall 2002).

Sprayers for open-field crops (Boom sprayers): Boom sprayers are the most common PPP application equipment used in agriculture. These sprayers utilize hydraulic pressure as a pump delivers the pressurized spray solution to a set of nozzles. They apply the spray liquid vertically or with a small angle with a horizontal boom located above the crop for low height crops. They carry large spray tanks and apply low or medium volumes of spray liquid from 10 to 150 L/ha or more thus allowing a relatively large area to be filled per filling, while the indicated spraying pressure is up to 5 bar (Johanningsmeier and Randall, 2002). Open-field sprayers are either mounted, or trailed, or self-propelled. Mounted boom sprayers include a spray tank with a capacity of 400 to 1500 L and a spray boom of 6 to 24 m. Trailed boom sprayers include a spray tank with a capacity of 800 to 2500 L and a boom of 12 to 45 m. Finally, self-propelled boom sprayers are special vehicles with built-in spraying systems. Their spray tank has a capacity of 2000 to 4000 L, or larger and a boom of up to 48 m. They usually utilize wide wheels to reduce spoil compression and enough height to spray tall crops such as corn and cotton (Tsatsarelis 2006).

Sprayers of 3D crops (Air-assisted sprayers): These sprayers distribute the spray liquid upwards and sideways with the help of an air current and are mainly used for spraying perennial crops, such as tree crops and bushes/vines. They are also referred to as nebulizers because of the very small droplets they create. In airblast sprayers the boom takes the form of a semicircle on which the nozzles are located. In the middle there is a fan that creates a strong air current which helps in applying the spray liquid at the highest points of trees and also penetrating the dense canopy of trees at low altitudes. The small droplets achieve better penetration and coverage of the foliage but they are prone to being transported out of target (spray drift). Airblast sprayers don't utilize the same type of nozzles throughout the whole boom, as it is sought for those that aim higher to produce larger droplets, thus minimizing the out of target deposition. Airblast sprayers can also be mounted or trailed, with a spray tank of 500 to 4000 L while the air supply ranges from 3 to 20 m^3/h (Gemtos and Cavalaris 2015, Tsatsarelis 2006).

Special sprayers: Specific spraying needs favored the construction of special spraying machines the nozzles of which are fixed upon special constructions to meet the needs of the operators. Such sprayers are orchard sprayers, vineyard sprayers, tunnel sprayers and more and are briefly described here.

Orchard (tower) sprayers: In applications on trees, sprayers with tall vertical booms can be used so that the nozzles are at their height. Thus, better coverage of the foliage is achieved. Spray is expressed towards the vegetation along a vertical plane and the droplets penetrate the canopy and deposit with the help of an air current.

Vineyard sprayers: Vineyard sprayers, in general, utilize special frames that surround the vine so that the nozzles/atomizers can apply the PPP from the lowest effective distance possible between them and the spray target and cover it with the support of an air current. For each treatment, the settings have to be adapted and optimized in order to suit crop development characteristics. Vineyard sprayers are similar to over-the-row fruit crop sprayers, which are equipped with a structure passing over the row and fitted with vertical elements holding nozzles and air spouts to spray both sides of the fruit crop's row at the same time (TOPPS 2013).

Tunnel sprayers: These sprayers are used for spraying vineyards and fruit trees. They can look like some vineyard sprayers, but the nozzles are placed inside a tunnel that surrounds the rows of vines or trees. Their main advantage is that they can reuse the spray liquid that has not been deposited on the vegetation after filtering it. Manufacturers claim that a reduced amount of crop protection agent of up to 35–40% and a spray drift reduction of up to 99% is achieved, thus, they can be used effectively in case of strong winds (Bourodimos 2014, Clemens 2020).

Multi-row sprayers: Multi-row fruit crop sprayers are machines that are able to apply on four or more rows in one single pass (TOPPS, 2013). They are usually based on a gantry with numerous fans or outlets spraying horizontally into the canopy. Most multi-row sprayers utilize modern technology, such as tracking drawbars, strainer/mixer and tank rinsing and some of particular interest have the ability to alter fan speed for varying canopy conditions (density and growth stage). Additionally, high-output hydraulics ensure rapid folding of the gantry system. Multi-row sprayers improve output by allowing better use of ideal spraying conditions, better timeliness, and fewer tractor/labour hours per acre. Multi-row sprayers reduce the number of passes over the ground, reducing compaction along many rows and confining compaction to the occasional row of travel.

Mist sprayers: Mist or Cannon sprayers are generally used for applications on high trees, but they are also used for spraying developed maize plants, vineyards, vegetables, greenhouses as well as for the control of mosquitoes, in livestock farming and more. They are characterized by high air velocities and use, in general, lower water volumes than conventional airblast sprayers. They consist of a radial fan conveying the air towards a single, large diameter air outlet (cannon) and hydraulic nozzles, which are positioned along the contour of the air outlet. In this way, the spray

136 *Modeling for Sustainable Management in Agriculture, Food and the Environment*

is propelled by a high-velocity air current which projects the droplets at distances of some dozens of meters from the spraying machine. This type of spraying equipment produces uncontrollable spray clouds which are very prone to spray drift thus they shall not be used in areas where it may cause risks (TOPPS 2013, Baker 2000).

Hooded sprayers: Hooded sprayers are boom sprayers for herbicide applications whose nozzles are located within special covers. These covers direct the sprayed liquid between the rows of the crop, thus limiting the spray drift while helping to get the liquid just on the intended targeted for weeding area and not on the crop. Hoods can be either plastic or aluminium.

Shielded sprayers: Shielded field crop sprayers utilize large shields on the boom to protect droplets from wind for a certain distance, whereby the effect of wind and consequently the spray drift is efficiently reduced. The disadvantage of these sprayers is the increased weight as well as the increased maintenance and cleaning time, especially when a different PPP is about to be applied next. Shields can also be designed to deflect the air flow and direct the droplets towards the ground (TOPPS, 2013).

Air-assisted field crop sprayers: Air-assisted field crop or air-curtain sprayers are open-field sprayers in which a generated air stream supports the transport of the spray droplets to the target. The air stream is generated by a fan and distributed over the boom with a cloth or plastic tube (sleeve). The tube has openings from which the air exits at a certain speed dragging the droplets on its way, thus helping them to more efficiently enter plants' canopy. These sprayers achieve a better distribution of the spray liquid, counteract against the effects of windy conditions including the wind generated from driving and thus can be used to prolong the period of acceptable spraying conditions (Bourodimos 2014, TOPPS 2013, Hardi 2020).

Greenhouse sprayers: For the application of PPPs in greenhouses two general types of sprayers are available, hydraulic and low-volume. In the hydraulic sprayers, the PPP is sprayed to the target with the help of a pump. The pump creates the pressure at 3–70 bar and the nozzles on the boom or handheld gun break the spray into small droplets and direct it to the canopy. In a low-volume (LV) sprayer, the spray liquid is injected into a high-speed air stream which is developed by a fan, blower or compressor. In the majority of LV sprayers, the concentrate PPP solution is injected into the air stream through a small pump. The speed of the air stream can reach 320 km/h. The aim is to replace the air within the foliage canopy with air that contains the PPP. In LV sprayers, as the size of the droplets is much smaller, positive results can be achieved with less active ingredient. There are many variations of these two general types of

Advanced Crop Protection Techniques and Technologies **137**

greenhouse sprayers, in order to fit particular crops or growing methods. Hydraulic sprayers include the aforementioned general-use small-scale sprayers the mobility of which is achieved by mounting them on rails or electric carts or by manually pulling them by hand or a compact tractor, knapsack sprayers and lightweight hand-held sprayers. Alternatively, three-way turrets with different nozzles for each application: irrigation, misting and PPP application are being used. Finally, the installation of a piping system that will deliver PPPs to every part of the greenhouse is also an option. In that case, PPPs preparation and filtration are done in a mixing area and a pump and piping that will handle the pressure developed are required. The disadvantage of using piping systems for PPP application is that the entire system must be drained and thoroughly cleaned before the application of a different PPP. Low-volume greenhouse sprayers include knapsack mist blowers, rotary disk sprayers, thermal and cold (mechanical) foggers. Knapsack mist blowers utilize a small gas engine and a fan which creates an air stream with a speed of 160-−320 km/h. The spray solution is injected into the air stream and is sprayed through it onto the target. Close attention must be paid to keep the spraying nozzle at least 2 meters away from the plants in order to avoid blast damage. Thermal foggers require a special carrier that is mixed with the PPP to improve the homogeneity of droplets' size and achieve even distribution of the spray solution. The carrier also decreases the molecular weight of the particles, allowing them to float in the air for up to 6 hours, thus making the greenhouse inaccessible to human intervention for that duration. A thermal fogger injects the PPP solution into a hot, fast-moving air stream which vaporizes it into fog particles. If transferred along the greenhouse, a thermal fogger can quickly and efficiently apply to its whole. Air circulation from a horizontal air flow (HAF) system will result in a more even distribution and better canopy penetration. Cold (also mechanical) foggers, use a high-pressure pump (70–210 bar) and atomizing nozzles to produce fog particles. The distribution of the spray solution is achieved through a hand-held gun or external fan units. Droplets in the 30-micron size drop out of the air fairly quickly but droplets in the 5-micron size may evaporate or float in the air currents for hours. Small particles cannot move through dense canopy, however, in most studies, good insect control has been achieved (Bartok 2020).

Aerial sprayers: Aerial spraying can be used to treat large areas quickly and, unlike ground spraying, can be carried out when field conditions prevent wheeled vehicle access, which enables the timing of spray treatments to be improved and soil compaction reduced. There are however, certain disadvantages associated with the "traditional" aircraft spraying. High wind speed and temperature inversion may limit treatment application whilst trees, waterways, environmental considerations and overhead power lines may also prevent some fields from being treated. Accurate deposition in dense crop canopies can also be more difficult to achieve with aircraft. Volatility and spray drift can be a problem with aerial spraying and environmental contamination can be significant if spraying is incorrectly executed (FAO 2001). Due to these reasons many countries have severely limited aerial application of PPPs, most notably, the European Union banned it outright with a few highly restricted exceptions in 2009, effectively ending the practice in all member states (EC 2017).

Alternatively, unmanned aerial vehicles (UAVs) can fly at lower height thus reducing the risk of spray drift, while avoiding any possible hazard for the sprayer operator. A UAV is an aircraft which can fly without a human pilot and if needed, can be controlled via radio channel. In the last two decades, various types of UAVs are being used in agriculture (Mogili and Deepak 2018) as they are characterized by high operational efficiency and low labor intensity. In order to improve their working efficiency, spraying systems on UAVs are configured to deliver highly concentrated low-volume spraying solutions. Spray rates for UAV systems are generally 1–2 L/ha, which is 25–50 times lower than conventional spray application systems. However, since highly concentrated PPP solutions are being used, operators must ensure that there are no gaps or overlaps in the spraying pattern, so to avoid insufficient coverage or phytotoxicity. UAVs fly at low heights of 3–5 m in order to diminish the risk of spray drift. The optimization of automatic guidance systems and the adoption of control algorithms have improved the accuracy of flight control and stability at these low altitudes (Xinyu Xue et al 2016). However, agricultural UAVs face numerous technical limitations such as battery efficiency, low flight time, communication distance and payload. These technical limitations must be resolved in order to provide the right approach for the next generation of agricultural solutions (Jeongeun Kim et al. 2019).

This chapter focuses mainly on open field and airblast sprayers which are the most commonly used in field operations. In different types of sprayers the parts may differ but the main components are: (i) the frame on which the various parts are being held, (ii) the spray tank in which the spray solution is stored, (iii) the filters which purify the water and they spray solution, (iv) the pump that generates the pressure in the spray solution, (v) the spray pressure control and adjustment system, (vi) the distribution tubes for the spray solution, (vii) the frame (boom) on which the nozzles are fitted and the (viii) the nozzles from which the spray solution is being sprayed

The principle of operation of the sprayers is, in general, the same. The spray solution which is stored in the tank gets purified through the filters and then is taken into the pump, which adds dynamic and kinetic energy to the liquid. At the pump's outlet, due to the non-free flow, the liquid develops pressure. It is then driven into a controller that includes

Advanced Crop Protection Techniques and Technologies **139**

the pressure regulator, according to which it relieves the pressure by returning a portion of the liquid back to the tank. The returning liquid helps in the constant stirring of the spray solution into the spray tank. The controller also utilizes manometers to check the pressure and control valves to control to which part of the machine the spray solution will be directed to.

After the controller, the solution is directed through the distribution tubes to the nozzles which split it into small drops, that is to say, spraying. As mentioned above, in open field sprayers nozzles are fitted on a straight boom while in orchard sprayers on a semicircular boom. In special sprayers they may have a different layout, e.g. for spraying in vineyards they are arranged on two vertical arms (Gemtos and Cavalaris 2015).

Problems within Plant Protection Products Application

Requisite for the plant disease control as they are, PPPs contain toxic substances that in case of excessive or incautious use could contribute in natural resources degradation and environmental (both flora and fauna) contamination. Several studies have proved that the final recipients of residual PPPs are groundwater and surface water reserves (Gonçalves et al. 2007, Guzzella et al. 2006, Hildebrandt et al. 2008, Papadopoulou-Mourkidou et al. 2004, Papastergiou and Papadopoulou-Mourkidou 2001, Rodriguez-Mozaz et al. 2004). PPPs can be washed away from the leaves and enter surface water bodies through different routes, most important are the losses of PPPs from point sources and diffuse sources (TOPPS, 2008).

Point Sources

Point sources represent the most important pathways of PPPs into surface water. Research has shown that if preventive measures are not taken, they can represent up to 40–90% of the contamination in surface water reserves. Although point sources contamination may occur due to multiple misusages during (a) sprayer cleaning, (b) sprayer filling, (c) management of remnants, (d) spills during PPP application, (e) PPP storage and (f) leakages during sprayer transport, they all have something in common. They can be entirely avoided by adopting the correct behavior when using and handling PPPs, given that the availability of adequate, in terms of safety, spray equipment and decent on-farm infrastructure is ensured (TOPPS 2006).

Diffuse Sources

On the other hand, diffuse sources originate from the application of PPPs in the field and are transferred to water via (a) the wind as spray drift during product application, (b) field run-off due to rainfall shortly after the application and (c) entries from subsurface water transfers through drainage. During PPP application, apart from some types of point source contamination (e.g. unintended spraying in / next to water courses and contamination of field access roads when turning the sprayer), diffuse sources are potentially the main contributors to water contamination if proper measures are not taken (TOPPS 2008). These measures include careful study of the weather conditions (wind, relative humidity, rainfall) in order to select the optimal application time (see Section 3.2) and cautious inspection and calibration of the spraying machinery prior to spraying.

Contrary to wide spread perceptions, spray drift is a rather minor entry route into surface water compared to other routes, but can be more important for certain crops. Applications in 3D crops (i.e. vineyards and orchard) are more critical concerning spray drift than in field crops due to type of sprayers used and the orientation of spray droplets that move horizontally through the orchard canopy and beyond it, as well as upwards above the canopy via direct spraying into the air or upward diffusion from the sprayed canopy (TOPPS 2020). Spray drift is defined as the quantity of plant protection product that is carried out of the sprayed area (treated) by the action of air currents during the application process (ISO 2005) and therefore spray drift generated during applications to 3D crops is complex and difficult to control (Miranda-Fuentes et al. 2018). This is where the optimization of spraying technology can be of assistance in minimizing spray drift during spraying applications, given that best management practices are nevertheless adopted.

Best Management Practices

Used and handled correctly, PPPs pose no unacceptable risks to water. But just a few drops of spilt concentrated PPP can break drinking water and environmental quality standards. The 3-year EU-Life programme project TOPPS (Train Operators to Promote best management Practices & Sustainability) (TOPPS 2020), created a series of manuals regarding the Best Management Practices (BMPs) in every step of the spraying application. BMPs are practical recommendations to follow in order to reduce point source pollution of water, spray drift, PPP runoff as also as recommendations regarding the management of remnant liquids contaminated with PPPs. According to the sequence of steps in the use of PPPs, 6 main processes are defined (TOPPS 2006):

Transport: Moving PPPs from suppliers to the farm is the first step where there might be risks for point source contamination and in many cases, farmers—correctly—rely on professional dealers/suppliers to ensure safe transport to the farm. Another transport step includes the transport of spray liquid in the spray tank from farm to field. There are prerequisites

Advanced Crop Protection Techniques and Technologies **141**

in order to not contaminate the storage, not to produce clean-up remnants of spills, to ensure no leakage and to not end up with unwanted stock.

On-farm Storage: Spills and accidental losses in PPP-storage facilities are very limited in occurrence, however, when they do occur the consequences might be significant both from a liability as from an environmental point of view, because in the storage room PPPs are usually concentrated in terms of chemical content. Safe storage has many benefits, such as enhanced safety for operators and farm dwellers, reduced pollution risk and reduced insurance fees, reduced risk of prosecution and fines from regulators, enhanced cross compliance and trade certification approval as also as risk reduction in environmental and water contamination.

Before spraying: Careful planning of the procedure to be followed during PPP application is mandatory prior to spraying. Planning includes marking of the fields to be treated and identification of the sensitive areas adjacent to them, careful selection of PPP according to various criteria and the likely weather forecast for the specific region at the time of the planned application. Regarding spraying equipment, they need to be inspected both by a third party and the operator, adjusted mainly regarding the liquid volume output rate, the spray profile and the air support and calibrated for operating parameters which ensures proper daily functioning. Lastly, it should be noted that the biggest point source risk before spraying is the filling and loading activity, as well as leakages when driving to the field and for that reason they should be performed with utmost care.

During spraying: Given that the previous process is properly executed, the spray activity itself should not impose a major risk on point source contamination, in contrary with the risk of diffuse source pollution. Transfers from diffuse sources may occur by a number of routes (e.g. runoff/erosion, spray and dust drift, leaching and drainage). The spray application process remains a mechanical and technology-driven process. Hence the operator should be knowledgeable about the spray application practice and remain vigilant during operation so that only the target area is treated. Older or intensively used (without appropriate maintenance) sprayers will trigger a higher risk of in-field problems, unless carefully maintained.

After spraying: The main point in the after spraying process is the management of the PPP fractions left at the end of the spray process both inside and outside of the sprayer. This includes (a) spray leftovers (spray solution surplus), (b) non sprayable solution (e.g. non-dilutable fractions), (c) pockets of PPP deposits in the spray tank, (d) deposits of PPPs on filter mesh and (e) external sprayer contamination due to spray drift which is often linked to sprayer design and concept. The careful rinsing of spray equipment, internally and externally, in the last treated field is one of the most important activities to minimize the risk of point source pollution.

Remnant management: The overall remnant disposal and waste management principle is to not produce waste. If in any given step remnants are produced, they should as far as possible be legally reused at once for the intended process. Despite all precautions some remnants (solid and/or liquid disposable fractions) will be produced as a result of the farming activity. It is important to find appropriate and efficient solutions at affordable cost to manage these so to maintain water quality standards. Some examples of these solutions are: physicochemical clean up, bioremediation (such as biobeds, biofilters, phytoremedation), reverse osmosis, photocatalysis and electrolytic breakdown. These solutions eventually result in a disposable liquid and/or solid fraction.

Spray Drift Reduction Techniques

As mentioned, spray drift can occur during the application of PPPs in the field. Spray drift is the transfer of small spray droplets out of the target area due to wind, poor calibration or application practices or incorrect nozzles. Spray drift reduction techniques (SDRTs) can be classified in direct and indirect (TOPPS, 2013). Direct measures aim to reduce spray drift at the source (formation and direction of the spray droplets) and are mainly addressed through application technologies, sprayer accessories designed to decrease spray drift generation and correct sprayer adjustment. Indirect measures, on the other hand, aim to reduce spray drift by measures to "capture spray drift" like buffer zones, no spray zones or barriers (e.g. windbreaks, hail nets, etc.).

Environmental Factors

Before starting an application, environmental factors relevant for spray drift risk should be considered. Most important is to know the distance from a crop to be sprayed to any sensitive area. Maps should be available where such information is documented and where indirect mitigation measures like buffer strips (e.g. hedges, windbreaks, other structures able to capture spray drift) are shown. Other major factors especially in 3D crops are (i) the canopy structure of the crop (height of field crops, planting, pruning and training system, canopy density, phenological stage), (ii) the evenness of canopy wall along the row (absence of space between adjacent plants) and (iii) growth stage/status of the crop, which largely determines the spray drift risk especially in the rows closer to sensitive areas. Key consideration is the leaf density and leaf area able to capture the spray and keep it in the target area. Environmental factors do not rapidly change and are therefore essential for any application plan and spray drift reduction strategy.

Advanced Crop Protection Techniques and Technologies **143**

Weather Conditions

Weather conditions are the main influencing factors for spray drift. These conditions cannot be directly influenced and predicted. Wind speed, wind direction, air humidity and temperature are the key factors which need consideration. In most countries critical values are recommended, indicating the limits to be respected for spraying. If one of the key variables exceeds the limit it is recommended not to spray. Wind speed influences the amount of fine droplets transported away from the target area. The wind direction determines the direction of the spray cloud and if it drifts towards a sensitive area. In situations where air humidity is low, water from the spray droplets is evaporated. This effect increases the amount of fine droplets and therefore increases the risk of unwanted transfer. If air temperature is too high, thermal effects tend to lift up small droplets and delay the sedimentation of the spray (thermal drift). Therefore the spray cloud is longer exposed to the transfer through wind. Decision Support Systems (DSS) for spray drift avoidance have been developed (see Section about "Decision Support Systems for Spraying Pesticide Applications" on page 123).

Drift Reduction Nozzles

Air induction: These nozzles are hydraulic type (part or an assembly of parts with an orifice through which the liquid is forced under pressure to produce a spray) provided with small orifices along its body enabling the suction of air within the liquid flux. The mixing of air and liquid allows the production of droplets containing air bubbles, therefore coarser droplets with respect to the ones produced by conventional nozzles. These nozzles reduce spray drift by 50 to 90% compared to a conventional nozzle. Both air induction nozzle types, flat fan and hollow cone, produce larger droplets by air induction, and are less prone to drift. Air induction hollow cone nozzles are especially recommended for conventional orchard/vineyard sprayers without deflectors.

Twin fluid nozzles: These nozzles are appliances in which the spray is produced by the action of a high-velocity airstream on the spray mixture. They allow changing of flow rate and droplet size independently. Droplet size can be adjusted to produce a coarse spray at field edges next to sensitive areas. Spray cross distribution from twin fluid nozzles tend to get more uneven if droplet size is increased too much.

Deflector nozzles: These nozzles are hydraulic type where droplets are generated by a small deflector into the nozzle body and then rebound towards the ground. These nozzles create a coarse droplet size with low kinetic energy and are typically used for application on bare soil. They feature a wide spray pattern and good overlapping between spray jets and therefore boom height can easily be lowered.

Sprayer Adjustment

Sprayer adjustment is largely related to the behavior of the operator and the adjustment options of the sprayer. According to the EU directive 2009/128 EC on the sustainable use of PPPs, operators are obliged to regularly calibrate their sprayers. Calibration is the validation that the sprayer can be operated according to the requirements of good agricultural practices. Therefore, the sprayer parameters should be adjusted in order to apply the correct amount of PPP to the target crop, implying that the potential losses of PPP to the environment are minimized. Various calibration manuals for different sprayer types exist on the web. EU Horizon 2020 Project INNOSETA has successfully created an online repository where various manuals regarding the sprayers' check can be freely accessed (INNOSETA 2020). Finally, these checks should be performed several times during the season as the crop composition changes throughout the year (e.g. leaf areas of the crops in plantation crops).

Sprayer Operation

Sprayers should be operated in such a way that the PPP is applied only on the desirable target area/crop. This requires special attention at field boundaries and if necessary the use of drift-reducing measures. Buffer zones and other non-target areas should not be sprayed. PPP labels refer to the required distance to water bodies and other sensitive areas. In 3D crops, when the outer row is being sprayed, the nozzles on the side of the sprayer without canopy should be closed. In these crop sprayers and especially for multi-row sprayers, a number of sections should be adaptable to the shape of the spray profile delivered by the sprayer (by shutting sections) and should fit the size of the field (for instance triangle shape). For field crop sprayers, the boom sections which apply PPP outside the target area should be switched off. The spraying operation should stop every time the sprayer reaches the field margin and turns to the next row. Field margins should be sprayed carefully and the use of drift-reducing technology is highly recommended (TOPPS 2013).

Conclusions

There are numerous types of spraying equipment for different applications in order to provide optimum PPP distribution and penetration in the crop canopy. The most used ones are boom and air-assisted sprayers and there are many problems (point and diffuse source) related to environmental and human health impacts that occur during preparation, application and cleaning/storing the sprayer. Therefore, there is a need to apply best management practices in all steps of PPP use and especially to avoid spray drift that its impact is completely uncontrolled when it takes place.

It can be seen that keeping the spraying machinery in a good condition, adjusting them on the specific field characteristics before PPP application and following specific protocols in preparation and closing steps can reduce that possibility of PPP contamination of natural resources and assist in more sustainable PPP use.

Technologies of Precision Spraying

Conventional sprayers provide almost homogeneous PPP application, which is a disadvantage if we consider the fact that pest dispersal is scattered. Therefore, the application of new technologies on spraying equipment to become more precise according to the spatial distribution of the pest under control seems to be a solution for even higher efficacy and efficiency of PPP application. The different types of technologies that are being used in precision spraying are various and every one of them has been developed in order to serve specific needs of crop protection applications. Aiming to categorize these technologies that nowadays are present as industrial solutions, we use the typology defined by Schwarz et al. (2011) that included Guidance, Recording and Reacting technologies, in this case specifically about crop protection activities (Fig. 6).

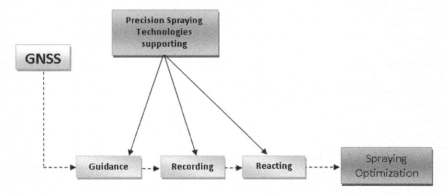

Figure 6. Sequence of Precision Spraying Technologies for spraying optimization.

Global Navigation Satellite System (GNSS)

Precision agriculture as a concept is based on the knowledge of exact spatial and temporal information that could be achieved only after the wide application of Global Navigation Satellite Systems (GNSS) (Lechner and Baumann 2000). This is the generic term for all geographical positioning based on satellites, like the American GPS, the Chinese BeiDou, the Russian GLONASS and the European Galileo. Real-time

146 *Modeling for Sustainable Management in Agriculture, Food and the Environment*

information supplied by GNSS can be obtained using a GNSS receiver which has to be mounted on the propelling equipment. Essentially this device receives radio signals that are transmitted by multiple satellites and based on that, GNSS receiver's position is calculated. In this way, location indications are available at any time but in order to be accurate, differential correction has to be applied. Built-in solutions such as Wide-Area Augmentation System (WAAS) and Real-Time Kinematic (RTK) correction improve the accuracy of the information supplied by the GNSS receiver or integrated guidance system. As we will see later in this section, GNSS services are involved almost in every step of the precision spraying procedure including recording and reacting.

As an example for the recording part, the accurate position and time information that is supplied by GNSS receivers on a continuous basis during spraying operations are useful data which can be collected and stored. Combining this information with the applicator's sensors data, it is possible to produce site- and time-specific records of spraying applications. As a result of this procedure, a map can be created containing all the previous history of applications and be used as history source for future applications. As regards the task of guidance systems in sprayers utilizing GNSS, the operator is able to precisely measure, map and respond, based on the unique spatial characteristics of each field. This leads to significant advantages like avoiding fatigue, reducing the time to complete the spraying process due to higher operation speeds and consequently reducing costs.

Technologies Supporting Guidance

In general, the term "guidance" in agriculture refers to the way of directing the movements of agricultural machinery and therefore the itineraries over the field. However, there are two main ways of performing spraying applications using either self-propelled sprayers or sprayers that are mounted on or trailed by a tractor (the vast majority). In both cases, in order to perform precision movements in the field, guidance systems are implemented either on the self-propelled machinery which simultaneously move and spray or on the tractor hitched with the sprayer (sometimes on the sprayer itself).

Driver Assistance Systems

The service of driver assistance is to help the operator to keep the vehicle in the right direction as steer the propelling equipment among the plant rows of the field area. It is not pre-installed and usually it needs to be set in the machinery's system.

Driver assistance systems constitute a major application of GNSS, as GNSS steering aids are commonly used by the farming community to

Advanced Crop Protection Techniques and Technologies **147**

improve guidance service. It provides farmers the capability of moving in precise straight lines and reducing the possibility of overlapping or missing areas. In addition, in PPP applications, GNSS-based guidance can replace the conventional way of marking using foam (Mcdougall et al. 2001). Among other advantages are the reduction of PPP and fuel costs, time, soil compaction and labor, while simultaneously field spraying efficiency is increased.

Lightbar and **auto-steer mode** can be selected by the operator. In both options, a GNSS receiver is used in order to identify the machinery's location in the field. Lightbar requires the driver to manually adjust steering, while on the other hand auto-steer technology can be connected to the steering wheel and automatically adjusts the steering. By choosing the automatic way, the operator is not busy with wheel steering requirements, but he is able to focus on monitoring the implemented field operations.

Machine Auto-guidance

Another substantial application of GNSS is on machine auto-guidance systems. These systems work in combination with on-board computer system and they are already integrated on the machinery, in contrast with the auto-steer technology. They can take over steering operations in a direct way, allow for headland steering, section control and accept both drive-maps and task maps to operate agricultural implements. More particularly about this technology, the signals for the navigation are received in a direct way from the hydraulics that handle the wheels of the sprayer. The operator is able to select the desired speed and upload the driving pattern, while a complete supervision is provided through a customized interface that is supported by the computer. In general, auto-guidance can help to optimize itineraries and therefore logistics, avoid fatigue and mistakes and increase the whole speed of the operation.

Elevation Maps

In general, the elevation characteristics of a cultivation influences spraying application and that is why there is need to monitor its variations (recording it and act accordingly). The main source for collection of soil elevation data are auto-steering systems or GNSS receiver. Using the latter, it is possible for a Digital Elevation Model to be produced that supply services of specific terrain attributes identification, such as slope, aspect, curvature, landscape water flow directions and topographic wetness indices. Typical application of elevation maps is present on uneven crop fields, where the proper way that the sprayer should enter the field, and the directions that should be followed to identify re-entry points can be defined based on them.

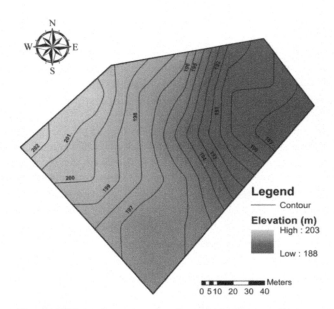

Figure 7. Elevation map of a vineyard in Drama, Greece.

Radar

Controlling the sprayer's travel speed is of critical role as deviations from the desirable one can lead to misapplication. That is why several solutions have been developed according to how low or high are these speeds. While for speeds lower than 8 km/h engine it is preferred to use rpms indications, for higher speeds digital speedometers using radar technology monitor speed with great accuracy (Beard and Deer 1999) (refspeeds). Radar's working principle is based on radio waves pulses that are being transmitted to the ground and received back (Zhang 2015). Recording the duration of the delay, it is possible to measure the frequency differences between every transmitted and received pulse (Zillmann et al. 2004). Due to the fact that this frequency is proportional to the speed, an indication of the sprayer speed is available (Paul and Speckmann 2004).

Technologies Supporting Recording (Canopy Mapping)

Extensive application of recording technologies is observed for the implementation of canopy mapping. Especially modern precision spraying systems that provide variable-rate spraying are based on technical data such as plant sizes and shapes, crop growth, canopy structures and the percentages of ground cover. Hence it is of critical role for efficient spraying that match crop structures, to acquire this information in an accurate way and improve PPP application methods via canopy characterization.

Advanced Crop Protection Techniques and Technologies   **149**

The means for achieving accurate recording are sensors which are used for crop canopy characteristics detection. Following vegetation spectroscopy principles (Suárez et al. 2015), canopy mapping is based on image (or video) data in order to deploy differences of reflectance in spectral bands. Normalized Differential Vegetation Index (NDVI) is a measurement between near infrared light reflected by vegetation and visible light. Healthier and more robust plants absorb more visible light and reflect more near infrared light, while the opposite happens for unhealthy or sparse vegetation. As regards soil, it does not perform intense reflection neither in the visible nor in the near-infrared region of the electromagnetic spectrum (Bannari et al. 1995). This index was designed in order to detect living vegetation and distinguish it from other materials such as soil, stones or dead vegetation. Therefore, a lot of sensors take measurements of the bands that crops are more sensitive, the red and the near-infrared, while others use different technologies. Some of the most efficient types of technologies that use spectral analysis and serve the above purpose are described below.

On-the-go Treatment Sensors

Spraying systems equipped with on-the-go technology do not use data from the crops that have been previously recorded. As the sprayer goes into the field, the sensors that are mounted on the sprayer boom and spatially precede the nozzles, collect all the information about the crop conditions. Therefore, the measurements of the sensors are combined with the applicator of the system and it is possible to have almost simultaneous recording and spraying application of the exact PPP quantity required.

WeedSeeker (Trimble, USA)[2] uses advanced optics to sense the possible presence of weeds. Infrared sensors are able to detect weeds from a brownish background (Fillols et al. 2013). It is a spot spray system that has been designed to allow annexation to conventional spraying tanks, pumps and plumbing. In case of detection, it sends a signal to the respective nozzle in order to apply the necessary quantity of chemical, spraying directly only the weed.

OptRx (AgLeader, USA)[3] is an NDVI sensor utilizing the reflectance of light emitted on the crops. The NDVI and NDRE (Normalized Difference Red Edge Index) crop vigor algorithms are available for small (i.e. early growth wheat) and large crops (i.e. corn) recording respectively. It is mounted on the sprayer's boom and its service is real-time data recording and measurements of crop conditions that will trigger immediate adjustment of PPP application.

---

[2] https://agriculture.trimble.com/product/weedseeker-spot-spray-system/
[3] https://www.agleader.com/blog/what-is-optrx/

WEED-IT Ag (Rometron, the Netherlands)[4] system utilizes sensors that emit red light towards the plants and as a result of the presence of chlorophyll the light is shifted to infrared and becomes detectable. According to the sensor that detected the infrared light of the weed, instant spraying through solenoid valve is conducted only to the desirable position. An advanced version named **WEED-IT Quadro**, utilizes four detection zones of every detection sensor used. The accuracy of the system is reinforced by the extra small zones with improved optics based on blue LED-lighting. Compared to the red LED-lighting, the blue one is less sensitive to background noise and more sensitive to weeds. Alongside, other factors that make the whole procedure more accurate and effective is the higher sampling frequency and communication speeds that are capable due to the dual core processor used. Individual flow control per nozzle is supported by PWM technology that is described in next section. Moreover, it can be built in any type and brand of sprayer.

Ultrasonic Sensors

Manual canopy characterization is expensive, time consuming and it is not non-destructive compared to the electronic alternative that can be combined with variable rate application (VRA) methods. An approach to achieve canopy detection is based on ultrasonic sensors which transmit sound waves of high frequency towards an object. By the time the ultrasonic waves return back, it is possible for these sensors to perceive the reflected echo. Recording the time difference between the sending and the receiving waves, the distance between the sensor and any object is calculated (Fig. 8). Sprayers equipped with ultrasonic sensors are widely used combined with VRA automatic control.

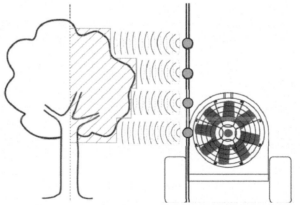

Figure 8. Ultrasonic sensors for canopy detection.

---

[4] https://www.weed-it.com/weedit-quadro

Advanced Crop Protection Techniques and Technologies 151

Canopy volume in vineyard crops and citrus can be measured utilizing and properly placing several ultrasonic sensors onto a sprayer (Balsari and Tamagnone 1998). Giles et al. (1989) after developing an algorithm, proceeded on an improved PPP application in apple and peach trees, supported by three ultrasonic sensors mounted on an air-blast orchard sprayer in different spots. They achieved to maintain satisfying coverage and penetration rates having reduce the spray volume in their applications. Ultrasonic sensors combined with electro-valves allowed to adapt the flow rate according to the crop structure.

However, ultrasonic sensors do not take measurements with high spatial resolution provided that they have limited penetration capability. They do not consist a source of big amount of information in comparison with other canopy mapping approaches, but besides their lower accuracy performance they are preferred when low cost is the objective.

Light Detection and Ranging (LIDAR) Sensors

LIDAR (Light Detection and Ranging) is a laser range sensor that records the elapsed time between the transmission of a laser beam pulse and the reception of its echo from a reflecting object. The duration of this procedure indicates the distance between an object and the laser and is called time-of-flight (TOF). LIDAR is very efficient when producing mathematical description of plant structure (Rosell et al. 2009). The applied algorithms and its measuring speed in relation with the objects in its surroundings allow the creation of 3D cloud points for accurate reconstruction of tree canopies, providing scanning capabilities (Fig. 9). In contrast with passive sensors, LIDAR is able to collect depth information penetrating the canopy and provide data about the density of the canopy and even for the inner structure of a tree.

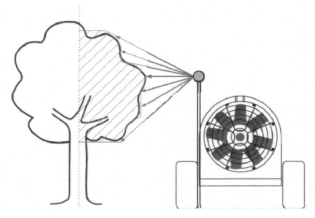

Figure 9. LIDAR sensor for canopy detection.

152 *Modeling for Sustainable Management in Agriculture, Food and the Environment*

Llorens et al. (2011) came to the conclusion that besides the fact that an ultrasonic sensor is an appropriate approach for canopy characterization, a LIDAR sensor supplies more accurate tree canopy data. The measurement beam of LIDAR is thinner and does not diverge a lot, while it is easy enough to be combined with a scanning mechanism. LIDAR can be mounted in several platforms in combination with an on board computer for data storage. As regards precision spraying it can either be attached on the sprayer (or the tractor) or Unmanned Aerial and Ground Vehicles (UAV and UGV) that are going to proceed with the PPP application procedure.

Balsari et al. (2008) focused their research in constructing a sprayer automatically able to adapt air distribution and spray according the characteristics of the diseased tree target. It has been observed that sprayers performing VRA in real time according to tree canopy utilizing LIDAR sensors, are capable of input savings of 40% (Colaço et al. 2018).

Cameras

There is a wide variety of camera types that are utilized in modern sprayers, in order to implement canopy mapping. Their main differences lie on the areas of electromagnetic radiation that their operation is based on. The full range of all frequencies of electromagnetic radiation (NASA 2015) is referred as electromagnetic spectrum and demonstrates the characteristic distribution of electromagnetic radiation absorbed or emitted by a particular object. The spectrum is divided into many bands, with the one that is visible to the human eye, being the shortest one (wavelength ranging from 390 to 700 nm) (Starr 2005). The visual spectrum is based on Red, Green and Blue bands and is called RGB region from their initials, while for wavelengths from 700 to 10000 nm, the band classification goes as, Near InfraRed (NIR), Middle InfraRed (MIR) and Far InfraRed (FIR) or Thermal. In general, canopy mapping techniques that are based on images cannot access the inner parts of the vegetation. Therefore, compared to LIDAR, they are affected a lot by the changing conditions of the surrounding lighting.

RGB (Red-Green-Blue): When recording with an RGB camera, the main operation is based on a CMOS (Complementary Metal-Oxide Semiconductor) or a CCD (Charged Coupled Device) image sensor, which depicts the colour existence percentages of the RGB model (Hirsch 2004) using appropriate filters. The image processing technique begins with a separation of plants from soil and continues with recognition of soil, texture and colour properties of plants. In this way, crop/weed or species classification is possible to be performed (Samseemoung et al. 2012). Stajnko et al. (2011) conducted a research applying PPPs in orchards via targeted spraying. A RGB camera-based machine vision system was responsible for detecting apple trees canopies and implement image

Advanced Crop Protection Techniques and Technologies

153

analysis. Using specific software all the data captured by RGB camera was processed and in real-time fed to a spraying arm. In addition there were three individually controlled sections, which adapted the pesticide spray flow to the canopy shape.

Multispectral: There is information in an image that human eye physiology does not allow to be captured and therefore RGB cameras cannot provide such kind of additional data. The role of multispectral cameras is to depict an object (crop or weed) by capturing data at determinate frequencies of the electromagnetic spectrum. Some of their capabilities that can be used for canopy mapping are: measurements of crop coverage (Rajan and Maas 2009), leaf diseases capturing (Bauer et al. 2011) and NDVI, Green NDVI and SRPI (Lebourgeois et al. 2012) calculation. When the preferred solution is based on remote sensing techniques (Schowengerdt 2007), multispectral cameras are ideal.

A typical example is the first exclusively automatic selective system that was constructed in order to spray diseased crops. Oberti et al. (2016) explored the case of grape vines infected by powdery mildew and their aim was to apply targeted spraying using a modular agricultural robot. This robot was based on a disease sensing system utilizing an R-G-NIR multispectral imaging, moving with six degrees of freedom and equipped with a precision spraying system. Automatically detection and spraying more than 85% of the diseased area within the canopy was among the greatest achievements of this effort. Alongside there was reduction of the PPP use from 65% to 85%, compared to a conventional homogeneous spraying of the canopy. Torres-Sanchez et al. (2015) conducted research about 3D modeling of tree canopy based on stereophotogrammetry principles using multispectral and RGB cameras mounted on an UAV. RGB results were better for fields with a pattern of tree-row plantation, while the images taken by the multispectral camera were superior for single tree plantation.

Hyperspectral: Very useful information is contained in hyperspectral images, which is collected by a hyperspectral sensor. In order to derive a continuous spectrum for each image cell, the sensors collects image data simultaneously in hundreds of narrow, adjacent spectral bands. Spectrometers can make spectral measurements of bands as narrow as 10 nm over a wide wavelength range, typically at least 400 to 2400 nm (visible through MIR wavelength ranges). Correlating crop characteristics to one or more of these bands is not possible by using only RGB or multispectral cameras.

An example of hyperspectral camera utilization of spraying application is the case of a UAV combined with an on board sprayer and RF controlled nozzles that was used by Meivel et al. (2016), in order to spray with PPPs in specific areas of crops that are not easily accessible by end-users. In order to obtain remote sensing images, the UAV was equipped with a multispectral camera and in this way it could identify the vegetation and the edges of the crop areas.

Thermal: Every object radiates energy at a wavelength corresponding to its surface temperature. In thermal images of crops, the energy that is radiated from their surface is captured through thermal cameras which form the images using infrared radiation (up to 14000 nm). The versatility, accuracy and high resolution of the infrared thermography makes it possible to identify the leaf characteristics of different crops on individual basis using thermal remote sensing (Kuenzer et al. 2013). Thermal cameras can also be applied for disease identification and estimating canopy temperatures, crop water stress indicators are available. As regards aerial spray application, Jiao et al. (2016) verified that infrared image processing algorithms combined with infrared thermal imaging method can be used to monitor PPP drift. Significant advantage of this procedure is that such kind of real-time measurements are characterized by speed, absence of contact and comprehensibility.

Technologies Supporting Reacting

Variable Rate Plant Protection Product Application

Sprayers enabled with variable rate (VR) PPP application technologies implement changes in the application rate that are proportional to the actual pest stress in the field and help to avoid application to undesired plant canopies and field areas (Karkee et al. 2013). They can also significantly reduce spray overlap (Batte and Ehsani 2006). It should be noted that VR technologies for PPP application can also be used to apply fertilizers at variable rates (Ess et al. 2001).

Automatic Section Control on Sprayers

Most of the sprayers enabled with VR application operate by selective control of small sections (containing several nozzles) of the spray boom (Christensen et al. 2009). Using a boom shut-off valve, the flow of product to the boom is shut on and off. When the sprayer is turning at the end of the field boundaries, these valves allow the operator to shut the sprayer on and off. Most agricultural sprayers have booms split into what are termed "boom-sections" allowing for independent control and giving the operator the ability to manually turn boom section off instead of the entire boom. This is possible using a switch box located in the operator's cabin. However, partial boom width may be required sometimes during the spraying procedure. Therefore, turning sections off can reduce overapplication of PPPs.

Advanced Crop Protection Techniques and Technologies   155

Based on the kind of input data that are being used, there are two types of VR PPP application technology, namely map-based and real-time sensor-based, while as regards the output side, there are four different types of applications; flow-based control, direct chemical injection, chemical injection with carrier control, and spraying nozzle control.

Map-based Variable Rate Plant Protection Product Application: This technology principle is to adjust the application rate utilizing an electronic map, named prescription or application map (Figure 10). Taking into account the field position from a GNSS receiver and a prescription map of desired rate, the input concentration is changed as the applicator moves through the field (Grisso et al. 2011).

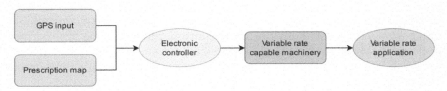

Figure 10. Flow chart of map-based variable rate PPP application.

Real-Time Sensor-Based Variable Rate Plant Protection Product Application: The input data of these systems are based both on contact (e.g. mechanical) and non-contact (e.g. camera) sensing in order to identify either the crop (canopy area) that needs to be protected or pests that have to be controlled (Fig. 11). For the efficient operation of this technology, various types of sensors can be used for the determination of color, shape, size, texture, reflectance, and temperatures of pests. As a result, canopy patterns or pest categorization patterns are created. The sensor input can also be used to control the direction and rate of chemical application (Karkee et al. 2013). RGB, multispectral, hyperspectral and thermal cameras, photodetectors, laser scanners and ultrasonic sensors are among the sensors that can be applied. They are mounted on a spray boom (or a bar) ahead of the spray nozzle and aimed at the ground. For example, when a chlorophyll (green) reflectance signal exceeds a threshold (set during calibration by the operator), a signal is sent from a controller to a solenoid-operated valve to release herbicide (Grisso et al. 2011). Both nozzle control systems and rate control systems can be used for VR of chemical application.

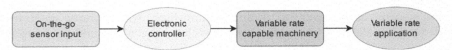

Figure 11. Flow chart of map-based variable rate PPP application.

In addition, sprayers that use information of the environment to reduce drift from the target are currently being developed. These sprayers use for example sensors which measure the wind speed and direction and change the sprayer settings (spray pressure, nozzle type) accordingly depending on where the sprayer is located in the field in relation to vulnerable areas based on GNSS (Doruchowski et al. 2009).

Flow-Based Control: Sprayers that use this type of control technology, aim to regulate the flow in order to vary the rate. More specifically, by varying the nozzle flow rate in direct proportion to the forward speed (Hloben 2007), they manage to keep the application rate constant. In relation with pressure-based systems the management of the flow-based ones is much easier and that is the reason why they are used more. These systems consist of a flow meter, a ground speed sensor, and a controllable valve (servo valve) with an electronic controller to apply the desired rate of the tank mix (Fig. 12). When it is possible for a communication link to be established between the controller and a 'map system', then a flow-based control system can also be used for VR applications in the zones of the field with their own characteristics and needs.

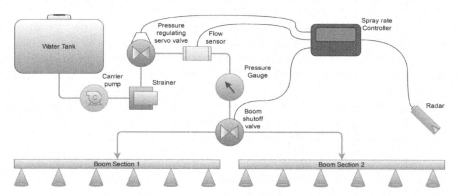

Figure 12. Flow-based controlled spraying system.

Direct Chemical Injection: These systems utilize a controller and a chemical pump to manage the rate of injection of a chemical into a stream of the carrier (water) rather than the flow rate of a tank mix. The flow rate of the carrier is usually constant, and the injection rate is varied to accommodate changes in ground speed or changes in the commanded application rate. If the controller is designed or modified to accept an external command, the system can be used for VR application (Fig. 13) (Humburg 2003). In direct chemical injection systems the chemical concentrate and the carrier are kept in separate tanks (Hloben 2007). Behind the carrier pump, the chemical can be injected into all boom sections (centralised), into only one section (decentralised), or directly into individual nozzles.

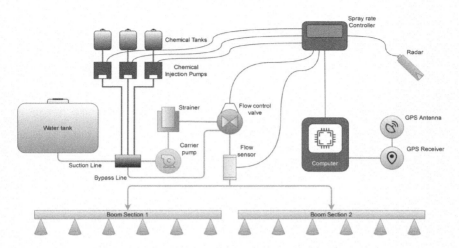

Figure 13. Direct chemical injection spraying system.

Chemical Injection with Carrier Control: This is about a combination of the two types of control technologies described above utilizing a control system that changes both the water carrier rate and the chemical injection rate in order to respond to ground speed or application rate changes (Fig. 14).

Spraying Nozzle Control: The key difference of this technology is that it requires the incorporation of direct-acting, in-line solenoid valves in the conventional sprayer nozzle assemblies, aiming to alternate the opening and the closing of the nozzle in high speeds (Fig. 15). The VR application is proportional to the flow rate, which is controlled by the duration of the time that the valve is open. Alongside, there are not changes in the spray pattern and the droplet size. Commercially available systems operate on 10 Hz frequency, which means they have ten on-off cycles per second. This provides a 100 ms time duration of one opening and closing operation for the solenoids mounted on each nozzle. However, as described in the next paragraph, using control technologies from the field of electronics (i.e. PWM), it is possible for a nozzle body to operate at 30 cycles per second. There are also different types of systems, controlling the flow rate either by mixing the fluid with air in the nozzles, which can reduce the flow by half, or varying the orifices of the nozzles. The latter can be achieved by a moving, steerable component within each nozzle or by combining several nozzles into one holder and switching between them (Weis et al. 2012). Although, individual nozzle control lead to more accuracy, most VR enabled sprayers with this output technology operate by selective control of a number of several nozzles (sections) of the spray boom.

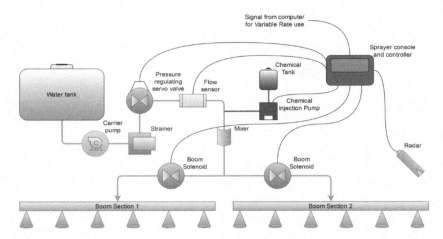

Figure 14. Chemical injection with carrier control spraying system.

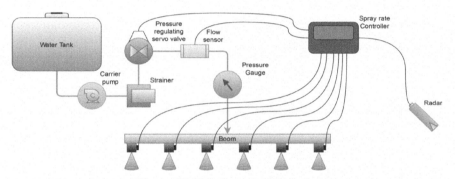

Figure 15. Nozzle control spraying system.

Pulse Width Modulation (PWM): The incorporation of PWM (Barr, 2001) technology for VR spraying application requires that each nozzle body is equipped with an electronic solenoid (shut-off valve). The valve turns on and off ten or more times every second, creating an intermittent, pulsed spray. The proportion of time that the valve is open, called the pulse width or duty cycle, can be electronically controlled. In Fig. 16 which depicts periodical pulse actuation signals, it is obvious that in such kind of systems, the duration of the pulse width (ON-mode) is going to be the regulator of the quantity of the spraying product.

The highlight of PWM technology is its ability to almost instantly alternate between on and off states, due to the short time needed for actuation response of the valve at each nozzle. In this way, the solenoid valve is actuated, the nozzle applies PPP at the desired pressure and as a result there is extreme product drain reduction (due to the duration of

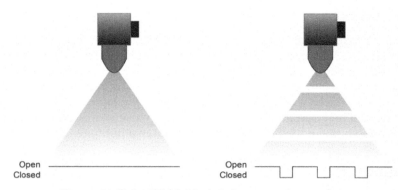

Figure 16. Pulse Width Modulation operation mode.

OFF-mode). In addition, the operator is able to control tip flow rate and droplet size independent of one another.

Applying liquid product at a specific pressure maintains uniform nozzle-to-nozzle overlap and droplet size. It is common that nozzles are paired in groups of two, with only one unit of the pair being in the ON-mode at any given moment. PWM nozzle technology allows for very fine grained as-applied maps, with application rates for each nozzle being recorded individually.

In flow-based systems, the pressure is affected during speed transitions or when a boom is actuated (Sharda et al. 2010). On the other hand, the PWM system is able to preserve the constant desired nozzle application pressure, without being affected by the number of nozzles that are or are not actuated (Mangus et al. 2016).

Boom Height Control: Although this is not a variable rate technology, it does improve in some way the precision of the spraying product application and makes it more uniform (Karkee et al. 2013). The main characteristic of this technology is that it uses real-time sensors in order to minimize the losses during spraying application that is caused by changes on e.g. ground speed or tire pressure. These sensors are able to maintain the balance and the distance between the sprayer boom and the ground by preventing boom oscillation above its horizontal axis.

Ultrasonic sensors measure (40 times per second) the distance to the ground. This information allows the control system to make responsive height adjustments. The system has shown reliable control with average speeds more than 29 km/h in all kinds of uneven terrain. Although boom height control is not a VRA technology as such, it eliminates streaks and improper overlaps, and improves coverage (Grisso et al. 2011). Similar control mechanisms can also be used to position the spray tower at an appropriate distance from the crop canopy in orchards and ornamental nurseries (Karkee et al. 2013).

Conclusions

Even if all the components of an optimum application of PPPs are in place (right PPP type and quantity, sprayer calibration and adjustment according to the crop sprayed, use of best management practices), it should be noticed that conventional spraying application cannot still provide PPP coverage in the best manner. Therefore, the technologies analyzed in this section and all related advancements are very useful in order to provide PPP in the parts of the field required and not in a homogeneous way.

Chapter Conclusions

This chapter provided information about the current trends on alternative product to synthetic PPPs and methods for optimized application of crop protection agents in order to significantly reduce PPP effects on the environment and humans. It is believed by the authors that a holistic crop protection strategy of maximum PPP efficacy and minimum residues is required to achieve this goal. Therefore, if this strategy starts from prediction models provided to the farmer in an easily accessible way through FMIS and DSS, then the primer idea of the situation in a specific field would become clearer in an early stage of development. This target would be assisted highly by the incorporation in the system of a detection tool for pest symptoms that could provide a better knowledge of the current situation. Having in mind the pest dispersal severity in the field, a crucial part would be to select the optimum combination of synthetic and biological PPPs from a large list of new product types that opens a new drive to pest management. However, the most crucial part that has not yet found the required attention, even if it is a very important aspect of PPP efficacy increment, is the in-field application using conventional or precision application sprayers. It is believed that this chapter has covered in a high extent the components of this holistic integrated pest management scheme to provide knowledge on how crop protection could be optimized in terms of efficacy, but also in terms of minimum environmental effects.

Acknowledgement

This work was supported by the EU H2020 programme through the project OPTIMA (Grant Agreement 773718 - H2020-SFS-2016-2017/H2020-SFS-2017-2).

References

Abdulridha, J., Y. Ampatzidis, R. Ehsani, and A. de Castro. 2018. Evaluating the performance of spectral features and multivariate analysis tools to detect laurel wilt disease and nutritional deficiency in avocado. Computers and Electronics in Agriculture 155, 203–211.

Abdulridha, J., O. Batuman and Y. Ampatzidis. 2019a. UAV-based remote sensing technique to detect citrus canker disease utilizing hyperspectral imaging and machine learning. Remote Sensing 11(11), 1373.

Abdulridha, J., O. Batuman and Y. Ampatzidis. 2019b. UAV-based remote sensing technique to detect citrus canker disease utilizing hyperspectral imaging and machine learning. Remote Sensing 11(11), 1373.

Abdulridha, J., Y. Ampatzidis, S.C. Kakarla and P. Roberts. 2019c. Detection of target spot and bacterial spot diseases in tomato using UAV-based and benchtop-based hyperspectral imaging techniques. Precision Agriculture (November), 1–24.

Ali, M.A., I. Rehman, A. Iqbal, S. Din, A.Q. Rao, A. Latif, T.R. Samiullah, S. Azam and T. Husnain. 2014. Nanotechnology, a new frontier in Agriculture. Adv. Life Sci. 1(3), 129–138.

Ampatzidis, Y., V. Partel and L. Costa. 2020. Agroview: Cloud-based application to process, analyze and visualize UAV-collected data for precision agriculture applications utilizing artificial intelligence. Computers and Electronics in Agriculture (in press).

Ampatzidis, Y. and V. Partel. 2019. UAV-based high throughput phenotyping in citrus utilizing multispectral imaging and artificial intelligence. Remote Sensing 11(4), 410, doi: 10.3390/rs11040410.

Ampatzidis, Y., V. Partel, B. Meyering and U. Albrecht. 2019. Citrus rootstock evaluation utilizing UAV-based remote sensing and artificial intelligence. Computers and Electronics in Agriculture 164, 104900, doi.org/10.1016/j.compag.2019.104900.

Ampatzidis, Y., A.C. Cruz, Roberto Pierro, Alberto Materazzi, Alessandra Panattoni, L. De Bellis and A. Luvisi. 2018. Vision-based System for Detecting Grapevine Yellow Diseases Using Artificial Intelligence. XXX International Horticultural Congress, II International Symposium on Mechanization, Precision Horticulture, and Robotics, 12–16 August, 2018, Istanbul Turkey.

Arivazhagan, S., R. Newlin Shebiah, S. Ananthi and S. Vishnu Varthini. 2013. Detection of unhealthy region of plant leaves and classification of plant leaf diseases using texture features. Agricultural Engineering International: CIGR Journal. Vol n pp

Baker, P. 2000. arizona Agricultural Pesticide Applicator Training Manual for Certification and Continuing Education. https://agriculture.az.gov/sites/default/files/Arizona_Agricultural_Pesticide_Applicator_Training%20Manual_az1149.pdf, accessed on April 3rd, 2020.

Balsari, P., G. Doruchowski, P. Marucco, M. Tamagnone, J.C. van de Zande and M. Wenneker. 2008. A System for adjusting the spray application to the target characteristics. Agric. Eng. Int. CIGR 10, 1–11.

162 *Modeling for Sustainable Management in Agriculture, Food and the Environment*

Balsari, P. and M. Tamagnone. 1998. An ultrasonic airblast sprayer. *In*: Proceedings of the International Conference on Agricultural Engineering AgEng, Oslo, Norway, 24–27 August, pp. 585–586.

Bamisile, B.S., C.K. Dash, K.S. Akutse, R. Keppanan and L. Wang. 2018. Fungal endophytes: Beyond herbivore management. Front. Microbiol. 9, 544, doi: 10.3389/fmicb.2018.00544. eCollection 2018.

Bannari, A., D. Morin, F. Bonn and A.R. Huete. 1995. A review of vegetation indices. Remote Sensing Review 13, 95–120.

Barbedo, Jayme Garcia Arnal. 2018. Impact of dataset size and variety on the effectiveness of deep learning and transfer learning for plant disease classification. Computers and Electronics in Agriculture 153, 46–53.

Barr, M. 2001. Introduction to Pulse Width Modulation (PWM). Barr Group.

Bartok, J.W. Jr. 2020. Greenhouse Sprayers and Spray Application Techniques. https://ag.umass.edu/greenhouse-floriculture/fact-sheets/sprayers-spray-application-techniques, accessed on April 5th, 2020.

Batte, M.T. and M.R. Ehsani. 2006. The economics of precision guidance with auto-boom control for farmer-owned agricultural sprayers. Computers and Electronics in Agriculture 53(1), 28–44.

Bauer, S.D., F. Korč and W. Förstner. 2011. The potential of automatic methods of classification to identify leaf diseases from multispectral images. Precision Agriculture 12(3), 361–377.

Bhattacharyya and Jha 2012. Plant growth-promoting rhizobacteria (PGPR): Emergence in agriculture. World J. Microbiol. Biotechnol, 28(4), 1327–1350.

Boller, T. and G. Felix. 2009. A renaissance of elicitors: Perception of microbe-associated molecular patterns and danger signals by pattern-recognition receptors. Annu. Rev. Plant Biol. 60, 379–407

Borah, B., R. Ahmed, M. Hussain, P. Phukon, S.B. Wann, D.Kr. Sarmah and B.S. Bhau. 2018. Suppression of root-knot disease in Pogostemon cablin caused by *Meloidogyne incognita* in a rhizobacteria mediated activation of phenylpropanoid pathway. Biological Control 119(1), 43–50.

Bourodimos, G. 2014. Crop Protection Machinery, Checks and Problems, MSc Thesis, University of Thessaly, https://ir.lib.uth.gr/xmlui/bitstream/handle/11615/43102/13505.pdf?sequence=1&isAllowed=y , accessed on March 21st, 2020 (in Greek).

Cabrera, J.C., A. Boland, P. Cambier, P. Frettinger and P. Van Cutsem. 2010. Chitosan oligosaccharides modulate the supramolecular conformation and the biological activity of oligogalacturonides in Arabidopsis. Glycobiology 20(6), 775–786.

Cardé, R.T. 2007. Using pheromones to disrupt mating of moth pests. pp. 122–169. *In*: M. Cogan and P. Jebson (Eds.). Perspectives in ecological Theory and Integrated Pest Management. Cambridge: Cambridge University Press, New York.

Christensen, S., H.T. Sogaard, P. Kudsk, M. Norremark, I. Lund, E.S. Nadimi and R. Jorgensen. 2009. Site-specific weed control technologies. Weed Research 49(3), 233–241.

Clemens, GmbH and Co. KG. 2020. | Weinbautechnik - Getränketechnik - Tankbau https://www.clemens-online.com/index.EN.php?cnt=p4250&nav=m206&dash=tsg, accessed on April 2nd, 2020.

Advanced Crop Protection Techniques and Technologies **163**

Cogoni, C., J.T. Irelan, M. Schumacher, T.J. Schmidhauser, E.U. Selker and G. Macino. 1996. Transgene silencing of the al-1 gene in vegetative cells of Neurospora is mediated by a cytoplasmic effector and does not depend on DNA-DNA interactions or DNA methylation. Eur. Mol. Biol. Organ. J. 15(12) 3153–3163.

Colaço, A.F., J.P. Molin, J.R. Rosell-Polo and A. Escolà. 2018. Application of light detection and ranging and ultrasonic sensors to high-throughput phenotyping and precision horticulture: Current status and challenges, Hortic. Res. 5(1), doi: 10.1038/s41438-018-0043-0.

Cook, M.S., Z.R. Khan and J.A. Pickett. 2007. The use of push-pull strategies in integrated pest management. Annu. Rev. Entomol. 52(1), 375–400.

Cruz, A., Y. Ampatzidis, R. Pierro, A. Materazzi, A. Panattoni, L. De Bellis and A. Luvisi. 2019. Detection of grapevine yellows symptoms in *Vitis vinifera* L. with artificial intelligence. Computers and Electronics in Agriculture, 157, 63–76.

Cruz, A.C., A. Luvisi, L. De Bellis and Y. Ampatzidis. 2017. X-FIDO: An effective application for detecting olive quick decline syndrome with novel deep learning methods. Frontiers, Plant Sci. 10 October 2017 | https://doi.org/10.3389/fpls.2017.01741.

Dalakouras, A., M. Wassenegger, E. Dadami, I. Ganopoulos, M.L. Pappas and K. Papadopoulou. 2020. Genetically modified organism-free RNA interference: Exogenous application of RNA molecules in plants. Plant Physiol. 182(1), 38–50.

Donatelli, M., R.D. Magarey, S. Bregaglio. L. Willocquet, J.P.M. Whish and S. Savary. 2017. Modelling the impacts of pests and diseases on agricultural systems. Agricultural Systems 155, 213–224.

Doruchowski, G., W. Swiechowski, R. Holownicki and A. Godyn. 2009. Environmentally-Dependent Application System (EDAS) for safer spray application in fruit growing. Journal of Horticultural Science & Biotechnology (special issue): 107–112.

Dubey, S.R. and A.S. Jalal. 2012. Adapted approach for fruit disease identification using images. International Journal of Computer Vision and Image Processing (IJCVIP) 2(3), 44–58.

EC. 2020a. The use of plant protection products in the European Union, Data 1992–2003, 2007 Edition, https://ec.europa.eu/eurostat/documents/3217494/5611788/KS-76-06-669-EN.PDF, accessed on 23 February, 2020.

EC. 2020b. http://ec.europa.eu/commfrontoffice/publicopinion/archives/ebs/ebs_354_en.pdf, accessed on 23 February, 2020.

EFSA, E. 2013. The 2010 European Union Report on Pesticide Residues in Food. EFSA Journal 11(3), 3130, https://www.pan- europe.info/old/Issues/documents/Food/EFSA%20monitoring%20residues%202010%20Mar%2013.pdf, accessed on 23 February, 2020.

El Asbahani, A., K. Miladi, W. Badri, M. Sala, E.H.A. Addi, H. Casabianca, A. El Mousadik, D. Hartmann, A. Jilale, F.N. Renaud and A. Elaissari. 2015. Essential oils: From extraction to encapsulation. Int. J. Pharm. 483(1-2), 220–243.

Electromagnetic spectrum. 2015. Imagine the Universe! Dictionary. NASA. Archived from the original on May 24, 2015. Retrieved June 3, 2015.

164 *Modeling for Sustainable Management in Agriculture, Food and the Environment*

Espejo-Garcia, B., N. Mylonas, L. Athanasakos, S. Fountas and I. Vasilakoglou. 2020. Towards weeds identification assistance through transfer learning. Computers and Electronics in Agriculture 171. https://doi.org/10.1016/j.compag.2020.105306.

Ess, D.R., S.D. Parsons and C.R. Medlin. 2001. Implementing site-specific management: Sprayer technology – Controlling application rate on the go. http://www.ces.purdue.edu/extmedia/AE/SSM-5-W.pdf.

European Commission EGTOP. 2011. Final report on plant protection products. https://ec.europa.eu/info/food-farming-fisheries/farming/organic-farming/co-operation-and-expert-advice/egtop-reports.

European Commission. 2017. Overview report: Sustainable use of pesticides. https://doi.org/10.2875/604951, accessed on April 5th, 2020.

FAO. 2001. Guidelines on good practice for aerial application of pesticides. http://www.fao.org/3/y2766e/y2766e00.htm, accessed on April 5th, 2020

Fletcher, S.J., P.T. Reeves, B.T. Hoang and N. Mitter. 2020. A perspective on RNAi-based biopesticides. Front. Plant Sci. 11, 51.

Fillols, E., C. Baillie, S. Underdown and T. Staier. 2013. Integrating the Weedseeker® technology into weed management strategies in sugarcane. Proceedings of the 35th Conference of the Australian Society of Sugar Cane Technologists held at Townsville, Queensland, Australia.

Fountas, S., D. Wulfsohn, S. Blackmore, H.L. Jacobsen and S.M. Pedersen. 2006. A model of decision making and information flows for information-intensive agriculture. Agricultural Systems 87, 192–210.

Fountas, S., C. Carli, C.G. Sørensen, Z. Tsiropoulos, C. Cavalaris, A. Vatsanidou, B. Liakos, M. Canavari, J. Wiebensohn and B. Tisserye. 2015a. Farm management information systems: Current situation and future perspectives. Computers and Electronics in Agriculture 115, 40–50.

Fountas, S., C.G. Sorensen, Z. Tsiropoulos, C. Cavalaris, V. Liakos and T. Gemtos. 2015b. Farm machinery management information system. Computers and Electronics in Agriculture 110, 131–138.

Gemtos, T. and C. Cavalaris. 2015. Machinery of plant maintainance (in Greek). https://repository.kallipos.gr/pdfviewer/web/viewer.html?file=/bitstream/11419/1324/1/02_chapter_01.pdf , accessed on March 28th, 2020.

Giles, D.K., M.J. Delwiche and R.B. Dodd. 1989. Sprayer control by sensing orchard crop characteristics: Orchard architecture and spray liquid savings. J. Agric. Eng. Res. 43, 271–289.

Grisso, R., M. Alley, W. Thomason, D. Holshouser and G.T. Roberson. 2011. Precision Farming Tools: Variable-Rate Application. Virginia Cooperative Extension Publication, pp. 442–505.

Guzzella, L., F. Pozzoni and G. Giuliano. 2006. Herbicide contamination in surficial ground water in Northern Italy. Environ. Pollut. 142, 344–353.

Hardi International A/S - Twin Force. https://hardi-international.com/sprayers/sprayer-components/twin-force, accessed on April 4th, 2020

Harihara, J., J. Fuller, Y. Ampatzidis, J. Abdulridha and A. Lerwill. 2019. Finite difference analysis and bivariate correlation of hyperspectral data for detecting laurel wilt disease and nutritional deficiency in avocado. Remote Sens. 11(15), 1748. https://doi.org/10.3390/rs11151748.

Advanced Crop Protection Techniques and Technologies

Hayles, J., L. Johnson, C. Worthley and D. Losic. 2017. Nanopesticides: A review of current research and perspectives. New Pestic. Soil Sens. 193–225.

Hildebrandt, A., M. Guillamón, S. Lacorte, R. Tauler and D. Barceló. 2008. Impact of pesticides used in agriculture and vineyards to surface and ground water quality (North Spain). Water Res. 42, 3315–3326.

Hirsch, R. 2004. Exploring Colour Photography: A Complete Guide. Laurence King Publishing. ISBN 1-85669-420-8.

Hloben, P. 2007. Study on the response time of direct injection systems for variable rate application of herbicides. Inaugural dissertation, Institut für Landtechnik der Rheinischen Friedrich-Wilhelms-Universität Bonn.

https://agriculture.trimble.com/product/weedseeker-spot-spray-system/

https://digitalcommons.usu.edu/cgi/viewcontent.cgi?referer=https://www.google.com/&httpsredir=1&article=1862&context=extension_curall

Humburg, D. 2003. Site-specific management guidelines: Variable rate equipment – Technology for weed control. Site-specific Management Guidelines (SSMG-7). Department of Agricultural and Biosystems Engineering, South Dakota State University.

INNOSETA Platform, Training Material, https://platform.innoseta.eu/list?s=calibration&type[]=4 , accessed on April 14th, 2020

INNOSETA webportal, http://www.innoseta.eu, accessed on April 14th, 2020.

ISO 22866. 2005. Equipment for crop protection—Methods for field measurement of spray drift. https://www.iso.org/standard/35161.html, accessed on April 10th, 2020.

Jaber, L.R. and S.E. Araj. 2017. Interactions among endophytic fungal entomopathogens (Ascomycota: Hypocreales), the green peach aphid Myzus persicae Sulzer (Homoptera: Aphididae), and the aphid endoparasitoid Aphidius colemani Viereck (Hymenoptera: Braconidae). Biol. Control 116(1), 53–61.

Jeongeun Kim, Seungwon Kim, Chanyoung Ju, Hyoung II Son. 2019. Unmanned aerial vehicles in agriculture: a review of perspective of platform, control, and applications. IEEE Access 7, 105100–105115 https://doi.org/10.1109/access.2019.2932119.

Jiao, L., D. Dong, H. Feng, X. Zhao and L. Chen. 2016. Monitoring spray drift in aerial spray application based on infrared thermal imaging technology. Comput. Electron. Agric. 121, 135–140, doi: 10.1016/j.compag.2015.12.006.

Johanningsmeier, J.S. and C.J. Randall. 2002. Pesticide Applicator Core Training Manual: Certification, Recertification and Registered Technician Training. Michigan State University.

Kairyte, K., A. Kadys and Z. Luksiene. 2013. Antibacterial and antifungal activity of photoactivated ZnO nanoparticles in suspension. J. Photochem. Photobiol. B. 128, 78–84.

Karkee, M., B. Steward and J. Kruckeberg. 2013. Automation of pesticide application systems. *In*: Zhang, G. and F.J. Pierce (Eds.). Agricultural Automation: Fundamentals and Practices. CRC Press, Boca Raton, FL, USA.

Katsuta, H., M. Nomura, T. Wakita, H. Daido, Y. Kobayashi, A. Kawahara and S. Banba. 2019. Discovery of broflanilide, a novel insecticide. Pestic. Sci. 44(2), 120–128.

Keith, S., A.E. David and G.A. El-Hiti. 2008. Role of modern chemistry in sustainable arable crop protection. Phil. Trans. R. Soc. Lond. B Biol. Sci. 363(1491), 623–637.

Kuenzer, C., J. Zhang, A. Tetzlaff and S. Dech. 2013. Thermal infrared remote sensing of surface and underground coal fires. pp. 429–451. *In*: Kuenzer, C. and S. Dech (Eds.). Thermal Infrared Remote Sensing – Sensors, Methods, Applications. Remote Sensing and Digital Image Processing Series 17, 572, ISBN 978-94-007-6638-9

Kwak, S.Y., T.T.S. Lew, C.J. Sweeney, V.B. Koman, M.H. Wong, K. Bohmert-Tatarev, K.D. Snell J.S. Seo, N.H. Chua and M.S. Strano. 2019. Chloroplast-selective gene delivery and expression in planta using chitosan-complexed single-walled carbon nanotube carriers. Nat. Nanotechnol. 14(5), 447–455.

Lechner, W. and S. Baumann. 2000. Global navigation satellite systems. Comput. Electron. Agric. 25(1–2), 67–85, doi: 10.1016/S0168-1699(99)00056-3.

Lebourgeois, V., A. Bégué, S. Labbé, M. Houlès and J.F. Martiné. 2012. A light-weight multi-spectral aerial imaging system for nitrogen crop monitoring. Precision Agriculture 13(5), 525–541.

Li, Guanlin, Z. Ma and Haiguang Wang. 2011. Image recognition of grape downy mildew and grape powdery mildew based on support vector machine. pp. 151–162. *In*: International Conference on Computer and Computing Technologies in Agriculture. Springer.

Liu, F., L.X. Wen, Z.Z. Li, W. Yu, H.Y. Sun and J.F. Chen. 2006. Porous hollow silica nanoparticles as controlled delivery system for water-soluble pesticide. Mater. Res. Bull. 41(12), 2268–2275.

Llorens, J., E. Gil, J. Llop and A. Escolà. 2011. Ultrasonic and LIDAR sensors for electronic canopy characterization in vineyards: Advances to improve pesticide application methods. Sensors 11(2), 2177–2194. doi:10.3390/s110202177.

Mangus, D., A. Sharda, A. Engelhardt, D. Flippo, R. Strasser and J.D. Luck. 2016. Analyzing nozzle spray fan pattern on an agricultural sprayer using pulse width modulated technology to generate an on-ground coverage map. Trans. Of ASABE. 60(2), 315–325.

McDougall, K., P. Gibbings and I. Wolski. 2001. Comparison of a d-GPS system and conventional guidance for spraying applications. In: 5th Precision Agriculture in Australasia Symposium: Information for Better Production and Environmental Management, 17-19 Jul 2001, Sydney, Australia.

Meivel, S., R. Maguteeswaran, N. Gandhiraj and G. Srinivasan. 2016. Quadcopter UAV Based Fertilizer and Pesticide Spraying System. International Academic Research Journal of Engineering Sciences 1, 8-12.

Meredith, A.N., B. Harper and S.L. Harper. 2016. The influence of size on the toxicity of an encapsulated pesticide: A comparison of micron- and nano-sized capsules. Environ. Int. 86, 68–74.

Miranda, M.Á., C. Barceló, F. Valdés, J.F. Feliu, D. Nestel, N. Papadopoulos, A. Sciarretta, M. Ruiz and B. Alorda. 2019. Developing and implementation of decision support system (DSS) for the control of olive fruit fly, bactrocera oleae, in mediterranean olive orchards. Agronomy, 9(10), Art. no. 620.

Miranda-Fuentes, A., P. Marucco, E.J. González-Sánchez, E. Gil, M. Grella and P. Balsari. 2018. Developing strategies to reduce spray drift in pneumatic

Advanced Crop Protection Techniques and Technologies

spraying in vineyards: Assessment of the parameters affecting droplet size in pneumatic spraying. Science of the Total Environment 616–617, 805–815. https://doi.org/10.1016/j.scitotenv.2017.10.242.

Mogili, Um Rao and B.B.V.L. Deepak. 2018. Review on application of drone systems in precision agriculture. Procedia Computer Science 133, 502–509. https://doi.org/10.1016/j.procs.2018.07.063.

Mondal, D. and D. Kole. 2016. A Time Efficient Leaf Rust Disease Detection Technique of Wheat Leaf Images Using Pearson Correlation Coefficient and Rough Fuzzy C-Means. 10.1007/978-81-322-2755-7_63.

Morris, J.S., A. Öhman and R.J. Dolan. 1998. Conscious and unconscious emotional learning in the human amygdala. Nature 393(6684), 467–470.

Murakami, E., A.M. Saraiva, L.C.M. Ribeiro, Jr. C.E. Cugnasca, A.R. Hirakawa and P.L.P. Correa. 2007. An infrastructure for the development of distributed service-oriented information systems for precision agriculture. Computers and Electronics in Agriculture 58(1), 37–48.

Napoli, C., C. Lemieux and R. Jorgensen. 1990. Introduction of a chimeric chalcone synthase gene into petunia results in reversible co-suppression of homologus genes in trans. Plant Cell 2(4), 279–289.

NIPHM. 2018. Hyderabad Pesticide Management Division, Pesticide Classification on Use, Chemical Nature, Formulation, Toxicity and Mode of Action etc. 1–123. https://niphm.gov.in/Recruitments ASO-PMD.pdf, accessed February 23rd, 2020.

Oberti, R., M. Marchi, P. Tirelli, A. Calcante, M. Iriti, E. Tona, M. Hočevar, J. Baur, J. Pfaff, C. Schütz and H. Ulbrich. 2016. Selective spraying of grapevines for disease control using a modular agricultural robot. Biosystems Engineering 146, 203–215. doi:10.1016/j.biosystemseng.2015.12.00.

Obolskiy, D., I. Pischel, B. Feistel, N. Glotov and M. Heinrich. 2011. *Artemisia dracunculus* L. (tarragon): A critical review of its traditional use, chemical composition, pharmacology, and safety. J. Agric. Food Chem. 59(21), 11367–11384.

Oerke, E.C. 2006. Crop losses to pests. The Journal of Agricultural Science 144(1), 31–43 https://doi.org/10.1017/S0021859605005708.

Ouda, S.M. 2014. Antifungal activity of silver and copper nanoparticles on two plant pathogens, *Alternaria alternata* and *Botrytis cinerea*. Res. J. Microbiol. 9(1), 34–42.

Owolade, O.F., D.O. Ogunleti and M.O. Adenekan. 2008. Titanium dioxide affects disease development and yield of edible cowpea. Elect. J. Environ. Agri. Food Chem. 7(5), 2942–2947.

Papadopoulou-Mourkidou, E., D.G. Karpouzas, J. Patsias, A. Kotopoulou, A. Milothridou, K. Kintzikoglou and P. Vlachou. 2004. The potential of pesticides to contaminate the ground water resources of the Axios River Basin in Macedonia, Northern Greece. Part I: Monitoring study in the north part of the basin. Sci. Total Environ. 321, 127–146.

Papastergiou, A. and E. Papadopoulou-Mourkidou. 2001. Occurrence and spatial and temporal distribution of pesticides in ground water of major corn-growing areas of Greece. Environ. Sci. Technol. 35, 63–69.

168 *Modeling for Sustainable Management in Agriculture, Food and the Environment*

Partel, V., L. Nunes, P. Stansley and Y. Ampatzidis. 2019. Automated vision-based system for monitoring Asian citrus Psyllid in orchards utilizing artificial intelligence. Computers and Electronics in Agriculture 162, 328–336.

Pasteris, R.J., M.A. Hanagan, J.J. Bisaha, B.L. Finkelstein, L.E. Hoffman, V. Gregory, J.L. Andreassi, J.A. Sweigard, B.A. Klyashchitsky, Y.T. Henry and R.A. Berger. 2016. Discovery of oxathiapiprolin, a new oomycete fungicide that targets an oxysterol binding protein. Bioorg. Med. Chem. 24(3), 354–361.

Paul, W. and H. Speckmann. 2004. Radar sensors: Emerging technologies for precision farming. Landtechnik 2, 92–93.

Pesticides. https://ec.europa.eu/food/plant/pesticides_en

Phillips, McDougall. 2018. Evolution of the crop protection Industry since 1960. CropLife. Available from: https://croplife.org/wp-content/uploads/2018/11/Phillips-McDougall-Evolution-of-the-Crop-Protection-Industry-since-1960-FINAL-REPORT.pdf

Phongpaichit, S., N. Rungjindamai, V. Rukachaisirikul and J. Sakayaroj. 2006. Antimicrobial activity in cultures of endophytic fungi isolated from Garcinia species. FEMS Immunol. Med. Microbiol. 48(3), 367–372.

Pérez, W., R. Arias, A. Taipe, O. Ortiz, G.A. Forbes, J. Andrade-Piedra and P. Kromann. 2020. A simple, hand-held decision support designed tool to help resource-poor farmers improve potato late blight management. Crop Protection 134, Article number 105186.

Pichersky, E. and J. Gershenzon. 2002. The formation and function of plant volatiles: Perfumes for pollinator attraction and defense. Curr. Opin. Plant Biol. 5(3), 237–243.

Prasad, R., V. Kumar and K.S. Prasad. 2014. Nanotechnology in sustainable agriculture: Present concerns and future aspects. Afr. J. Biotechnol. 13(6), 705–713.

Rai and Ingle 2012. 2012. Role of nanotechnology in agriculture with special reference to management of insect pests. Appl. Microbiol. Biotechnol. 94(2), 287–293.

Rajan, N. and S.J. Maas. 2009. Mapping crop ground cover using airborne multispectral digital imagery. Precision Agriculture 10(4), 304–318.

Rodriguez-Mozaz, S., M.J. López de Alda and D. Barceló. 2004. Monitoring of estrogens, pesticides and bisphenol A in natural waters and drinking water treatment plants by solid-phase extraction–liquid chromatography–mass spectrometry, J. Chromatogr. A 1045, 85–92.

Rodriguez-Saona, C., N. Vorsa, A. Singh, J. Johnson-Cicalese, Z. Szendrei, M. Mescher and C. Frost. 2011. Tracing the history of plant traits under domestication in cranberries: Potential consequences on anti-herbivore defences. J. Exp. Bot. 62(8), 2633–2644.

Romano, N. and G. Macino. 1992. Quelling: Transient inactivation of gene expression in *Neurospora crassa* by transformation with homologous sequences. Mol. Microbiol. 6(22), 3343–3353.

Rosell, J.R., J. Llorens, R. Sanz, J. Arnó, M. Ribes-Dasi, J. Masip, A. Escolà, F. Camp, F. Solanelles, F. Gràcia, E. Gil, L. Val, S. Planas and J. Palacín. 2009. Obtaining the three-dimensional structure of tree orchards from remote 2D terrestrial LIDAR scanning. Agric. For. Meteorol. 149, 1505–1515.

Rossi, V., T. Caffi and F. Salinari. 2012. Helping farmers face the increasing complexity of decision-making for crop protection. Phytopathol. Mediterr. 51, 457–479.

Samseemoung, G., P. Soni, H.P.W. Jayasuriya and V.M. Salokhe. 2012. Application of low altitude remote sensing (LARS) platform for monitoring crop growth and weed infestation in a soybean plantation. Precision Agriculture 13(6), 611–627.

Sankaran, S. and R. Ehsani. 2013. Comparison of visible-near infrared and mid-infrared spectroscopy for classification of Huanglongbing and citrus canker infected leaves. Agricultural Engineering International: CIGR Journal 15(3), 75–79.

Scarfato, P., E. Avallone, P. Lannelli, V. De Feo and D.J. Acierno. 2007. Synthesis and characterization of polyurea microcapsules containing essential oils with antigerminative activity. J. Appl. Polym. Sci. 105(6), 3568–3577.

Schowengerdt, R.A. 2007. Remote sensing: Models and Methods for Image Processing (3rd ed.). Academic Press. ISBN 978-0-12-369407-2.

Schwarz, J., L. Herold and B. Pollin. 2011. Typology of PF Technologies. Deliverable 7.1. FP7 Project Future Farm. www.futurefarm.eu.

Schwessinger, B. and P.C. Ronald. 2012. Plant innate immunity: Perception of conserved microbial signatures. Annu. Rev. Plant Biol. 63, 451–482.

Sciarretta, A., M.R. Tabilio, A. Amore, M. Colacci, M.A. Miranda, D. Nestel, N.T. Papadopoulos and P. Trematerra. 2019. Defining and evaluating a decision support system (DSS) for the precise pest management of the Mediterranean Fruit Fly, Ceratitis capitata, at the farm level. Agronomy 9(10), Art. no. 608.

Sharda, A., J.P. Fulton, T.P. McDonald, W.C. Zech, M.J. Darr and C.J. Brodbeck. 2010. Real-time pressure and flow dynamics due to boom section and individual nozzle control on agricultural sprayers. Trans. ASABE 53, 1363–1371. doi:10.13031/2013.34891

Shtienberg, D. 2013. Will decision-support systems be widely used for the management of plant diseases? Annu. Rev. Phytopathol. 51, 1–16.

Sivasakthi, S., G. Usharani and P. Saranraj. 2014. Biocontrol potentiality of plant growth promoting bacteria (PGPR) – Pseudomonas fluorescens and Bacillus subtilis: A review. Afr. J. Agric. Res. 9(16), 1265–1277.

Slattery, M., B. Harper and S. Harper. 2019. Pesticide encapsulation at the nanoscale drives changes to the hydrophobic partitioning and toxicity of an active ingredient. Nanomaterials (Basel) 9(1), 81.

Sørensen, G.C., S. Fountas, E. Nash, L. Pesonen, D. Bochtis, S.M. Pedersen, B. Basso and S.B. Blackmore. 2010. Conceptual model of a future farm management information system. Computers and Electronics in Agriculture 72, 37–47.

Sooväli, P., M. Koppel, E. Lauringson and L. Talgre, L. 2017. The advantage of decision support system for managing spring barley disease in Estonia. Agronomy Research 15(5), 2134–2143.

Stajnko, D., P. Vindis and B. Mursec. 2011. Automated system for targeted spraying in orchards by using RGB imaging. In: DAAAM International Scientific Book 2011 (DAAAM International Vienna, Vienna 2011) https://doi.org/10.2507/daaam.scibook.2011.23.

170 *Modeling for Sustainable Management in Agriculture, Food and the Environment*

Starr, C. 2005. Biology: Concepts and Applications. Thomson Brooks/Cole. p. 94. ISBN 0-534-46226-X.

Suárez, L., N. Restrepo-Coupe, A. Hueni and L. Chisholm. 2015. Vegetation spectroscopy, p. 13.

Sumitomo Chemical News Release on Feb. 25, 2019. https://www.sumitomo-chem.co.jp/english/news/detail/20190225e.html.

Tesh, S.A., J.M. Tesh, I. Fegert, R. Buesen, S. Schneider, T. Mentzel, B. van Ravenzwaay and S. Stinchcombe. 2019. Innovative selection approach for a new antifungal agent mefentrifluconazole (Revysol®) and the impact upon its toxicity profile. Regul. Toxicol. Pharmacol. 106, 152–168.

TOPPS. 2006. Best Management Practices: Prevent Water Contamination through Point Sources, 1, 1–57. http://www.topps-life.org/uploads/8/0/0/3/8003583/_topps_best_management_practices_findoc_070613.pdf, accessed on April 10th, 2020.

TOPPS. 2008. Best Management Practices to Reduce Point Sources. http://www.topps-life.org/uploads/8/0/0/3/8003583/point_of_source_engl-template.pdf, accessed on April 10th, 2020.

TOPPS. 2013. Best Management Practices to Reduce Spray Drift, 52. http://www.topps-life.org/uploads/8/0/0/3/8003583/en_drift_book. pdf, accessed on April 2nd, 2020.

TOPPS. 2015. http://www.topps-life.org/spray-drift.html, accessed on April 10th, 2020.

Torres-Sánchez, J., F. López-Granados, N. Serrano, O. Arquero and J.M. Peña .2015. High-throughput 3-D monitoring of agricultural-tree plantations with Unmanned Aerial Vehicle (UAV) technology. PLoS One 10(6), 1–20, 2015, doi: 10.1371/journal.pone.0130479.

Tsatsarelis, K. 2006. Agricultural Machinery Management. Giahoudis Publishing (in Greek).

Umetsu, N. and Y. Shirai. 2020. Development of novel pesticides in the 21st century. Pestic. Sci. 45(2), 1–21.

Valdés-Gómez, H., M. Araya-Alman, C. Pañitrur-De la Fuente, N. Verdugo-Vásquez, M. Lolas, C. Acevedo-Opazo, C. Gary and A. Calonnec. 2017. Evaluation of a decision support strategy for the control of powdery mildew, Erysiphe necator (Schw.) Burr. *In*: Grapevine in the Central Region of Chile. Pest Management Science 73(9), 1813–1821.

Vallad, G.E. and R.M. Goodman. 2004. Systemic acquired resistance and induced systemic resistance in conventional agriculture. Crop Sci. 44(6), 1920–1934.

Verma, J.P., J. Yadav and K.N. Tiwari. 2009. Effect of Mesorhizobium and plant growth promoting rhizobacteria on nodulation and yields of chickpea. Biol. Forum – An Int. J. 1(2), 11–14.

Vet, L.E.M. and M. Dicke. 1992. Ecology of infochemical use by natural enemies in a tritrophic context. Annu. Rev. Entomol. 37, 141–172.

von Rad, U., M. Mueller and J. Durner. 2005. Evaluation of natural and synthetic stimulants of plant immunity by microarray technology. The New Phytologist 165(1), 191–202.

Waghmare, H., R. Kokare and Y. Dandawate. 2016. Detection and classification of diseases of grape plant using opposite colour local binary pattern feature

Advanced Crop Protection Techniques and Technologies **171**

and machine learning for automated decision support system. *In*: 2016 3rd International Conference on Signal Processing and Integrated Networks (SPIN), IEEE. 513–518.

Waghunde, R., R. Shelake and A. Sabalpara. 2016. Trichoderma: A significant fungus for agriculture and environment. Afr. J. Agric. Res. 11(22), 1952–1965.

Walters, D.R., J. Ratsep and N.D. Havis. 2013. Controlling crop diseases using induced resistance: Challenges for the future. J. Exp. Bot. 64(5), 1263–1280.

Walters, D.R., A.C. Newton and G.D. Lyon. (eds.). 2014. Induced Resistance for Plant Defense: A Sustainable Approach to Crop Protection. 2nd ed. Oxford, UK: Wiley-Blackwell.

Wang, F.W., R.H. Jiao, A.B. Cheng, S.H. Tan and Y.C. Song. 2007. Antimicrobial potentials of endophytic fungi residing in Quercus variabilis and brefeldin A obtained from Cladosporium sp. World J. Microbiol. Biotechnol. 23(1), 79–83.

Wang, P., E. Lombi, F.J. Zhao and P.M. Kopittke. 2016. Nanotechnology: A new opportunity in plant sciences. Trends Plant Sci. 21, 699–712.

Weis, M., M. Keller and V.R. Ayala. 2012. Herbicide reduction methods. *In*: Alvarez-Fernandez, R. (Ed.). Herbicides – Environmental Impact Studies and Management Approaches. Intech, Rijeka, Croatia.

Wilson, R.C. and J.A. Doudna. 2013. Molecular mechanisms of RNA interference. Annu. Rev. Biophys. 42, 217–239.

Xinyu Xue, Yubin Lan, Zhu Sun, Chun Chang, W. Clint Hoffmann. 2016. Develop an unmanned aerial vehicle based automatic aerial spraying system. Computers and Electronics in Agriculture 128, 58–66. https://doi.org/10.1016/j.compag.2016.07.022.

Zhang, Qin. 2015. Precision Agriculture Technology for Crop Farming. CRC Press, ISBN 9781482251074.

Zillmann, E., H. Lilienthal, T. Schrage and E. Schnug. 2004. Significance of radar remote sensed imagery for agricultural applications. Landbauforschung Völkenrode 4(54), 199–210.

CHAPTER

6

Remote Sensing in Agricultural Production Assessment

Nicolas R. Dalezios[1]* and Ioannis N. Faraslis[2]
[1] Department of Civil Engineering, University of Thessaly, Volos, Greece
[2] Department of Environmental Sciences, University of Thessaly, Volos, Greece

Introduction

Meteorological forecasts for agriculture may overlap with agrometeorological forecasts, such as weather forecasts for farm operations, i.e. spraying pesticides or deciding on actions due to adverse weather (Togliatti et al. 2017, Dumont et al. 2014). Moreover, national institutions issue forecasts, such as weather, or frost warnings, which are vital to the farming community (Dalezios 2015, WMO 2010). Nevertheless, operational forecasting is conducted for different spatial scales (Wu et al. 2015, Gorski and Gorska 2003). At the micro-scale, there is the field or the farm level. Data are usually available with acceptable accuracy at this scale, such as the breed or the known variety, and so are the yield and the environmental conditions, including soil type, soil depth, or the rate of application of inputs. The micro-scale is the scale of on-farm decision making by individuals, or irrigation plant managers.

The macro-scale is essentially the regional scale (Dabrowska-Zielinska et al. 2002). Regional forecasts are issued at the scale of agricultural statistics addressed to users, such as national food security managers, or market planners and traders (Johnson et al. 2016, Kolotii et al. 2015, Kuri et al. 2014, Dempeworlf et al. 2014). At the macro-scale, many variables are meaningless, such as soil water holding capacity (Singh et al. 2017, Wang et

---

*Corresponding author: dalezios.n.r@gmail.com

Remote Sensing in Agricultural Production Assessment **173**

al. 2014, Kussul et al. 2014, Manatsa et al. 2011). The spectrum from macro-to micro-scales is covered and the two extremes are very well defined in terms of users and methods. Several applications are at an intermediate scale. They would include, for instance, certain types of crop insurances. There are also links between forecasting and monitoring. Specifically, monitoring and within-season yield assessment is implemented by observing the environmental conditions that are conducive (or not) to the development of organisms, such as for pests and diseases, or by direct observation of the stage and condition of the organisms being monitored (Basso and Liu 2019, Peralta et al. 2016, Li et al. 2015, Dumont et al. 2015, Johnson 2014). Forecasting may be considered when data are collected to assess environmental conditions. Agricultural production assessment involves methods, which attempt to quantitatively assess the impact of weather variations and variability mainly on regional crop yields throughout the growing season (Sharma et al. 2017). Remote sensing is a useful tool to analyze the vegetation dynamic on local, regional, or global scales (Kogan 2001) and to determine the impact of climate on vegetation (Wang et al. 2003). Satellite remote sensing is contributing to agricultural studies, since early seventies using optical data for the classification of agricultural crops and monitoring crop growth and crop development.

In general, the application of remote sensing to agriculture falls broadly into three categories (Steven and Jaggard 1995): (1) land classification and crop mapping; (2) monitoring and forecasting of crop production; and (3) identification of stress in crops and generally vegetation. Also, data from remote sensing platforms can be used to complement weather data in crop yield assessments, among others (Quarmby et al. 1993, Hayes and Decker 1996, Dalezios et al. 2001, Tsiros and Dalezios 2010). Satellite data can be used to monitor the onset of the agrometeorological conditions to vegetation and provide details about its condition. In addition, satellite systems provide temporally and spatially continuous data over the globe (Tucker and Choudhury 1987) and thus, they are potentially better and relatively inexpensive tools for regional applications, such as monitoring vegetation's condition, or crop yield estimation than conventional weather data. Studies have been carried out for several parts of the world (Wu et al. 2015, Johnson et al. 1993) showing the potential of satellite-based data in crop monitoring and assessment.

Accurate production assessment on regional to national scales at a significant time period before harvesting is becoming increasingly important in developing and developed countries (Figueiredo et al. 2016, Machakaire et al. 2016, Sharma et al. 2015, Kowalik et al. 2014, Tsiros et al. 2009). Predictive relationships are quite difficult to derive, whereas the incorporation of the vegetation physiology with the spectral signatures depends on several logistical factors, such as the cost and the temporal and spatial resolution of the associated satellite data (Campos et al. 2018,

174 *Modeling for Sustainable Management in Agriculture, Food and the Environment*

Fieuzal et al. 2017, Bu et al. 2017, Al-Gaadi et al. 2016, Bolton and Friedl 2013, Das et al. 1993). Usually, the methods for estimating crop production are based on objective techniques, such as crop growth modelling and remote sensing (Holzman and Rivas 2016, Geipel et al. 2014, Bandyopadhyay et al. 2014, Bouman 1994). Although the farmers have a direct knowledge of the crop condition, crop prediction modelling can provide indirect benefits in terms of stability and quality of the advice offered by agricultural support services. Also, farmers are interested in knowing in time problems regarding their crops. Satellite data can provide a better understanding of the spatial and temporal evolution of the parameters incorporated into models. Crop monitoring and prediction of crop yield over extended areas require repetitive and consistent high-quality information on the state of the crops, as well as on the occurrence, duration and impact of stress conditions. In order the reflected or emitted radiation values recorded by the satellite sensors to be applicable, conversion in useful information is required. The development of vegetation indices can provide valuable information in stress management, for example in assessing irrigation demand, disease, pest and weed control, and crop nutrition although for this, high resolution is required (Steven and Jaggard 1995).

In this chapter, remote sensing features and components in agricultural production modelling are initially considered. Then, agricultural production assessment methodologies are described incorporating remote sensing data and methods. Finally, applications and case studies are presented.

Remote Sensing Features in Agricultural Production Assessment

This section presents the current remote sensing technology that is applicable to the field of agricultural production assessment. The information presented is applicable for monitoring and assessment of agricultural crops and grasslands and their impact on agricultural production mainly at regional and national levels.

There is a gradually increasing trend for the use of remote sensing in production assessment, and specifically for the detection of several spatial and temporal features at different scales (Dalezios 2015). Moreover, a major consideration for remote sensing use in agriculture, is the extent to which operational users can rely on a continued supply of data (Thenkabail et al. 2004, García-Berná et al 2020). Indeed, satellite systems provide temporally and spatially continuous data over the globe and, thus, they are potentially better and relatively inexpensive tools for regional applications, such as crop yield modelling, monitoring and assessment, than conventional environmental and weather data. For these types of applications, appropriate remote sensing systems are weather radars and satellites that provide low spatial and high temporal resolution data, since daily coverage and data acquisition are necessary. The series of geosynchronous, polar-orbiting meteorological satellites fulfil the above requirements and there are already long series of data sets. This section presents a brief description of remote sensing systems and their potential in crop yield assessment.

The remote sensing technology is accessible to both developed and developing countries and the cost for acquiring the imageries and data from orbiting and geostationary satellite systems have been reduced over the past decade. Some of the imagery is now available without cost to the global user community. However, there is still a great need for training of technical personnel to develop products that are usable to the farmers and managers. The interpretation and timely access to remote sensing products for use in agriculture follows the development of sensors and the acquisition of data.

Satellite Systems for Agrometeorological Analysis

Several criteria can be used to classify satellite systems. A basic criterion is the wavelength of the electromagnetic radiation, which classifies the systems as being sensitive to visible, infrared and microwave radiation regions of the spectrum. Another criterion classifies the satellite systems into passive and active. Specifically, passive satellite systems record the naturally reflected or transmitted radiation. In agricultural production assessment, two types of passive remote sensing systems are considered, namely meteorological and environmental or resource satellites. The main differences between the two types of satellites are their spatial and temporal resolution. More specifically, meteorological satellites have a rather coarse spatial resolution, but high temporal re-occurrence, thus, being suitable mainly for operational applications, such as crop monitoring and crop-weather relationships. Environmental satellites have fine spatial resolution, but low temporal re-occurrence, being basically used for land-use classification, such as quantitative crop simulation during the phenological cycle. On the other hand, active satellite systems transmit energy and record the returned signal. Such systems are weather radars and SARs (Synthetic Aperture Radar), which operate in the microwave portion of the electromagnetic spectrum and are considered all-weather systems, since they can penetrate clouds without signal attenuation. Active satellite systems are very useful in agricultural analysis, since precipitation detected by weather radar is a key parameter, as well as soil moisture can be detected from SAR images (Liu Chang-an et al. 2019).

Every year new satellite systems are being launched and the number is steadily increasing with a continuous improvement of the spatial resolution. There is also a tendency to increase the number of available bands in these satellites providing additional valuable information. One of the advantages of using remotely sensed data is that they allow for a high-resolution spatial coverage and are updated frequently to allow for near real time analyses, whereas the main drawbacks are the relatively short record of available data sets. New remote sensing systems offer online open information for web platforms and are also utilized for monitoring and detecting environmental variables and parameters. Such systems are NASA's new online satellites for climate change, Global Precipitation Measurement Core Observatory, Orbiting Carbon Observatory-2, and active-passive Soil Moisture, as well as the European Copernicus system with six Sentinel satellites (2014–2021) to monitor land, ocean, emergency response, atmosphere, security and climate change (ESA 2014). Moreover, massive cloud computing resources and analytical tools for working with big data sets make it possible to extract new information from environmental satellites' imagery with varying spatial resolution, such as Landsat-8 imagery (15m), RapidEye (5m), Worldview-3 (.31m) or Pleiades (.5m). Thus, digital data processing of crop status, including satellite imagery, and crop monitoring throughout the growing season, including decision support systems (DSS), could be incorporated into a dynamic web platform for crop production assessment. Table 1 presents a list of current active and passive meteorological and environmental satellite systems.

Large Area Coverage Sensors and Systems

Copernicus: A new European satellite system, namely the Sentinel system, has been launched in 2014 and expected to continue up to 2021, based on the initial plan (ESA 2014). Table 2 presents a brief description of the functions of the different satellites, which constitute components of the Sentinel system. Indeed, the Sentinel satellites are a family of satellites, which are expected to replace the ENVISAT Satellites and to provide additional spatial instruments and capabilities of earth observation. They are a part of the Copernicus program, from the European Space Agency (ESA 2014). The Sentinel-2 mission is a land monitoring constellation of two satellites that provide high resolution optical imagery and continuity of existing systems, such as SPOT and Landsat. The mission is designed to provide global coverage of the Earth's land surface every 10 days with one satellite and 5 days with 2 satellites, making the data of great use for monitoring and operational applications. The satellites are equipped with the state-of-the-art MSI (Multispectral Imager) instrument that offers high-resolution optical imagery (ESA 2014). The first of the two satellites (Sentinel-2A) has been launched in April 2015, and the second one (Sentinel-2B) has been launched in 2017. They are both planned to be

Table 1. An indicative list of active-passive meteorological-environmental satellites

Passive	Active	Passive-Active
Landsat 1-8	Sentinel-1A, 1B	Sentinel-3A, 3B
Sentinel-2A, 2B	RADARSAT-1, 2	SEASAT
Sentinel-4A, 4B	SMOS: Soil Moisture and Ocean Salinity	ERS-1, ERS-2
Sentinel-5 Precursor	GPM: Global Precipitation Measurement	ENVISAT
METEOSAT	CloudSat	JERS-1
AVHRR/3 (NOAA-15 through 19)	GCOM-W1	SMAP: Soil Moisture Active Passive
TERRA (MODIS-ASTER)	ADM-Aeolus	TRMM: Tropical Rainfall Measuring Mission
SPOT 4, 5, 6 & 7	SAOCOM-1A	JPSS: Joint Polar Satellite System (Suomi-NPP and NOAA-20)
GOSAT-2: Greenhouse gases Observing SATellite-2		GCOM-C, GCOM-W: Global Change Observation Mission - Climate
RapidEye		MetOp-C: Meteorological operational satellite
ALOS		Aqua (EOS PM-1)
IKONOS		Aura (EOS CH-1)
QuickBird		
WorldView-1, 2 & 3		
GeoEye-1		
Pleiades-1A, 1B		
IRS-1A, 1B, 1C, 1D		

(Contd.)

Table 1. (Contd.)

Passive	Active	Passive-Active
ResourceSat-1, 2		
Cartosat-1, 2, 2A, 2B		
Cartosat-2C, 2D, 2E		
GEO-KOMSAT-2A		
GOES-R: Geostationary Operational Environmental Satellites		
Formosat-5		
VenµS		
EnMAP: Environmental Mapping and Analysis Program		
PRISMA		
OCO-2: Orbiting Carbon Observatory-2		

operational for at least 7.25 years and have an initial weight of 1,100 kg. They also have a sun-synchronous orbit at 786 km of altitude, with 98.5° of inclination. They have a spatial resolution ranging from 10 to 60 meters (ESA 2014). They are designed for: land observation, including vegetation, soil and water cover, inland waterways and coastal areas; land use and change detection maps; providing support in generating land cover; disaster relief support; and climate change monitoring.

Table 2. Copernicus: European Sentinel Satellites

Satellite	Type of sensor carrying on	Applications
Sentinel-1A Sentinel-1B	C-band radar medium spatial resolution	Land, ocean monitoring, ice detection, oil spill monitoring, ship detection tracking, flood mapping, monitoring of land-surface motion risks, mapping land-surface, forest, water and soil, agriculture
Sentinel-2A Sentinel-2B	Optical multispectral medium to moderate spatial resolution instruments	Land-cover, usage and change detection maps, geophysical variable maps (leaf chlorophyll content, leaf water content, leaf area index etc.), risk mapping, disaster relief
Sentinel-3A Sentinel-3B	Optical ocean and land colour moderate spatial resolution instrument, sea and land temperature radiometer, altimeter and microwave radiometer	Sea and land applications, sea and land temp, sea-surface and land-ice topography, coastal zones, in land-water and sea ice topography
Sentinel-4A Sentinel-4B	Optical and microwave low resolution sensors	Geostationary atmospheric chemistry missions
Sentinel-5A Sentinel-5B	UV-VIS-NIR-SWIR push broom grating spectrometer - TROPOMI moderate resolution sensor	Low earth orbit atmospheric chemistry missions
Sentinel-6A Sentinel-6B	Altimetry sensors	Altimetry mission

Geostationary Meteorological Satellites: There is a worldwide network of operational geostationary meteorological satellites, which provides visible and infrared images of the Earth's surface and atmosphere. Countries/regions with current geostationary operational meteorological satellites are the USA (GOES series), Europe (METEOSAT series), Japan (GMS series, including the recently launched GMS-5), India (INSAT series) and Russia (GOMS).

NOAA-AVHRR: These instruments are exhibiting large-scale swath size and a daily revisit capability, which explain their extended use for large-scale land monitoring and vegetation analysis. The current series of operational polar orbiting meteorological satellites is provided by NOAA. Two satellites are maintained in polar orbit at any time, one in a "morning" orbit and the other in an "afternoon" orbit. The series provides a wide range of data of interest, including sea surface temperature, cloud cover, data for land studies, temperature and humidity profiles and ozone concentrations.

VEGETATION satellite operated by France provides similar bands as SPOT high-resolution data with similar daily coverage and resolution as NOAA-AVHRR. TERRA: On February 24, 2000, Terra began collecting what has ultimately become a new 15-year global data set, on which to base scientific investigations about our complex home planet. These spacecrafts help scientists unravel the mysteries of climate and environmental change.

Microwave Sensors and Systems

Some indicative microwave sensors and systems are presented:

Copernicus Sentinel-1: The Sentinel-1 comprises a constellation of two polar-orbiting satellites. Sentinel-1A was launched on 3 April 2014 and Sentinel-1B on 25 April 2016. Their mission is to acquire, day and night, C-band synthetic aperture radar imaging, regardless of the weather, for land and ocean services. In addition, active microwave techniques are used for monitoring global landmasses-oceans, coastal zones and shipping routes in European waters at regular intervals.

ERS series: ERS-1 was launched by ESA in July 1991; ERS-2 was launched in April 1995. This series concentrates on global and regional environmental issues, making use of active microwave techniques that enable a range of measurements to be made of land, sea and ice surfaces independent of cloud cover. In addition, the ATSR instrument on these missions provides images of the surface or cloud top. The GOME instrument on ERS-2 provides atmospheric chemistry measurements.

RADARSAT: RADARSAT is an advanced Earth observation satellite project developed by Canada to monitor environmental change and to support resource sustainability. With RADARSAT's launch in early 1995, Canada and the world have access to the first radar satellite system capable of large-scale production and timely delivery of data. These data meet the needs of commercial, government and scientific programs and provide a source of reliable and cost-effective data for environmental and resource professionals worldwide.

Remotely Sensed Crop Yield Modelling

Remote sensing capabilities provide a viable method to offset any loss of information. However, there are dissimilarities in temporal and spatial averages as envisioned by modelling efforts, as exist in the real world and as measured by remote sensing systems. Thus, remotely sensed data in order to be useful for monitoring crops and assessing crop production must be compatible with mathematical modelling of the corresponding quantification schemes. Moreover, new sensors have higher spatial resolution to overcome shortcoming in existing products. Novel noise reduction and other atmosphere correction algorithms improve the thematic accuracy of remote sensing data sets.

Remote sensing systems have difficulties in meeting the simultaneous requirements for high spatial and temporal resolution through the growing season to monitor individual fields. The type of satellite data appropriate for crop monitoring and crop production assessment, crop monitoring and climate impact assessment are from remote sensing systems that provide low spatial and high temporal resolution data, since daily coverage and acquisition of data is needed for such applications. Also, long-series databases should be available. Satellite data that fulfill the above requirements are NOAA/AVHRR. In most cases, daily data is aggregated to weekly or ten-day composite images.

Remote Sensing Components in Crop Yield Modelling

Remote sensing can contribute to mapping and monitoring of agronomic conditions, which include mapping vegetation type and land cover, and monitoring vegetation condition, moisture availability and soil moisture. All these applications are achieved with reflective remote sensing, thermal remote sensing or the combination of those two, except from soil moisture, which is monitored with microwave remote sensing.

Satellite techniques in monitoring agroclimate are based on satellite derived parameters and indices. There are several approaches which can be categorized as following: (1) only remotely sensed imagery; (2) combination of remote sensing products with meteorological variables; and (3) crop yield modelling. The first two approaches are usually preferred in monitoring, assessment, trend analysis and agroclimatic classification applications.

The interest for the remote sensing approach in crop yield modelling has been increased mainly during the last decades and is still under steady improvement. Satellite data can provide a better understanding of the spatial and temporal evolution of the parameters incorporated into models. Remote sensing methods can be divided (Vossen 1994) in: statistical, deterministic and combined. The statistical approach is based on indices derived from satellite sensors averaged over a region or country and entered in a regression analysis. The deterministic approach consolidates the computation of Normalized Difference Vegetation Index (NDVI), Leaf Area Index (LAI), Absorbed Photosynthetically Active Radiation (APAR) or Fraction Photosynthetically Active Radiation (FPAR) and biomass before yield assessment. The combined methods integrate remotely sensed information into crop growth models. The latter two methods require large amount of data, such as plant physiology, soil and site-specific characteristics, or daily weather conditions, whereas the statistical methods have the minimum data requirements (Vogt 1994).

International Operational Systems

There are a few established international operational systems, which are briefly presented:

GIEWS: The Global Information and Early Warning System on Food and Agriculture was established in the wake of the world food crisis of the early 1970s. GIEWS remains the leading source of information on food production and food security for countries around the world. In the past 25 years, the system has become a worldwide network, which includes governments, Non-Governmental Organizations (NGOs) and numerous commercial, research and media organizations. Over the years, a unique database on global, regional, national and subnational food security has been maintained, refined and continuously updated. GIEWS has invested in innovative methods for collecting, analyzing, presenting and disseminating information, making full use of the revolution in information technology and the advent of computer communications. The system supports national- and regional-level initiatives to enhance food information and early warning systems. GIEWS provides policy makers and relief agencies throughout the world with the most up-to-date and accurate information available. Objective information and early warning will continue to have a crucial role in ensuring that timely and appropriate action can be taken to avoid suffering. In this regard, GIEWS has repeatedly demonstrated its capacity to alert the world to emerging food shortages.

FEWS NET: The goal of the Famine Early Warning System Network (FEWS NET) is to strengthen the abilities of African countries and regional organizations to manage threats of food security through the provision of timely and analytical early warning and vulnerability information. Objectives are to determine the geographical extent of ground-derived data, to fill in information for inaccessible areas, and to detect some problems early. Satellite imagery products can be used to get a "bird's eye view" of the situation. One of the greatest strengths of the FEWS project is the ability to combine information gathered on the ground, such as field observations, market information, and weather station data, etc., with the "big picture" view provided by the satellite imagery. Over the years, some problems with imagery products used by FEWS have developed, been noted and characterized. This situation creates a challenge to use the imagery products wisely, so that accurate conclusions are drawn. The Normalized Difference Vegetation Index (NDVI) is used to monitor vegetation conditions in the Sahel, where climate conditions are favorable for its use, i.e. no clouds. In recent years, FEWS' mandate has expanded into regions, where the seasonal weather conditions are not as favorable for satellite monitoring. NDVI is not as useful in East Africa, the Horn and southern Africa due to long periods of clouds and haze during the most critical parts of the growing season.

RFE: Meteosat Rainfall Estimates (RFE) is used to monitor rainfall amounts over most of the African continent. Its strength is that it shows widespread rainfall patterns rather than amounts at one point (ground station data). Every 30 minutes the Meteosat satellite observes and measures the temperature of clouds. A rough relation has been established between the duration of cold (below 235K) cloud tops and the amount of rainfall. The RFE combines the satellite cold cloud duration (CCD) data with ground station data in a sophisticated model that also incorporates other parameters (humidity, wind direction, and topography). The moisture index (CWS) is a third parameter that is generated by FEW and is the ratio of water supply to water demand. The "supply" is represented by the sum of the decadal Meteosat RFE and water stored in the soil (excess water stored from previous rainfall events). The demand side is represented by an estimate of potential evapotranspiration derived from data provided by NOAA from a global weather forecast model. The moisture index is computed every 10 days and can be used to monitor the moisture situation throughout the agricultural season. The product relates moisture demand of the atmosphere (estimated by potential evapotranspiration) to the moisture supply available from rainfall to meet this demand. The estimate is based on a moisture "accounting system" calculating the "supply" versus "demand" for moisture.

Agricultural Production Assessment

Crop biomass production has been addressed several years ago, with the development of detailed bio-physical models (De Wit 1965). The introduction of new space research programs, such as the USDA-AgRISTARS (Wilson and Sebaugh 1981), or the ISRO-CAPE (Navalgund et al. 1991), has emerged new assessment opportunities for international agricultural production. At the present time, crop yield/production forecasts are widely used at global, national, regional and field levels, however, there are different objectives, methodologies, data needs, timeliness, costs and reliability (Rembold et al. 2013). The objective of crop yield and production forecast activities should be the reduction of the risks associated with local or national food systems. Indeed, the food system involves various components, such as natural resources and inputs, primary and secondary production, transport, storage and exchange, consumption, or health and nutrition, and agents, such as policymakers, producers, inputs sellers, output buyers, farm advisors, or researchers (Pinstrup-Andersen and Watson 2011). Risk reduction should contribute to improved outcomes in terms of the environment, such as better access to natural capital, socioeconomic aspects, such as increased wealth, income, employment, and economic growth, and health and nutrition, such as reduced diseases, morbidity, and mortality rates.

The selection of the spatiotemporal scale affects the interests of the actors of the food system. At the farmer level, "prescriptive farming" is applied in the USA with the objective to perform in-field yield modeling to improve management techniques and boost actual yield. Moreover, the GEOGLAM project (www.geoglam-crop-monitor.org), which has been resulted from the 2011 G20 summit, monitors current year conditions and contributes national crop production forecasts (for wheat, soybeans, corn, and rice) computed by 30 national partners to the AMIS Outlooks on a monthly basis. Similarly, the Agricultural Model Inter-comparison and Improvement Project (AGMIP) (Rosenzweig et al. 2013) attempts to improve agricultural models for the medium- and long-term effects of climate change on crop yields. Furthermore, the choice between forecasting yield or production should be considered. Institutions obtain the production forecast by multiplying expected yield by the crop area, whereas farmers may derive the yield by dividing production by crop extension. The recent development of Crop Data Layers (CDL) is an efficient solution in regions with large field sizes. ESA has recently initiated the operational production of 20m monthly land cover maps of Africa from Sentinel 2, which is a free-of-charge solution for the African continent (54 countries).

The evaluation criteria include properties of models, such as reliability, objectivity, consistency with scientific knowledge, adequacy to scales, minimum cost and simplicity (Wilson and Sebaugh 1981). At the present time, timeliness is essential. Specifically, an advance of one month with respect to the harvest date is usually chosen for food security monitoring, however, economic actors expect several annual outlooks. In other words, the announced publication dates are of primary importance, since issuance of this information generally influences international commodity markets. Moreover, the model's simplicity and structure (Donatelli et al. 2010) and the minimum data sets (MDS) required (Basso et al. 2013) affect the forecasting system's costs, such as human resources, data purchase, hardware and software. Open-source model frameworks, such as BIOMA and DSSAT (http://dssat.net/), should be favoured, since they will provide solutions whose robustness is guaranteed by the large community of users. Due to climate change, extreme weather events are becoming more frequent, and historical data poorly represent the growing conditions obtaining after the year 2000. The sensitivity to extreme events has thus become an issue of high priority, as "normal" years are less in need of reliable forecasts.

Operational Modelling Methods

Two modelling approaches currently compose the core of operational crop yield forecast models: statistical models and process-based models. Statistical models are usually regression models (simple or multiple, linear or non-linear, static or dynamic) that link the variables of interest (i.e. the yields) to the predictors known for the current season. Based on parameters estimated from historical data, they are used to infer the most probable current-year outcome. The predictors are chosen from the meteorology (pluviometry, temperature, solar radiation) and/or the remote sensing (vegetation indices, LAI, soil moisture) domains. Statistical crop models are simple and entail low costs; several authors have claimed to achieve over 75 percent of variance explanation. The models' main drawback is that they have the smallest prediction interval around the average of the reference dataset, whereas actors of the food system are mostly interested in abnormal years. In addition, these models cannot be extrapolated in time or space.

Process-based models are based on mechanistic models and replace the theoretical relations with empirical functions. The level of approximation, the choice of modelled processes and the datasets retained, has led to the current diversity of models, whose bench making remains a challenge. Most models require information on crop management, such as planting dates, phenology, or variety, nutrient availability, such as soil parameters, or fertilization, water availability, such as soil moisture, or evapotranspiration and energy received, such as solar radiation. Models are mostly deterministic, although some recent developments refer to stochastic approaches (Chipanshi et al. 2015). At the present time, most models make use of remote sensing information, such as crop phenology, and reference validated datasets are becoming available for meteorological data (NCAR 2014), soil information (FAO 2009), satellite imagery (USGS 2015) and land cover mapping (Basso et al. 2014). It should also be recalled that most yield models perform crop yield assessments, however, very few of them report on the biomass production of pastures land, although grasslands occupy 70 percent of agricultural land. Among the main reasons for this is the complexity introduced by multi-species aspects, competition with scrubs and trees, and grazing or periodical cuttings. Although most of the solutions proposed refer to the regression of pasture biomass with remote sensing vegetation indices (Donald et al. 2010), some process-based models have also been developed (Taubert et al. 2012).

Future Trend in Crop Production

The main uncertainty with regards to the future of crops production is related to the effects of climate change and, specifically, the extent and rapidity of these changes. It is recognized that real-time crop estimation constitutes one of the challenges, which could be even more significant if the crop optimal location is known, or the management techniques or diseases progress at a greater speed. For instance, during the last decades in China, double or triple seasons cropping has moved 100 km to the north, enabling a dramatic increase in rice and wheat production due to changes in crop areas. Similarly, models based on past observations are expected to become less relevant, especially when genetics, which is the current basis for the selection of varieties, will be replaced by synthetic biology. Moreover, it will be important to identify the impacts of climate variability and extreme events on the output of models. Even if forecasts may withstand greater uncertainty than estimation methods, limits exist beyond which results will no longer be useful.

Another challenge derives from the role of the private sector in model development and applications. Specifically, profit maximization by ascertaining consumer preferences, the best production places by considering soil quality, radiation and pluviometry and future market evolution, are expected to be only partially satisfactory. The public sector will have to finance the developments corresponding to the applications at national and regional level, whereas the private sector is likely to boost the research at local level, aiming to perform field-level simulations and comparing the results of various types of management practice.

Application: Remotely Sensed Annual Cotton Crop Production Assessment

This is an application of remotely sensed assessment of annual cotton crop production in Thessaly Greece (Domenikiotis et al. 2004a, b, 2005). Two indices, namely the vegetation condition index (VCI) (Kogan 2001) and the Bhalme and Mooley drought index (BMDI) (Oladipo 1985), are utilized to evaluate the meteorological effects on cotton production in Thessaly, Greece. The development of the proposed approach is based on the VCI data, which is incorporated in the development of the BMDI methodology. This methodological approach integrates the accumulated meteorological effects, as they are expressed by the VCI, on agricultural areas. Then, the developed new index, namely Bhalme and Mooley vegetation condition index (BMVCI), is applied to the region of Thessaly, which is the main cotton production area of Greece. Figure 1 presents a map of Greece for the development of the BMVCI, where Thessaly in the central part of the country. An empirical relationship between BMVCI and cotton production is developed for the assessment of the cotton production before the harvest at the end of August.

Figure 1. Map of Greece showing the sampling areas for the development of the Bhalme and Mooley Vegetation Condition Index (BMVCI) (from Domenikiotis et al. 2004b).

Satellite derived BMVCI: The derived BMDI is an index that provides a satisfactory measure of the current status of agricultural drought. Unlike other meteorological drought indices, such as the Palmer Drought Severity Index (PDSI), BMDI is designed to evaluate the degree of severity and frequency of prolonged periods of abnormally dry conditions. Remotely sensed derived vegetation condition index (VCI) is based on NDVI, which is obtained by combining the Channels 1 and 2, visible and near infrared respectively of NOAA/AVHRR (Kogan 2001, Dalezios et al. 2014). NOAA is a series of meteorological satellites having several instruments on board, such as AVHRR, which is a multi-spectral scanner with medium spatial resolution. The swath is 3000 × 6000 km, which produces overlaps of the same area and the daily coverage of the whole earth. The NDVI is given by the following equation:

$$NDVI = (Ch1 - Ch2) / (Ch1 + Ch2) \qquad (1)$$

where Ch1 and Ch2 are the radiances of the first two channels of NOAA/AVHRR. NDVI is a quick and efficient way for the estimation of vivid vegetation. After a stressed condition, significant reduction in NDVI of the field is expected and values corresponding to complete lack of chlorophyll elements are sometimes anticipated. Previous studies (Schultz and Halpert 1993) showed that normalized difference vegetation index (NDVI) is well correlated with 2–3 months cumulative rainfall. The model development consists of the following steps:

Step 1: Filtering – maximum value composite (MVC). For the purposes of estimating the impact of the weather on vegetation, the nonweather effects should be filtered out. Kogan proposed spatial filtering to eliminate that portion of noise incorporated into NDVI (Kogan 1990). Additionally, the daily maps of NDVI can be composited over a ten-day period (decadal), saving those values that have the largest difference between radiance for near infrared and visible wave bands during the ten days, for each map shell. With this procedure MVC images can be estimated. The combination of the filtering and the MVC can significantly reduce the noise from residual clouds, fluctuating transparency of the atmosphere, target/sensor geometry, and satellite orbital drift (Goward et al. 1991). Other noise can be related to processing, data errors, or simple random noise (Kogan 1995b). Such fluctuations must be removed before NDVI would be used for monitoring. This can be achieved with a "5342 compound twice" filter applied to remove the noise of the NDVI series (Van Dijk et al. 1987).

Step 2: Vegetation index. This step consists of the comparison of any year's NDVI with the absolute maximum and minimum NDVI values in the archive, which defines the ecosystem resources (Kogan 1990, 1994, 1995a). The entire procedure is given by the expression of the VCI:

$$VCI = 100 \times (NDVI - NDVI_{min}) / (NDVI_{max} - NDVI_{min}) \qquad (2)$$

where NDVI, $NDVI_{max}$ and $NDVI_{min}$ are the smoothed (ten-day) MVCs normalized difference vegetation index, its multi-year maximum and its multi-year minimum, respectively, for each pixel, in a specific area. The VCI varies from zero, for extremely unfavorable conditions, to 100, for optimal conditions. VCI separates the short-term weather signal in the NDVI data from the long-term ecological signal (Kogan 1997, Kogan and Sullivan 1993).

Step 3: Anomaly index M. Computation of monthly VCI values is achieved by estimating the maximum values of the three dekadals consisting each month. Long-term mean monthly VCI and the standard deviation, s, for each examined point are estimated in order to evaluate the variation of VCI values in time. The percentage departure of monthly VCI from the long-term mean is then used to compute the VCI anomaly index, M, given by

$$M = 100 \times (VCI - VCI_{mean})/s \qquad (3)$$

Averages of the highest accumulated values of the negative M values during successive sequence of months are then obtained for all sampling areas. The accumulated value of M is used to express the duration of anomaly in time. For unfavorable conditions the anomaly is negative, which means that the accumulated value is more negative compared to other cases, expressing the duration of this anomaly in time.

Step 4: Least-square equation. Highest anomalies of all areas are estimated and the average value of the highest negative anomaly for all the areas is computed. This process expresses the spatial behavior of all the areas under consideration. This step provides a relative measure of regional anomalies, since it permits numerical designation of extreme values of VCI in various parts of the study region. The extreme unfavorable condition from the monthly highest accumulated negative M value is given by a least-square equation:

$$\sum_{i=1}^{k} Mt = a + bk \qquad (4)$$

where k is the number of months. According to the Bhalme and Mooley methodology, the equation of the line corresponding to the extreme case (same as Palmer) is given as

$$BMVCI_k = 4\sum_{i=1}^{k}[M_t/(a+bk)] \qquad (5)$$

where $BMVCI_k$ is the derived index value of the kth month (Fig. 2). The constants a and b characterize the study area. Equation (5) depicts VCI departures expressed in both space and time, where the space component is incorporated at the constants a and b, while the time component is incorporated at M_t for each month.

Step 5: Difference between successive months. As results from Equation (5), a negative value of M is required to make $BMVCI_k$ more negative and maintain the existing condition in successive months. Thus, for all months following an initial month with law values, an additional term is

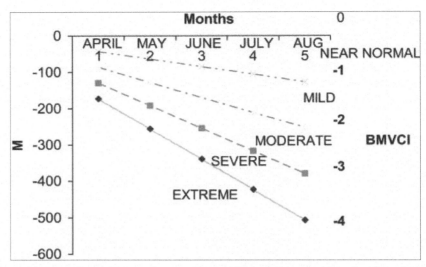

Figure 2. Family of lines corresponding to four Bhalme and Mooley Vegetation Condition Index (BMVCI) categories (from Domenikiotis et al. 2005).

introduced to account for any carry-over effect of the antecedent condition, rearranging Eq. (5) to

$$\Delta_{BMVCIk} = 4\,[\,M_k/(a+b)\,] + c\,BMVCI_{k-1} \qquad (6)$$

where $\Delta_{BMVCIk} = BMVCI_k - BMVCI_{k-1}$, and c a constant that depends on the impact of the antecedent condition. Hence, the final stress severity index for a given month k is given by

$$BMVCI_k = 4\,[M_k/(a+b)] + (1+c)\,BMVCI_{k-1} \qquad (7)$$

The index values are calibrated to nine classes as shown in Table 3.

Table 3. Classification of weather using Z-index (from Palmer, 1965)

Z-index (and BMVCI)	Environmental conditions
I ≥ 4	Extremely favor conditions
3.99 ≥ I ≥ 3	Very favor conditions
2.99 ≥ I ≥ 2	Moderately conditions
1.99 ≥ I ≥ 1	Slight conditions
0.99 ≥ I ≥ 0.99	Near normal
–1 ≥ I ≥ –1.99	Mild unfavorable conditions
-2 ≥ I ≥ -2.99	Moderate unfavorable conditions
3 ≥ I ≥ –3.99	Severe unfavorable conditions
–4 ≥ I	Extreme unfavorable conditions

Results: A time series of NOAA/AVHRR NDVI images for Thessaly, with 8 x 8 km² resolution, in successive years (1981–1999), is obtained and the VCI is estimated. The data set consists of 654 dekadals which correspond to the NDVI for the period 1981–1999. The obtained data consist of MVC images for eighteen years. NDVI map generated for each day during the growing season. Values of dekadals of VCI are converted to monthly, getting the maximum VCI value of the three corresponding dekadals from April to August. Based on step 4 a time series of BMVCI values, in successive years (1982–1997), is obtained. The data set consists of 16 years x 5 months, which correspond to the monthly BMVCI of 1981–1997. The constants a and b take the values 80.9 and 114.17, respectively. An empirical relationship between the cotton production and the index is developed to validate the sensitivity of the BMVCI to the effects of meteorological conditions during the growing season. For the model development the total production of Thessaly is utilized. Area coverage and production data are provided by the National Statistical Service of Greece. The empirical relationship developed for Thessaly in Central Greece is given by the equation:

$$\text{Cotton production (tons)} = 163{,}018 \times \text{BMDVI} + 389{,}619 \qquad (8)$$

Equation (8) is developed based on the time series 1982–1997. The correlation between BMVCI and cotton production over Greece is 86% (R^2 = 73%). It seems that BMVCI can demonstrate very well the meteorological and other related phenomena to cotton production. The proposed methodology could give an estimate of the total cotton production every year at the end of August when BMVCI could be estimated. The two following years 1998 and 1999 are utilized in order to validate the methodological approach. In order to predict the cotton production for 1998 the Eq. (8) is applied. The BMVCI variable in this equation results from incorporating the satellite data of 1998 to the previous data set (1982–1997) using the steps 1–5. The real cotton production for the year 1998 in Thessaly is 542,498 tons and the method applied predicts 553,618 tons that is 2% higher than the real value (Table 4). The same process is repeated for the prediction of cotton production in 1999. Incorporating the satellite data

Table 4. Percentage departure of real versus predicted cotton production in Thessaly

Real/Predicted production	Year	
	1998	1999
Real cotton production (tons)	537,380	542,498
Predicted cotton production (tons)	512,826	553,618
Percentage departure (%)	–5%	+2%

of 1999, the cotton production in Thessaly is estimated to be 512,826 tons which is 5% lower than the real production (537,380 tons). The estimated values (Table 4) for 1998 and 1999 as resulted from the validation process seem to be very satisfactory.

Summary and Conclusions

Remote sensing features and components in agricultural production modelling are considered. Moreover, agricultural production assessment methodologies are described incorporating remote sensing data and methods. It has been observed that sophisticated crop simulation systems cannot delineate and forecast crop yield mainly due to the complexity of the models with many components and many inputs, as well as the uncertainty in the climate system. Furthermore, it has been indicated that in agricultural production assessment there is an increasing trend and demand for new remotely sensed-based technological tools with steadily improving results. It seems that very good results can be obtained with relatively simple simulation models, especially when dealing with regional scales, where more emphasis is provided to the precise selection of "value-added" agrometeorological parameters than to the processing of large volumes of input data. Remote sensing data and methods help in that approach also due to their improving reliability and data availability.

An application is presented describing a methodological approach for quantifying the sequence of the meteorological effects on the cotton production during the growing season in Thessaly, Greece. BMVCI can be a useful tool for assess meteorological impacts on cotton. The advantage of BMVCI is its independence of the surface type and its availability for regions, where a sparse weather observing network exists. For the validation of the extracted BMVCI index the relationship between the cotton production of Thessaly and the BMVCI values is derived. The correlation coefficient indicates that the proposed index encompasses the meteorological conditions, which affect the final production. Therefore, BMVCI depicts and gives a consistent indication of cotton productivity in Thessaly. Year by year, the index is expected to improve the ability for incorporating extreme cases into the total process.

Acknowledgments

This research has been partly funded by PRIMA 2018 SUPROMED project (2019-2020) and PRIMA 2019 HubIS project (2020-2023).

References

Al-Gaadi, K.A., A.A. Hassaballa, E. Tola, A.G. Kayad, R. Madugundu, B. Alblewi and F. Assiri. 2016. Prediction of potato crop yield using precision agriculture techniques. PLOS ONE 11(9), e0162219. https://doi.org/10.1371/journal. pone.0162219.

Bandyopadhyay, K.K., S. Pradhan, R.N. Sahoo, Ravender Singh, V.K. Gupta, D.K. Joshi and A.K. Sutradhar. 2014. Characterization of water stress and prediction of yield of wheat using spectral indices under varied water and nitrogen management practices. Agricultural Water Management 146, 115–123, doi.org/10.1016/j.agwat.2014.07.017.

Basso, B., D. Cammarano and E. Carfagna. 2013. Review of crop yield forecasting methods and early warning systems. Report to the Global Strategy to Improve Agricultural and Rural Statistics. FAO Publication. Rome.

Basso, B., U. Schulthess and E. Carfagna. 2014. A comprehensive evaluation of methodological and operational solutions to improve crop yield forecasting. FAO Contract Report. Rome.

Basso, B. and Lin Liu. 2019. Seasonal crop yield forecast: Methods, applications, and accuracies. Advances in Agronomy 154, 201–255. ISSN 0065-2113.

Bolton, D.K. and M.A. Friedl. 2013. Forecasting crop yield using remotely sensed vegetation indices and crop phenology metrics. Agric. For. Meteorol. 152, 223–232.

Bouman, B. 1994. Yield prediction by crop modeling and remote sensing. pp. 91–104. In: Proceedings of Workshop for Central and Eastern Europe on Agrometeorological Models: Theory and Applications in the Mars Project, 21-25 November 1994, Ispra-Italy.

Bu, H., L.K. Sharma, A. Denton and D.W. Franzen. 2017. Comparison of satellite imagery and ground-based active optical sensors as yield predictors in sugar beet, spring wheat, corn, and sunflower. Argon. J. 109, 299–308.

Campos, I., Laura González-Gómez, Julio Villodre, Jose González-Piqueras, Andrew E. Suyker and Alfonso Calera. 2018. Remote sensing-based crop biomass with water or light-driven crop growth models in wheat commercial fields. Field Crops Research 216, 175–188.

Chipanshi, A., Y. Zhang, L. Kouadio, N. Newlands, A. Davidson, H. Hill, R. Warren, B. Qian, B. Daneshfar, F. Bedard and G. Reichert. 2015. Evaluation of the ICCYF model for in-season prediction of crop yield across the Canadian agricultural landscape. Agricultural and Forest Meteorology 206: 137–150.

Dabrowska-Zielinska, K., F.N. Kogan, A. Ciolkosz, M. Gruszczynska and W. Kowalik. 2002. Modelling of crop growth conditions and crop yield in Poland using AVHRR-based indices. International Journal of Remote Sensing 23, 1109–1123.

Dalezios, N.R. 2015. Agrometeorology: Analysis and Simulation (in Greek). KALLIPOS: Libraries of Hellenic Universities (also e-book), ISBN: 978-960-603-134-2: 481.

Dalezios, N.R., A. Blanta, N.V. Spyropoulos and A.M. Tarquis. 2014. Risk identification of agricultural drought in sustainable agroecosystems. Natural Hazards and Earth System Sciences 14, 2435–2448.

Dalezios, N.R., C. Domenikiotis, A. Loukas, S.T. Tzortzios and C. Kalaitzidis. 2001. Cotton yield estimation based on NOAA/AVHRR produced NDVI. EGS Journal of Physics and Chemistry of the Earth – Part B, 26(3), 247–251.

Das, D.K., K.K. Mishra and N. Kalra. 1993. Assessing growth and yield of wheat using remotely-sensed canopy temperature and spectral indices. International Journal of Remote Sensing 14(17), 3081–3092, DOI: 10.1080/01431169308904421

De Wit, C.T. 1965. Photosynthesis of Leaf Canopies. Agricultural Research Report No. 683. Center for Agriculture Publications and Documentation. Wageningen, The Netherlands.

Dempewolf, J., B., Adusei, I. Becker-Reshef, M. Hansen, P. Potapov, A. Khan and B. Barker. 2014. Wheat yield forecasting for Punjab province from Vegetation Index Time Series and Historic Crop Statistics. Remote Sens. 6, 9653–9675.

Domenikiotis, C., M. Spiliotopoulos, E. Tsiros and N.R. Dalezios. 2004a. Early cotton yield assessment by the use of the NOAA/AVHRR derived drought Vegetation Condition Index in Greece. International Journal of Remote Sensing 25, 2807–2819.

Domenikiotis, C., M. Spiliotopoulos, E. Tsiros and N.R. Dalezios. 2004b. Early cotton production assessment in Greece based on the combination of the drought Vegetation Condition Index (VCI) and Bhalme and Mooley Drought Index (BMDI). International Journal of Remote Sensing 25(23), 5373–5388.

Domenikiotis, C., M. Spiliotopoulos, E. Tsiros and N.R. Dalezios. 2005. Remotely sensed estimation of annual cotton production under different environmental conditions in central Greece. Physics and Chemistry of the Earth 30, 45–52.

Donald, G.E., S.G. Gherardi, A. Edirisinghe, S.P. Gittins, D.A Henry and G. Mata. 2010. Using MODIS imagery, climate and soil data to estimate pasture growth rates on farms in the south-west of Western Australia. Animal Production Science 50(6), 611–615.

Donatelli, M., G. Russell, A.E. Rizzoli, M. Acutis, M. Adam, I.N. Athanasiadis, M. Balderacchi, L. Bechini, H. Belhouchette, G. Bellocchi, J.-E. Bergez, M. Botta, E. Braudeau, S. Bregaglio, L. Carlini, E. Casellas, F. Celette, E. Ceotto, M.H. Charron-Moirez, R. Confalonieri, M. Corbeels, L. Criscuolo, P. Cruz, A. di Guardo, D. Ditto, C. Dupraz, M. Duru, D. Fiorani, A. Gentile, F. Ewert, C. Gary, E. Habyarimana, C. Jouany, K. Kansou, R. Knapen, G.L. Filippi, P.A. Leffelaar, L. Manici, G. Martin, P. Martin, E. Meuter, N. Mugueta, R. Mulia, M. van Noordwijk, R. Oomen, A. Rosenmund, V. Rossi, F. Salinari, A. Serrano, A. Sorce, G. Vincent, J.-P. Theau, O. Thérond, M. Trevisan, P. Trevisiol, F.K. van Evert, D. Wallach, J. Wery and A. Zerourou. 2010. A component-based framework for simulating agricultural production and externalities. In: Brouwer, F. and van Ittersum, M. (eds.). Environmental and Agricultural Modelling: Integrated Approaches for Policy Impact Assessment 63–108. Springer.

Dumont, B., B. Basso, V. Leemans, B. Bodson, J.P. Destain and M.F. Destain. 2015. A comparison of within-season yield prediction algorithms based on crop model behaviour analysis. Agric. For. Meteorol. 204, 10–21.

Dumont, B., V. Leemans, S. Ferrandis, B. Bodson, J.-P. Destain and M.-F. Destain. 2014. Assessing the potential of an algorithm based on mean climatic data to predict wheat yield. Precis. Agric. 15, 255–272.

ESA. 2014. Sentinel, Earth online - ESA. <https://earth.esa.int/web/guest/missions/esa-future-missions/ sentinel-1>, 06/04/2014.

FAO. 2009. Harmonized World Soil Database. FAO, Rome and IIASA, Laxenburg (Austria).

Fieuzal, R., C.M. Sicre and F. Baup. 2017. Estimation of corn yield using multi-temporal optical and radar satellite data and artificial neural networks. Int. J. Appl. Earth Obs. Geoinf. 57, 14–23.

Figueiredo, Gleyce Kelly Dantas Araújo, Brunsell, Nathaniel Allan, Higa, Breno Hiroyuki, Rocha, Jansle Vieira, and Lamparelli, Rubens Augusto Camargo. 2016. Correlation maps to assess soybean yield from EVI data in Paraná State, Brazil. Scientia Agricola, 73(5), 462–470. https://dx.doi.org/10.1590/0103-9016-2015-0215.

García-Berná, José A., Sofia Ouhbi, Brahim Benmouna, Ginés García-Mateos, José L. Fernández-Alemán, and José M Molina-Martínez. 2020. Systematic mapping study on remote sensing in agriculture. Applied Sciences 10(10), 3456.

Geipel, J., J. Link and W. Claupein. 2014. Combined spectral and spatial modeling of corn yield based on aerial images and crop surface models acquired with an unmanned aircraft system. Remote Sens. 6, 10335–10355.

Gorski, T. and K. Gorska. 2003. The effects of scale on crop yield variability. Agricultural Systems 78(3): 425–434.

Goward, S.N., B. Markham, D.G. Dye, W. Dulaney and J. Yang. 1991. Normalized difference vegetation index measurements from advanced very high resolution radiometer. Remote Sensing of Environment 35(2&3), 259–279.

Hayes, M.J. and W.L. Decker. 1996. Using NOAA AVHRR data to estimate maize production in the United States corn belt. International Journal of Remote Sensing 17, 3189–3200.

Holzman, M.E. and R.E. Rivas. 2016. Early maize yield forecasting from remotely sensed temperature/vegetation index measurements. IEEE J. Sel. Top. Appl. Earth Obs. Remote Sens. 9, 507–519.

Johnson, M.D., W.E. Hsieh, A.J. Cannon, A. Davidson and F. Bedard. 2016. Crop yield forecasting on the Canadian prairies by remotely sensed vegetation indices and machine learning methods. Agric. For. Meteorol. 218, 74–84.

Johnson, D.M. 2014. An assessment of pre- and within-season remotely sensed variables for forecasting corn and soybean yields in the United States. Remote Sens. Environ. 141, 116–128.

Johnson, G. E., V.R. Achutuni, S. Thiruvengadachari and F. Kogan. 1993. The role of NOAA satellite data in drought early warning and monitoring selected case studies. pp. 31–49. In: Drought Assessment, Management and Planning Theory and Case Studies. Kluwer Academic, Boston.

Kogan, F.N. 1990. Remote sensing of weather impacts on vegetation in non-homogenous area. International Journal of Remote Sensing 11, 1405–1419.

Kogan, F.N. 1994. NOAA plays leadership role in developing satellite technology for drought watch. Earth Observation Magazine September: 18–21.

Kogan, F.N. 1995a. Application of vegetation index and brightness temperature for drought detection. Advance in Space Research 15(11), 91–100.

Kogan, F.N. 1995b. Droughts of the late 1980s in the United States derived from NOAA polar orbiting satellite data. Bulletin – American Meteorological Society 76(5), 655–668.
Kogan, F.N. 1997. Global drought watch from space. Bulletin – American Meteorological Society 78, 621–636.
Kogan, F.N. 2001. Operational space technology for global vegetation assessment. Bulletin of the American Meteorological Society 82: 1949–1964.
Kogan, F.N. and J. Sullivan. 1993. Development of global drought watch system using NOAA/AVHRR data. Advances in Space Research 13(5): 219–222.
Kolotii, A., N. Kussul, A. Shelestov, S. Skakun, B. Yailymov, R. Basarab, M. Lavreniuk, T. Oliinyk and V. Ostapenko. 2015. Comparison of biophysical and satellite predictors for wheat yield forecasting in Ukraine International Archives of the Photogrammetry. Remote Sensing and Spatial Information Sciences, ISPRS Archives 40(7W3), 39–44.
Kowalik, W., K. Dabrowska-Zielinska, M. Meroni, T.U. Raczka and A. de Wit. 2014. Yield estimation using spot-vegetation products: A case study of wheat in European countries. Int. J. Appl. Earth Obs. Geoinf. 32, 228–239.
Kuri, F., A. Murwira, K.S. Murwira and M. Masocha. 2014. Predicting maize yield in Zimbabwe using dry dekads derived from remotely sensed vegetation condition index. Int. J. Appl. Earth Obs. Geoinf. 33, 39–46.
Kussul, N., A. Kolotii. S. Skakun. A. Shelestov, O. Kussul and T. Oliynuk. 2014. Efficiency estimation of different satellite data usage for winter wheat yield forecasting in Ukraine. IEEE Geoscience and Remote Sensing Symposium, Quebec City, QC, 5080–5082. doi: 10.1109/IGARSS.2014.6947639
Li, Z., M. Song, H. Feng and Y. Zhao. 2015. Within-season yield prediction with different nitrogen inputs under rain-fed condition using CERES-wheat model in the northwest of China. J. Sci. Food Agric. 96, 2906–2916.
Liu, Chang-an, Chen, Zhong-xin, Shao Yun, Chen, Jin-song, Tuya Hasi and Pan Hai-zhu. 2019. Research advances of SAR remote sensing for agriculture applications: A review. Journal of Integrative Agriculture 18(3), 506–525.
Machakaire, A.T.B., J.M. Steyn, D.O. Caldiz and A.J. Haverkort. 2016. Forecasting yield and tuber size of processing potatoes in South Africa using the LINTUL-potato-DSS model. Potato Res. 59, 195–206.
Manatsa, D., I.W. Nyakudya, G. Mukwada and H. Matsikwa. 2011. Maize yield forecasting for Zimbabwe farming sectors using satellite rainfall estimates. Nat. Hazards 59, 447–463.
Navalgund, R.R., J.S. Parihar, Ajai and P.P. Nageshwara Rao. 1991. Crop inventory using remotely sensed data. Current Science 61: 162–171.
NCAR, 2014. Precipitation Data Sets: Overview & Comparison Table. Available at: https://climatedataguide.ucar.edu/climate-data/precipitation-data-sets-overview comparison-table. Accessed on 4 September 2015.
Oladipo, E.O. 1985. A comparative performance analysis of three meteorological drought indices. Journal of Climatology 5, 655–664.
Palmer, 1965. Meteorological Drought, Office of Climatology. US Weather Bureau, Research Paper No. 45, Washington DC: 58. http://www.ncdc.noaa.gov/temp-and-precip/drought/docs/palmer.pdf.

Peralta, N.R., Y. Assefa, J. Du, C.J. Barden and I.A. Ciampitti. 2016. Mid-season high-resolution satellite imagery for forecasting site-specific corn yield. Remote Sens. 8, 848.
Pinstrup-Andersen, P. and D.D. Watson II. 2011. Food policy for developing countries: The role of government in global, national, and local food systems. Cornell University Press. Ithaca, USA.
Quarmby, N.A., M. Milnes, T.L. Hindle and N. Silleos. 1993. The use of multi-temporal NDVI measurements from AVHRR data for crop yield estimation and prediction. International Journal of Remote Sensing 14, 199–210.
Rembold, F., C. Atzberger, I. Savin and O. Rojas. 2013. Using low resolution satellite imagery for yield prediction and yield anomaly detection. Remote Sensing 5(4), 1704–1733.
Rosenzweig, C., J.W. Jones, J.L. Hatfield, Alex Ruane, K.J. Thornburn, J.M. Antle, G.C. Nelson, C. Porter, S. Janssen, B. Basso, F. Ewert, D. Wallach, G. Baigorria and J.M. Winter. 2013. The Agricultural Model Intercomparison and Improvement Project (AgMIP): Protocols and pilot studies. Agricultural and Forest Meteorology 170, 166–182.
Schultz, A.P. and S.M. Halpert. 1993. Global correlation of temperature, NDVI and precipitation. Advances in Space Research 13(5), 277–280.
Sharma, L.K., S.K. Bali, J.D. Dwyer, A.B. Plant and A. Bhowmik. 2017. A case study of improving yield prediction and sulfur deficiency detection using optical sensors and relationship of historical potato yield with weather data in maine. Sensors 17, 1095.
Sharma, L.K., H. Bu, A. Denton and D.W. Franzen. 2015. Active-optical sensors using red NDVI compared to red edge NDVI for prediction of corn grain yield in North Dakota, U.S.A. Sensors 15, 27832–27853.
Singh, P.K., K.K. Singh, P. Singh, R. Balasubramanian, A.K. Baxla, B. Kumar, A. Gupta, L.S. Rathore and N. Kalra. 2017. Forecasting of wheat yield in various agro-climatic regions of Bihar by using CERES-wheat model. J. Agrometeorol. 19, 346–349.
Steven, M.D. and K.W. Jaggard. 1995. Advances in crop monitoring by remote sensing. In: Danson, F.M. and Plummer, S.E. [eds.]. Advances in Environmental Remote Sensing, Wiley.
Taubert, F., K. Frank and A. Huth. 2012. A review of grassland models in the biofuel context. Ecological Modelling 245, 84–93.
Thenkabail, S. Prasad, A. Eden Enclona, S. Mask Ashton and Bauke Van Der Meer. 2004. Accuracy assessments of hyperspectral waveband performance for vegetation analysis applications. Remote Sensing of Environment 91(3-4), 354–376.
Togliatti, K., S.V. Archontoulis, R. Dietzel, L. Puntel and A. VanLoocke. 2017. How does inclusion of weather forecasting impact in-season crop model predictions? Field Crop Res. 214, 261–272.
Tsiros, E., C. Domenikiotis and N.R. Dalezios. 2009. Sustainable production zoning for agroclimatic classification using GIS and remote sensing. IDŐJÁRÁS (Quarterly Journal of the Hungarian Meteorological Service) 113(1–2), 55–68.
Tsiros, E. and N.R. Dalezios. 2010. Remotely sensed indices in crop yield modeling. In: L. Toulios and G. Stancalie [eds.]. Satellite Data availability, methods and

challenges for the assessment of climate change and variability impacts on agriculture. COST Action 734, European Union 29–44.

Tucker, C.J. and B.J. Choudhury. 1987. Satellite remote sensing of drought conditions. Remote Sensing of Environment 23, 243–251.

USGS. 2015. Landsat 8 (L8) Data Users Handbook. LSDS-1574 Version 1.0. USGS Publication.

Van Dijk, A., L.S. Callis and M.C. Sakamoto. 1987. Smoothing vegetation index profiles: An alternative method for reducing radiometric disturbance in NOAA/AVHRR data. Journal of Photogrammetric Engineering & Remote Sensing 63, 1059–1067.

Vogt, J., 1994. The use of low resolution satellite data for crop state monitoring. Possibilities and limitations. pp. 223–240. In: Proceedings of Workshop for Central and Eastern Europe on Agrometeorological Models: Theory and Applications in the Mars Project, 21-25 November 1994, Ispra-Italy.

Vossen, P. 1994. An overview of methods for national crop yield forecasting. pp. 13–19. In: Proceedings of Workshop for Central and Eastern Europe on Agrometeorological Models: Theory and Applications in the Mars Project, 21-25 November 1994, Ispra-Italy.

Wang, M., F. Tao and W. Shi. 2014. Corn yield forecasting in Northeast China using remotely sensed spectral indices and crop phenology metrics. Journal of Integrative Agriculture 13(7), 1538–1545, https://doi.org/10.1016/S2095-3119(14)60817-0.

Wang, J., P.M. Rich and K.P. Price. 2003. Temporal responses of NDVI to precipitation and temperature in the central Great Plains, USA. International Journal of Remote Sensing 24, 2345–2364.

Wilson, W. and J.L. Sebaugh. 1981. Established criteria and selected methods for evaluating crop yield models in the AgRISTARS Program. pp. 24-31. In: American Statistical Association 1981. Proceedings of the Section on Survey Research Methods.

WMO, 2010. Guide to Agricultural Meteorological Practices. WMO – No. 134, 799 p.

Wu, B., René Gommes, Miao Zhang, Hongwei Zeng, Nana Yan, Wentao Zou, Yang Zheng, Ning Zhang, Sheng Chang, Qiang Xing and Anna van Heijden. 2015. Global crop monitoring: A satellite-based hierarchical approach. Remote Sens. 7, 3907–3933. doi:10.3390/rs70403907.

CHAPTER

7

Integrating Agriculture-related Data Provided by Thematic Networks into a High Impact Knowledge Reservoir

Hercules Panoutsopoulos[1]*, Borja Espejo Garcia[1], Philip E.G. Verbist[2], Spyros Fountas[1], Pieter Spanoghe[2] and Christopher Brewster[3]

[1] Department of Natural Resources Management and Agricultural Engineering, Agricultural University of Athens, Greece
[2] Department of Plants and Crops, Faculty of Bioscience Engineering, University of Ghent, Belgium
[3] Institute of Data Science, Maastricht University, Netherlands

Introduction

Knowledge is conveyed through digital artifacts that people create as part of their everyday activities. Making these artifacts widely available may involve the use of database systems able to handle their storage and management. These systems deploy database models explicitly defining the internal database structure. Database models are specific types of data models, whose role is to formally describe entities, as well as their associations, and further enable data type specifications, relation definitions and constraints identification (Umanath and Scamell 2014). However, technology provides a wide spectrum of possibilities for the creation of digital artifacts and data generation. The abundance of the technologies and tools available allow for the production of data in a variety of formats. In many cases, knowledge is communicated through semi-structured and unstructured data rather than structured data. This has direct implications for the data store system to adopt the respective database models. The relational database management systems (RDBMSs)

*Corresponding author: hpanoutsopoulos@aua.gr

are not the optimal solution for the storage and management of semi-structured and unstructured data, especially when large volumes of such kinds of data need to handled. As a consequence, a new paradigm of database technologies and models has emerged (da Silva et al. 2015).

The aim of this chapter is to illustrate the initial attempts towards a formal definition of the concept of Thematic Networks, through a specially designed ontology, and a database model for storing Agriculture-related data into a centralized data store. The book chapter's focus is EURAKNOS[1], which is an EU-funded, H2020[2] research project collating Agriculture-related data, in various formats, in order to make it available to any interested parties and stakeholders for further analysis or development. The data considered in EURAKNOS is disseminated by Thematic Networks, which, in the project's context, are conceptualized as Knowledge Reservoirs.

EURAKNOS is a Thematic Network itself and as other Thematic Networks its overarching goal is to aggregate and further disseminate data conveying useful information and knowledge to a range of stakeholders targeted (namely, farmers, foresters, and advisors). In other words, its aim is to create a so called "High Impact Knowledge Reservoir". To this end, a data repository is going to be developed as the core component of the EURAKNOS digital platform. A similar approach has also been taken by the other Thematic Networks, which allow access to agricultural data stored into their own repositories. As an example we can mention: (i) the Inno4Grass[3] Thematic Network's "Encyclopedia pratensis" data repository[4]; (ii) The Smart-AKIS[5] Thematic Network's "Smart Farming Technologies Platform"[6]; and (iii) the 4D4F[7] Thematic Network's "Technology Warehouse"[8]. In addition, we may also refer to cases of Thematic Networks (e.g. AFINET[9]) that make their data available via general-purpose repositories such as Zenodo[10]. A thorough analysis of the repositories of the existing Thematic Networks, already undertaken in EURAKNOS, has revealed a number of design-related issues and inconsistencies with regard to the provision of the data to the user. More specifically, by taking account of the different scope of each Thematic Network, there is a great variance in the information and content needed

---

[1] https://www.euraknos.eu/
[2] https://ec.europa.eu/programmes/horizon2020/en/what-horizon-2020
[3] https://www.inno4grass.eu/en/
[4] https://www.encyclopediapratensis.eu/
[5] https://www.smart-akis.com/
[6] https://smart-akis.com/SFCPPortal/#/app-h/technologies
[7] https://www.4d4f.eu/
[8] https://www.4d4f.eu/content/technology-warehouse
[9] https://euraf.isa.utl.pt/el/afinet
[10] https://zenodo.org/

to conveyed, with a range of data formats being used. However, apart from the variance in the content/information and the data formats being used, the major deficiency, inherent to the design of all the existing Thematic Network repositories, is the inconsistency in the categorization and characterization of the data. In other words, there is no commonly accepted framework for the classification of the data disseminated by Thematic Networks, which, in turn, makes any attempt to proceed to a process of cataloguing them a difficult endeavor. This issue has direct implications for the annotation of data with metadata and the facilitation of the data search and retrieval process in compliance with contemporary recommendation and guideline frameworks such as the FAIR principles (Wilkinson et al. 2016). EURAKNOS aspires to help close this gap and contribute to a solution to the problem of the observed, design-related variances and inconsistencies by proposing a robust model that efficiently captures the entire spectrum of the data types and formats available by Thematic Networks.

Given the above, the efficient management of data heterogeneity and the need to structure data in an efficient manner, are core challenges for EURAKNOS and the various Thematic Networks, in the agricultural sector, which cover a range of activities, and topics, from dairy farms to agroforestry. This chapter begins with an outline of the concept of Thematic Networks and the rationale behind them. After that, a description of the EURAKNOS project takes place with an emphasis on the methodology adopted for identifying, collating and making available Thematic Network outputs (i.e. data) of interest. The ontology of Thematic Networks, aimed to be used for the needs of metadata definition, is presented next. From a technical perspective, the implementation of the High Impact Knowledge Reservoir will be based on an appropriately-designed digital platform. So, after an overview of the digital platform's architecture, a number of design-related considerations are discussed. These relate to: (i) the retrieval and integration of the Thematic Network outputs; (ii) the EURAKNOS data store and database model; (iii) the search technologies to be considered; and (iv) the user interaction. The chapter concludes with a summary of the key points of the work undertaken, its key contributions and limitations, as well as the steps to be taken next.

The Role of Thematic Networks as Multipliers of Agriculture-related Knowledge

EURAKNOS is a Thematic Network. Thematic Networks are a particular format of Multi-Actor projects, promoted by EIP-AGRI and funded by EU's Horizon 2020 programme, working on specific themes. They bring people from both the science and practice domains together to create practical and useful outputs. The concept of Thematic Networks is at the core of EURAKNOS. It has stemmed from the need to efficiently address Agriculture-/Forestry-related problems of ever-increasing complexity and identify novel solutions. The dynamic agricultural landscape calls for out-of-the-box thinking and challenges the top-down, linear model of knowledge transfer from the research community to practitioners. Scientists can no longer be viewed as the only innovation brokers in the Agri-food value chain. This means that other stakeholders also have an important role to play. In other words, solutions to problems need to occur as an outcome of coordinated, joint efforts of various actors bringing different perspectives and values to the process and, consequently, contributing to synergies between research and practice.

The above described approach is core to what the agricultural European Innovation Partnership (EIP-AGRI) calls an *"interactive innovation model"*[11] and constitutes the foundation of the Multi-Actor projects (EIP-AGRI 2017). The use of the term *"interactive"* is indicative of the way in which innovation is conceptualized as it is expected to occur from bottom-up processes involving seminal interactions among the various stakeholders (e.g. farmers, advisors, SME and NGO representatives, researchers) and aims to further the already existing knowledge. Thematic Networks are a particular format of Multi-Actor projects (EIP-AGRI 2016) and as such they:

- relate to specific themes (e.g. sustainable cropping systems, animal production systems, plant health, rural dynamics and policies, knowledge and innovation systems) and focus on real problems of practitioners;
- bring together partners with complementary backgrounds and expertise to collaborate, during the entire project lifecycle, and come up with innovative solutions to problems;
- collect, further develop, as well as disseminate ready-to-apply recommendations and practices and, thus, serve as multipliers of the Agriculture-related knowledge.

The key characteristics and properties of Thematic Networks are summed up in the following definition, which has been developed with the aim to facilitate the ontology creation:

Thematic networks are multi-actor projects collecting existing knowledge[12] and best practices on a given theme, which relates to a domain. Their aim is to produce outputs, having a specific purpose and addressing a particular topic, which are of different kinds (e.g. text, software, images,

---

[11] https://ec.europa.eu/eip/agriculture/en/eip-agri-concept
[12] In the context of EURAKNOS project, the term knowledge is used to denote the data that convey agricultural knowledge.

audio, video, and datasets) and formats. Outputs target end-users (e.g. farmers, foresters, advisors) and are produced by output creators, engaged in the Thematic Network, which can be distinguished into organizations (e.g. universities, SMEs, NGOs, research institutes), having different kinds of involvement in the Thematic Network (participatory or leading), and individual actors (e.g. farmers, livestock breeders, advisors).

EURAKNOS: A Meta-Thematic Network for Collecting, Compiling and Enabling Access to Existing Best Practices and Knowledge

The goal of the EURAKNOS project[13] is to collate, store and further disseminate already created, Agriculture-related data. It is a Thematic Network aiming to strengthen agricultural knowledge and promote innovation across Europe. By bringing together academic organizations, research institutes, advisory centers, government bodies, SMEs, NGOs and farmer organizations, EURAKNOS embraces the Multi-Actor approach and acts as an "umbrella" project aiming to connect all Thematic Networks. It can be considered as a Thematic Network about Thematic Networks, i.e. a meta-Thematic Network. Through the coordinated efforts of a consortium of 17 organizations from 11 European countries, with an extensive expertise in innovation in Agriculture and Forestry, EURAKNOS aims to attain a number of objectives relating to:

- the establishment of connections with existing Thematic Networks and the increase of their impact as creators and multipliers of Agriculture-related knowledge;
- the collection, analysis and evaluation, on the basis of well-established quantitative/qualitative criteria, of the knowledge and tools available by Thematic Networks;
- the development of guidelines and technical specifications for a centralized repository of agricultural knowledge, as well as recommendations for future Thematic Network-related initiatives;
- the development of a platform consisting of the EURAKNOS Thematic Network repository, search engine, and a web-based environment for querying and accessing Agriculture-related data;
- the promotion, sustainability and longevity of the project by making use of fit-for-purpose communication and dissemination channels and also pursuing links with other Thematic Networks, research projects (at the EU and national levels), as well as educational/training programs.

---

[13] The EURAKNOS project receives funding from the European Union's Horizon 2020 research and innovation programme under grant agreement No 817863.

Methodology for Agriculture-related Data Collection, Storage and Dissemination

Methodology Overview and Involved Steps

As mentioned earlier, a term core to the project is that of "Knowledge Reservoir" (KR). EURAKNOS considers all Thematic Networks as KRs. A KR is a collection of digital artifacts conveying practical, ready-to-apply knowledge able to contribute to innovative solutions for a sustainable Agriculture and Forestry. The aim of EURAKNOS is to build a High Impact Knowledge Reservoir (HIKR), namely a KR that uses a content structuring model tailored to needs of the end-users targeted. The activities for the data collection, storage and dissemination are described in a four-phase methodology. The phases of the EURAKNOS methodology relate to: (i) Evaluating, (ii) Determining, (iii) Exploring, and (iv) Widening. Descriptions of the activities involved in each phase are provided in Table 1.

After having mentioned the phases of the methodology adopted in EURAKNOS and the activities involved in it, it is helpful to proceed to the presentation of the expected, from the Thematic Networks' evaluation, outcomes and the description of what the recommendations for an HIKR should be about.

State-of-the-Art Review and Recommendations for a High Impact Knowledge Reservoir

The first two methodology phases (namely, "Evaluating" and "Determining") set the ground for the development of the technical specifications and the creation of the EURAKNOS platform. As mentioned earlier, the "Evaluating" phase involves a rigorous analysis of how Thematic Networks have addressed the issues of: (i) data storage and management; (ii) KR design; (iii) communication, dissemination and exploitation; and (iv) Multi-Actor engagement. To attain this goal, a number of specially designed, fit-for-purpose tasks (namely, "data impact assessment", "design of knowledge reservoirs", "dissemination, communication and information strategies" and "Multi-Actor approach") have been executed. These tasks have involved a combination of desktop study and face-to-face interviews of Thematic Network representatives. Table 2 below lists all the tasks involved in the specific methodology phase together with references to the research tools used and the outcomes expected.

The "Evaluating" phase gives input to the "Determining" phase. This input is required for the creation of recommendations for developing the EURAKNOS HIKR. In order to better illustrate the synergy between

Table 1. Phases of EURAKNOS methodology, description of their scope and alignment with project work packages

#	Phase	Involved activities
1	Evaluating	• Definition of the qualitative and quantitative criteria (based on cultural, socio-economic and environmental aspects) for ranking Thematic Network outputs with regard to their applicability at the local, regional, national and EU level. • Evaluation of the ongoing and completed Thematic Networks. Operational Groups[1] and other relevant Multi-Actor projects are also taken into consideration. • Evaluation focused upon the knowledge and tools produced, as well as the communication and dissemination channels employed for reaching out to the end-users and maximizing the impact of Thematic Networks. • Evaluation of the Multi-Actor approaches (employed by Thematic Networks) with the aim to estimate the short-, medium-, and long-term involvement of the different types of actors.
2	Determining	• Development of recommendations and guidelines for: • The collection, storage and sharing of ready-to-be-used agricultural knowledge; • The set-up of an HIKR, tailored to the needs of the end-users targeted, allowing for easy access to high quality content; • The communication and dissemination of innovative knowledge to the end-users; • Interoperable KRs in future Thematic Network efforts.
3	Exploring	• Development of an ontology for describing the Thematic Networks domain. • Development of an architecture and technical specifications for the EURAKNOS platform. • Development of the EURAKNOS digital platform comprising: - A data repository, built on the basis of Open and FAIR data principles, for storing agricultural knowledge related digital artifacts; - A search engine for executing queries on the knowledge stored; - A user interface enabling the querying and access of the knowledge available.
4	Widening	• Design and execution of communication, dissemination, exploitation, and networking activities to maximize the impact of EURAKNOS.

(Contd.)

Table 1. (*Contd.*)

#	Phase	Involved activities

4	Widening	• Development of a strategy for reaching out to a variety of audiences with special attention being paid to the EURAKNOS platform's end-users (e.g. farmers, foresters, advisors).
		• Synergies and connections with other Thematic Networks and Multi-Actor projects so as to:
		  - Contribute to the maximization of the impact of the existing Thematic Networks; and
		  - Guide and structure future efforts in Knowledge Reservoirs' development.
		• Pursuit of the sustainability and longevity of EURAKNOS by drawing links with training initiatives and educational programs at various sectors (e.g. academic, advisory, farm sectors) and levels (local, regional, national, and EU level).
		• Connection of EURAKNOS with EIP-AGRI to help develop links with the existing and future Thematic Networks, Operational Groups and Focus Groups.

Table 2. Tasks in the "Evaluating" phase of the EURAKNOS methodology, the research tools employed and the outcomes expected

#	Task name	Task description	Research tools employed and outcomes
1	Data impact assessment	• Investigation and analysis of the methods used for data generation and collection. • Investigation of the tools and technologies used for data storage. • Investigation of the data formats and types, as well as the content of the knowledge sources and tools available. • Estimation of the produced knowledge completeness and identification of potential knowledge gaps.	Desktop study — Research of Thematic Network websites to get insights into content provision and information architecture. Evaluation of the variations identified with regard to the different sectoral themes addressed by the Thematic Networks (e.g. livestock, crop production, forestry). Face-to-face interviews — Interviews of Thematic Network representatives (e.g. coordinators, WP/Task leaders, technical infrastructure administrators).
2	Design of knowledge reservoirs	• Investigation and analysis of: - The design of existing KRs; - The database models used for structuring knowledge; - The websites and data store systems of well-known international organizations (e.g. FAO, OECD, EFSA, etc.) contributing to the provision and dissemination of agricultural knowledge. • Analysis based on the principles for open access to knowledge provided by initiatives such as the OpenAIRE project.	Desktop study — Research existing KRs for data and knowledge formats, and the means for making it available to end-users. Research has focused upon: (i) open source software solutions; (ii) format of the data and knowledge available; (iii) search engines used; (iv) user interaction and experience. Face-to-face interviews — Interviews of Thematic Network representatives involved in the design of the KRs (e.g. software/database engineers, technical infrastructure administrators).

(Contd.)

Table 2. (Contd.)

#	Task name	Task description	Research tools employed and outcomes	
3	Dissemination, communication and information strategies	• Review of the state-of-the-art in communication and dissemination practices and tools. • Special attention on how specific types of end-users, of particular interest to EURAKNOS (e.g. farmers, foresters and advisors), have been reached. • Special consideration of social media.	Desktop study	Quantitative and qualitative evaluation of the dissemination and communication tools and material by taking account of the particular needs of the different end-user types, age, geographic location of end-users, frequency of use, etc.
			Face-to-face interviews	Interviews of the Thematic Network representatives involved in the development and implementation of the Thematic Networks' communication, dissemination, and exploitation strategies.
4	Multi-Actor approach	• Focus on the Multi-Actor approach employed by the existing Thematic Networks. • Investigation of how Multi-Actor approaches have been conceptualized, put into motion and executed. Emphasis upon the post-execution phase. • Specific issues taken into consideration: - The number and type of actors (e.g. in terms of the sector and organization represented, the geographic location, etc.); - The methods of approaching different actor types; - The delivery of the input by the actors involved; - The benefits in the short-, medium- and long-term.	Desktop study	Quantitative and qualitative analysis of the information retrieved from the Thematic Network websites.
			Face-to-face interviews	Interviews of Thematic Network partners and actors (in particular farmers, foresters and advisors) to further refine the outcomes of the desktop study.

these two methodology phases, Table 3 provides the description of the tasks involved in the "Evaluating" phase and their links to tasks of the "Determining" phase.

Towards an Ontology of Thematic Networks

Knowledge Representation is dedicated to domain-specific knowledge modeling. Two widely adopted Knowledge Representation models are database models and ontologies. Despite the fact that they have some differences (with many of them being just historical), these two constructs share a strong semantic heritage by using different formalisms, such as logic, to build conceptual models of some subject matter. Ontologies are explicit specifications of a conceptualization (Gruber 1993) with their aim being to represent meaning rather than data. They are based on Description Logic, a low-level Knowledge Representation technique able to be documented through various markup languages such as RDF, RDFS, OWL and OWL-DL. Ontologies can provide solutions to data heterogeneity and interoperability problems and, for that reason, they have played a significant role in the Semantic Web's development (Grimm et. al. 2011).

In order to develop the database model for the data representation in EURAKNOS, an ontology of Thematic Networks has been decided to be developed. More specifically, NOTICE (oNtology Of ThematIC nEtworks) is an ontology providing a formal description of the Thematic Networks' domain. The initial work undertaken on this ontology's development is presented in this chapter. NOTICE helps identify key entities related to the concept of Thematic Networks, the key attributes of the entities, as well as the relations between them. The NOTICE ontology, created on the basis of the methodology proposed by Noy and McGuiness (2001), aims to facilitate the definition of metadata for the annotation of data in the EURAKNOS data store. Figure 1 illustrates the major steps involved in the ontology creation process.

Figure 1. Methodology employed for building the NOTICE ontology (adapted from Noy and McGuiness 2001).

To the best of our knowledge, no systematic efforts regarding the creation of formal, explicit descriptions of the concept of Thematic Networks (based on some kind of Knowledge Representation structure) exist. Therefore, the NOTICE ontology has been built from scratch. The

Table 3. Tasks involved in the "Determining" phase of EURAKNOS methodology and their links to the "Evaluating" phase tasks

#	Task name	Task description	Alignment with task of the "Evaluating" phase
1	HIKR data best practices and methodologies	• Definition of the best methodologies and practices to generate, select, collect and store knowledge and data as the outputs of Thematic Networks. • Decisions about the data to be integrated in the EURAKNOS HIKR (decisions will be based on cultural, socio-economic, and relevant environmental aspects). • Recommendations for the development of a database model and data structuring specifications for the HIKR.	Data impact assessment
2	Design of HIKR	• Recommendations and guidelines for the EURAKNOS HIKR design by taking account of: - The needs of the end-users targeted; - Technology issues (e.g. ingestion of the data into the HIKR, data querying and access scenarios, data validation, user authentication and data security)	Design of knowledge reservoirs
3	HIKR dissemination, communication and exploitation strategies	• Identification and selection of the tools to communicate the project-related work, inform the end-users and disseminate the project's outcomes. • Exploitation of the tools identified with regard to best information, communication and dissemination channels to make the proposed innovation known to a wide range of potential end-users. • Proposal of a new format for practice abstracts.	Dissemination, communication and information strategies
4	HIKR Multi-Actor approach	• Identification and selection of the tools for Multi-Actor engagement and knowledge creation at different project phases, namely: conceptualization, initiation, execution and post-execution of the project. • Evaluation of the stakeholder needs with regard to the knowledge needed to be produced and stored in the HIKR.	Multi-Actor approach

identification of key terms, leading to the extraction of domain-related entities (which are, in turn, modeled as the ontology's classes and subclasses) and relations between them, has been based on the definition of the concept of Thematic Networks provided earlier. From that textual description, a number of statements containing references to domain-related entities, properties of those entities and relations between entities, have been extracted. In the statements presented below, the potential entities and entity properties are denoted with the use of bold characters and potential relations are highlighted with italicized characters. More specifically:

- A **Thematic Network** *is about* a **theme**.
- The **theme** (of a Thematic Network) *relates to* a **domain**.
- An **output** of a Thematic network *targets* **end – users**.
- An **output** *serves* a **purpose**.
- An **output** *addresses* a **topic**.
- An **output** *has* a **format**.
- A **topic** *relates to* a **theme** (namely, the theme of the Thematic Network).
- An **output** *is produced by* an **output creator**.
- An **output creator** *is distinguished into* **individual actor** and **organization**.
- An **individual actor** *belongs to* an **organization**.
- An **organization** *has* a specific **type of involvement** (namely, leading or participating organization) in the Thematic Network.

The above statements have helped to come up with a set of ontology classes, subclasses, and their properties all listed in Table 4 that follows.

The definition of the NOTICE classes, their subclasses, and a number of their properties has been based on the following schema.org types: *Thing, CreativeWork, DigitalDocument, MediaObject, AudioObject, ImageObject, VideoObject, PresentationDigitalDocument, SoftwareApplication, Person* and *Organization*. As mentioned in its official website[14], schema.org offers a vocabulary, able to be used with various encodings, for the definition of entities, relationships between entities and actions. The definition of the different kinds of digital artifacts, disseminated by Thematic Networks, has been based on the list of the media types (termed as Multipurpose Internet Mail Extensions or MIME types) provided by the Internet Assigned Numbers Authority[15]. The types included in this list are: *application, audio, example, font, image, message, model, text* and *video*. In order to propose an as inclusive as possible list of the Thematic Network—related output kinds, specifically tailored to the ontology's design needs, the {*application, audio, image, text, video*} MIME types sublist has been adopted and enriched

---

[14] https://schema.org/
[15] https://www.iana.org/

Table 4. The NOTICE ontology classes, subclasses and their properties

Class name	Class definition	Class properties	Subclasses	Subclass properties
Thematic Network	See definition provided in the section "The role of Thematic Networks as multipliers of Agriculture – related practical knowledge".	Acronym FullName Url	–	–
Theme	The subject a Thematic Network is about.	Title Domain	–	–
Output Creator	The actor or group of actors whose activity/-ies have led to the creation of a Thematic Network's output.	Name Description Country	IndividualActor A person who has been involved in the creation of a Thematic Network's output.	Email Type
			Organization An organization which has been involved in the creation of a Thematic Network's output.	AreaServed ContactPoint Involvement Type
Output	A digital artifact produced in the context of a Thematic Network.	Abstract Aggregate Rating dateCreatedinLanguage IsAccessibleForFree Keywords Purpose Size Title	AudioObject An audio file.	Duration Format PlayerType Transcript Type

Dataset	A body of structured information describing some topic(s) of interest.[1]	Format
		Issn
		Measurment Technique
		Type
		Variable Measured
Digital Document	A document available in a digital format with its content being mostly text.	Format
		Type
Image Object	An image file.	Height
		Format
		Type
		Width
Presentation Digital Document	A file containing slides or used for a presentation.[2]	Format
		Type
Software Application	Software designed to perform a group of coordinated functions, tasks, or activities for the benefit of the user.[3]	AvailableOnDevice
		Download Url
		Format
		MemoryRequirements
		OperatingSystem
		SoftwareRequirements
		SoftwareVersion
		StorageRequirements
		Type

(Contd.)

Table 4. The NOTICE ontology classes, subclasses and their properties

Class name	Class definition	Class properties	Subclasses	Subclass properties
			VideoObject A video file.	duration format playerType transcript type videoFrameSize videoQuality
Topic	The subject that an output of a Thematic Network is about.	Title	-	-
EndUser	The human individual that uses any computing-enabled device/appliance.[4]	Type	-	-

[1] Definition provided by schema.org; https://schema.org/Dataset
[2] Definition provided by schema.org; https://schema.org/PresentationDigitalDocument
[3] Definition provided by Wikipedia (https://en.wikipedia.org/wiki/Application_software)
[4] Definition provided by Technopedia: https://www.techopedia.com/definition/610/end-user

with the *presentation* and *dataset* types. Table 5 below lists all the kinds of potential Thematic Network outputs distinguished in NOTICE, which are modeled as subclasses of the "Output" class. It needs to be stressed that each output serves a specific purpose (namely, *access to data, best practice presentation, communication, decision support, dissemination, educational material, innovative practice presentation, training material*). This leads to another way of categorizing the different kinds of outputs, by taking account of the purpose-related types proposed. In other words, each subclass of the "Output" class has a property named "type" assigned to it, with its values relating to the purpose that the output serves.

Table 5. Subclasses of the "Output" class and respective values of the purpose-related "type" property

Subclasses of the "Output" class	Values of "type" property
AudioObject	{Advertising podcast, educational/training podcast, event capturing podcast, informational podcast, interview, on-demand seminar, tutorial}
Dataset	{Auditory data, crop-related data, geospatial data, graph-related data, imagery data, input-related data, network-related data, temporal data, textual data, video data, yield-related data}
DigitalDocument	{Article in conference proceedings, best practice guide, book, booklet, chapter in edited volume, deliverable report, factsheet, handbook/manual, journal article, milestone report, newsletter, practice abstract, press release, spreadsheet, review document, technical article, tutorial}
ImageObject	{Chart/graph, figure/image, info graphic}
Presentation-DigitalObject	{Demonstration, educational/training presentation, informational presentation, tutorial}
Software-application	{AI software, business software, data repository/database, decision support tool, educational/training software, Farm Management Information System (FMIS), game, scientific software, simulation}
VideoObject	{Advertising video, demonstration video, educational/training video, event capturing video, informational video, interview, testimonial, tutorial}

Distinguishing among different types of end-users is also important given that specific platform functionalities and solutions will be able to be provided given each user type's needs. On this basis, the following end-user types are defined: *adviser, bee keeper, consumer, distributor, entrepreneur, farmer, fisherman, forester, instructor, livestock breeder, policy maker, researcher, student*, *trader*, *trainer*, and *university professor*. As far as the relations between the ontology's classes are concerned, these are summarized in Table 6 that follows.

Table 6. The NOTICE ontology relations and the ontology classes participating in them

Referencing class	Relation	Referenced class
Thematic Network	*engages*	Output Creator
	is About	Theme
	is Coordinated By	Organization
Topic	*relates To*	Theme
Output	*addresses*	Topic
	is Produced By	Output Creator
	targets	End User
Individual Actor	*affiliated With*	Organization

All the ontology-related details are summarized in the diagrammatic representation of NOTICE illustrated in Fig. 2. However, it needs to be stressed again, that the work presented in NOTICE is preliminary. There are issues that need to be further taken care of such as the establishment of links between NOTICE and widely adopted, Agriculture-related ontologies and vocabularies for the needs of providing values to the domain and theme of Thematic Networks, as well as the topic of Thematic Network outputs.

Architecture of a Digital Platform for Agriculture-related Data

Architecture Overview

The EURAKNOS digital platform constitutes the technical implementation of the HIKR. The platform description is based on a three-layer architecture consisting of the data persistence layer, the application layer, and the presentation layer. The data persistence layer relates to the storage and management of the data. It is the layer where the data store is. The application layer is concerned with the actual logic of the platform. This is the layer where the EURAKNOS search engine resides. It handles data exchange between the presentation and data persistence layers and does not have to do with data persistence or how data is actually displayed to the end-user. However, it may well support multiple user interfaces (for instance, a web application and a mobile app). Finally, the presentation layer (in other words, the user interface) is what the end-users see. It is the part of the application that the end-users interact with. It displays the

Integrating Agriculture-related Data Provided by Thematic Networks... **217**

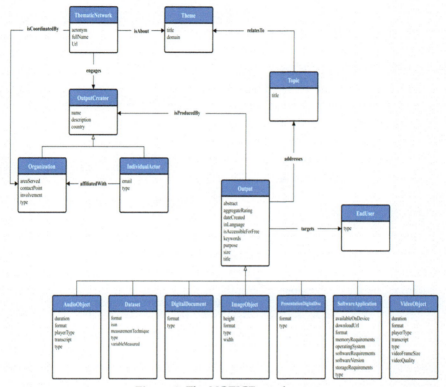

Figure 2. The NOTICE ontology.

data and receives requests from the end-users. This layer is not concerned with any logic and it just relies on the data. In order to make this stack of layers work, every layer needs to provide an Application Programming Interface (API) so that the other layers can communicate with it. So, for example, the EURAKNOS Search Engine may provide a REST Service and an OpenAPI (Swagger) specification upon which a user interface may be built. An overview of the EURAKNOS platform's architecture is provided in Fig. 3.

Issues Related to Data Collection and Ingestion into the EURAKNOS Data Store

EURAKNOS aims to collect and organize agricultural knowledge-related outputs available by existing Thematic Networks. Such outputs have so far been developed and managed in a decentralized and unstructured way. So, in order to make the data in the EURAKNOS data repository searchable and identifiable, indexes need to be built. Apart from that, a collection of large amounts of unstructured data will need to be based on

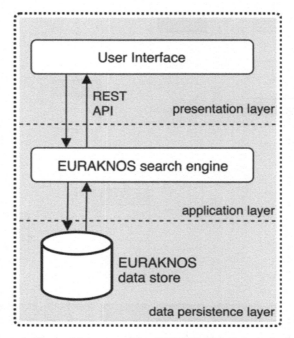

Figure 3. The architecture of the EURAKNOS digital platform.

some kind of automated process. Thematic Network outputs need to be aggregated into a single structured search index so that it can be searched. This is where web crawlers come into play. A web crawler is a program or automated script that browses the World Wide Web. It is usually employed to collect information, but it can also be used for automating maintenance tasks such as checking for dead links on a website or testing websites for errors.

A point to consider is that it is important not to "harm" the website that is being crawled. To this end, politeness policies are used to prevent the crawled website from being heavily affected. So, a polite web crawler should:
- respect the rules defined in the website's robots.txt file;
- avoid degrading the performance of the website it is crawling; and
- identify itself and its creator with contact information.

Humans are able to easily understand the content of a web page by just seeing it. However, it is not that easy for search engines to also interpret that same raw data. In order to help this interpretation process, a crawler collects metadata from the website. Search indexes can use metadata to interpret and link documents. The most obvious metadata provided by a web page are title-tags, the meta description, and keywords. It needs to be stressed that, quite often, web pages provide also descriptions for images. In the case of lack of metadata, web crawlers can resort to other ways of data interpretation.

The EURAKNOS Data Repository and Database Model

Thematic Networks compile information in many different ways. Therefore, it is hard to define a strict schema for data collection. One way to address this problem with an RDBMS is to employ the EAV/CR model (namely, Entity Attribute Value with Classes and Relationships). RDBMSs are highly consistent, but this comes at the cost of not being able to horizontally scale. NoSQL systems, on the other hand, allow for horizontal scalability, yet, at the cost of consistency. Horizontal scaling refers to the use of clusters of commodity hardware to store data, with each piece of hardware being responsible for the execution of processes such as look-ups and read/write operations on the data stored in it (Lake and Crowther 2013). This specific capacity of NoSQL data stores is pointed out in the definition of Cattell (2010) according to which NoSQL systems are *"designed to provide good horizontal scalability for simple read/write database operations distributed over many servers"* (p. 12). However, the advantages of NoSQL systems go beyond scalability-related issues. According to Vaish (2013), NoSQL data stores allow for schemaless data representation, which means that application developers can dynamically integrate changes in their design without needing to define a fixed data structure in advance. Schemaless data representation reduces the development time given that data access can be handled by application code rather than complex SQL queries. As a consequence, there is potential to develop applications able to efficiently respond to various workloads and deliver results very quickly.

The solution intended to be adopted for the deployment of the EURAKNOS data repository is MongoDB. MongoDB[16] belongs to the document-oriented category of NoSQL systems. By being a specific type of NoSQL data stores, document-oriented databases allow for the adoption of a dynamic and changeable schema, or no schema at all; a feature that makes them ideal for the storage of content changing over time (Vaish 2013). MongoDB is an open-source database management system providing high read and write throughput, as well as the ability for horizontal scaling and automatic failure recovery (Banker 2012). MongoDB has become popular mostly because of its capacity to efficiently represent and retrieve hierarchically structured information without a need to execute resource-intensive table joins (Banker 2012). Moreover,

---

[16] https://www.mongodb.com/

according to Banker (2012), MongoDB supports ad hoc queries[17] and data indexing. It also provides automatic data replication, which means distribution of data across nodes of a cluster with the aim to eradicate data loss due to hardware or network failure. Distribution of the data across nodes is internally handled by a mechanism called auto-sharding.

The model employed by MongoDB for data storage is called "document" and is based upon the JSON (i.e. JavaScript Object Notation) data exchange format. More specifically, MongoDB makes use of a binary representation of JSON called BSON (Lake and Crowther 2013). BSON documents can have a maximum size of 16 MBs; however, larger documents can also be stored with the help of the GridFS API. MongoDB's document can be better conceptualized if considered as the counterpart of a table row in an RDBMS. A document is made up of property names and values. Values can be of any BSON compatible data type (e.g. string, number, Boolean, date), as well as array, document (called embedded document) and array of documents. Thus, MongoDB can offer great flexibility for modeling complex data structures (Banker 2012). A "collection" is a group of documents and can be considered as the equivalent of a relational database's table. It needs to be highlighted that MongoDB allows for documents with different fields in the same collection.

Based on NOTICE, the database model proposed for the Agriculture-related data representation and storage is shown in Fig. 4.

Searching for Agriculture – Related Practical Knowledge

The primary aim of a search engine is to retrieve the most relevant documents to user queries, excluding other general content (Brin and Page 1998). To achieve this goal, a search engine usually instantiates crawlers that visit links, appearing in web pages, and download documents represented by those links. After that, an indexer parses the content of the documents (either textual or binary) and organizes it with the help of an index. Indexing is the method of storing data in index files and in a format helping the fast and efficient text searching. There are different index types each of which has strengths and weaknesses. The most popular index type is the inverted index, which is a data structure that stores mappings from terms to a set of documents. Apache Lucene[18] is the most popular open source library for document indexing. By also enabling query submissions, it allows the retrieval of query-matching results. The index can be stored in the file system or memory and can be

---

[17] According to Technopedia (https://www.techopedia.com/definition/30581/ad-hoc-query-sql-programming), an ad hoc query is *"a loosely typed command/query whose value depends upon some variable. Each time the command is executed, the result is different, depending on the value of the variable."*
[18] https://lucene.apache.org/

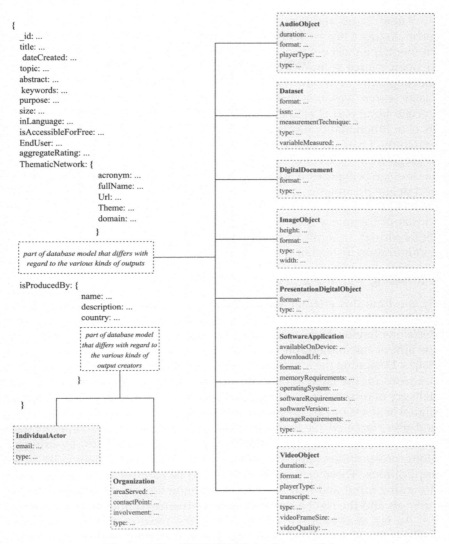

Figure 4. The EURAKNOS database model.

used to search the web, databases, and ontologies. Prior to storing data in index files, data is analyzed and parsed. Given Lucene's efficiency and precise search algorithms, it is widely adopted for being at the core of a search engine. The effectiveness of a search engine can be measured by two popular performance metrics, namely precision (i.e. the fraction of retrieved documents that are relevant) and recall (i.e. the fraction of relevant documents that have been retrieved).

There is no right or wrong choice with regard to search engine technologies. Choices depend on the application requirements and, based on them, the most efficient solution can be determined. Among a number of open source solutions available, the leading one, also qualifying for the deployment of the EURAKNOS search engine, is Elasticsearch[19]. Elasticsearch was first released in 2010 and is built upon the Apache Lucene library. It is stable and has a well-documented reference guide. Its core functionality has been enriched beyond simple text indexing and searching. Over the years, features such as faceting (currently known as aggregations), field collapsing, and language detection have been included. Elasticsearch exposes a REST API that allows, among others, to query and delete documents, as well as to create and manage indexes by using the HTTP GET, DELETE, POST and PUT methods. As far as the output format of the query results is concerned, Elasticsearch makes use of the JSON format. In terms of scalability, Elasticsearch uses a modern cluster configuration instead of the old-fashioned Master-Slave architecture.

Interacting with the EURAKNOS Digital Platform

By the time this chapter was authored, some preparatory work on the platform's back-end design had been done without, however, any final decisions having been made with regard to user interaction. Therefore, the aim of this paragraph is to highlight a number of interaction-related issues. Designing the interaction with the platform is heavily focused upon decisions for the facilitation of input provision from the end-user and the delivery of results. On one hand, the EURAKNOS repository will integrate digital artifacts of various formats and types waiting to be searched by the end-users targeted. On the other hand, the end-users come to interact with the system, with the expectation to get what is looked for, by bringing along presumptions and experiences from their interactions with other applications. These critical issues need to be carefully considered when designing input and output interfaces aiming to provide straightforward prompts and the right amount of clearly structured information.

As far as user input is concerned, the most commonly employed design pattern is that of a search box accompanied by a dedicated search button. Enabling users to submit free-text queries is the most commonly employed practice providing a great degree of freedom. In that case, the use of tools able to facilitate query syntax and submission needs to be investigated. According to Rosenfeld et al. (2015), such tools are spell checkers, which automatically correct misspelled query terms; stemming tools for retrieving results that contain terms sharing the same stem with terms in queries; Natural Language Processing tools having the capacity

---

[19] https://www.elastic.co/products/elasticsearch

to provide results after a syntactic analysis of the query; controlled vocabularies and thesauri enabling the search for results containing semantically similar terms; and autocompletion/autosuggestion tools able to significantly enhance the query development process.

Despite the intuitive nature of the free-text search and the advanced features that sophisticated add-ons can provide, the results yielded may not always be those expected. As a consequence, it is very important to investigate ways of further supporting the end users' searching endeavors. A solution to this direction is to provide the user with advanced search functionalities, able to lead to more specific queries, through the exploitation of logical operators. However, the use of this feature should be opted by the user (e.g. in cases where there are difficulties in retrieving the results required). So, in terms of design, access to this kind of functionality should be made available through separate interfaces. In this context, an option that is worth investigating is that of the interface segmentations called search zones (Rosenfeld et al. 2015), which offer search functionalities targeting at different user needs.

The design of search results display is also critical especially when the diversity of the Thematic Network outputs comes into play. A question requiring attention relates to the kind and amount of the results-related information needed to be displayed to the end-user. As Rosenfeld et al. (2015) point out, it is necessary to strike a balance between the display of representational information (for instance, the title, the creator and the date of creation of the result obtained) and descriptive information (in other words, information like the one mentioned above plus a content summary and maybe some keywords), aiming to help users not quite certain of the results they need. In addition to all the above, it should not be neglected that there also needs to be a focus on the order of the results display. Sorting and ranking are two popular options with the former appearing to be appropriate in cases where the user needs to make decisions or take actions, and the latter allowing for the establishment of a better understanding and learning purposes (Rosenfeld et al. 2015).

Conclusions and Further Steps

The aim of this chapter has been to present a systematic, ongoing effort for collecting Agriculture-related data and making them available. This process takes place within the context of EURAKNOS, a project that focuses on data disseminated by Thematic Networks. EURAKNOS is a Thematic Network itself aspiring to provide a single-point-of-access for Agriculture-related data available by the existing Thematic Networks. To this end, a fit-for-purpose methodology is implemented. Yet, there are many challenges that need to be addressed in order to conclude to a unified collection of Thematic Networks' outputs. For instance, there is a great diversity in the themes addressed by Thematic Networks, as well as in the types and formats of the outputs produced. In addition, there is no single technology used for the development of the existing Thematic Networks' Knowledge Reservoirs, and no consensus exists with regard to the data modeling approaches employed. As a consequence, the collation, storage, and provision of Thematic Network—related agricultural data, through a centralized repository, requires a robust and flexible data model. In this context, EURAKNOS makes a unique contribution by proposing the NOTICE ontology for the purpose of capturing, and formally describing, an extensive list of entities, entity properties, and relations tightly associated with any output (i.e. data object) disseminated by a Thematic Network. The ultimate goal of this Knowledge Representation structure is to help towards the identification and definition of a set of metadata for efficiently annotating the Thematic Network – related outputs in compliance with the FAIR data principles.

However, there are also some considerable limitations having mostly to do with EURAKNOS's scope. More specifically, EURAKNOS focuses solely on Thematic Networks and the data available by them. Thematic Networks are just a small fraction of Multi-Actor Projects and cannot be considered, in any case, as the sole sources of Agriculture-related knowledge. There are many more research-related efforts resulting in the creation of useful data that need to be considered. The NOTICE ontology is the first systematic attempt towards a formal, holistic description, and categorization, of agricultural data, but it cannot capture the full array of the characteristics and particularities of the data created in any Agriculture-related (research) effort. Therefore, by building upon the work conducted in EURAKNOS, further initiatives need to be taken towards this knowledge mapping direction[20].

In order to contribute to the realization of the main goal and objectives of EURAKNOS, there is a number of steps that need to be further taken. These steps relate to:

- The establishment of links between the NOTICE ontology and well-known Agriculture-related ontologies and vocabularies for the needs of providing values to the domain and theme of Thematic Networks, as well as the topic of the outputs of Thematic Networks.
- The facilitation of both human- and machine-enabled access to data through the achievement of compliance with the FAIR (i.e. "Findable",

---

[20] EUREKA (https://www.h2020eureka.eu/) is the follow-up project of EURAKNOS that extends upon its work through the adoption of a broader perspective (EUREKA focuses on the data objects produced by the entire set of Multi-Actor Projects. The EUREKA project receives funding from the EU's Horizon 2020 research and innovation programme under the grant agreement No 862790.

"Accessible", "Interoperable", and "Reusable") guiding principles and open data initiatives such as the OpenAIRE project[21].
- The development of the technical specifications necessary to assemble a robust system based on cutting-edge software solutions.
- The finalization of user interaction-related issues and the architecture of the information to be provided through the EURAKNOS digital platform, given the various end-user types targeted and their respective needs.

The work that has already been conducted together with the advancements expected, as the result of the steps to be taken next, will lead to the development of a body of knowledge of significant impact at both the small- and large-scale levels. At the small-scale level, EURAKNOS will frame the context for the future Thematic Networks by proposing and delivering a complete set of recommendations about their conceptual design and technology-related choices. By being exploited as it is or extended upon a fit-for-purpose basis, the NOTICE ontology is going to be a point-of-reference for the future Thematic Networks' conceptual design. In addition to that, the EURAKNOS platform's architecture and technical design will play a catalytic role to the creation and deployment of robust technological infrastructures capable of accurately serving the Thematic Network community members' needs. At the large-scale and long-term level, the achievements envisioned in EURAKNOS can also have implications for future policies. The benefits than can be reaped from the systematic exploitation of the unified EURAKNOS framework for Agriculture-related data collection and delivery may gradually lead to the establishment of standards and their embracement by policy-related authorities at the regional, national, and, probably, the international level.

References

Agricultural European Innovation Partnership. 2016. Thematic Networks under Horizon 2020: Compiling knowledge ready for practice. Retrieved from https://ec.europa.eu/eip/agriculture/sites/agri-eip/files/eip-agri_brochure_thematic_networks_2016_en_web.pdf

Agricultural European Innovation Partnership. 2017. Horizon 2020 multi-actor projects. Retrieved from https://ec.europa.eu/eip/agriculture/sites/agri-eip/files/eip-agri_brochure_multi-actor_ projects_2017_en_web.pdf

Banker, K. 2012. MongoDB in action. Manning Publications Co. New York. USA.

Brin, S. and L. Page. 1998. The Anatomy of a Large-Scale Hypertextual Web Search Engine. *In*: Seventh International World-Wide Web Conference (WWW 1998), Brisbane, Australia.

---

[21] https://www.openaire.eu/

Cattell, R. 2010. Scalable SQL and NoSQL data stores. Acm Sigmod Record 39(4), 12–27.
da Silva, A.R., A. Silva and A. Ribeiro. 2015. Data modeling and data analytics: A survey from a big data perspective. Journal of Software Engineering and Applications 8(12): 720–726.
Grimm, S., A. Abecker, J. Völker and R. Studer. 2011. Ontologies and the Semantic Web. *In*: Domingue, J., D. Fensel and J.A. Hendler. [eds.]. Handbook of Semantic Web Technologies. Springer, Berlin, Germany.
Gruber, T.R. 1993. Toward principles for the design of ontologies used for knowledge sharing. Technical Report KSL 93–04, Knowledge Systems Laboratory, Stanford University.
Lake, P. and P. Crowther. 2013. Concise Guide to Databases. Springer, London. UK.
Noy, N.F. and D.L. McGuinness. 2001. Ontology development 101: A guide to creating your first ontology. Retrieved from https://protege.stanford.edu/publications/ontology_development/ ontology101.pdf
Rosenfeld, L., P. Morville, and J. Arango. 2015. Information Architecture: For the Web and Beyond. O'Reilly Media, Inc., Sebastopol, CA.
Umanath, N.S. and R. W. Scamell. 2014. Data Modeling and Database Design. Delmar Learning, New York, USA.
Vaish, G. 2013. Getting Started with NoSQL. Packt Publishing Ltd, Birmingham. UK.
Wilkinson, M.D., M. Dumontier, I.J. Aalbersberg, G. Appleton, M. Axton, A. Baak, N. Blomberg, J.W. Boiten, L.B. da Silva Santos, P.E. Bourne and J. Bouwman. 2016. The FAIR Guiding Principles for scientific data management and stewardship. Scientific Data 3(1), 1-9.

CHAPTER
8

A Multicriteria DEA Model for Estimating the Efficiency of Agricultural Production Process

Anna Kalioropoulou*, Basil Manos and Thomas Bournaris
Aristotle University of Thessaloniki, Department of Agricultural Economics, Thessaloniki 541 24, Greece

Introduction

The aim of the present paper is the optimization and the better discrimination of agricultural production performance at the seven prefectures (DMUs) of the region of Central Macedonia in Northern Greece considering five inputs and two outputs. To this end, a multicriteria DEA approach was implemented at a regional level. The results achieved were compared with those of the conventional DEA model.

The conventional DEA model, known as CCR model, is a model of constant returns-to-scale (CRS) introduced by Charnes et al. (1978). The CCR model later was extended by Banker et al. (1984) to the model of variable returns-to-scale (VRS), known as BCC model. Several variations of conventional or more advanced DEA related models are widely applied for agricultural efficiency evaluation, such as malmquist productivity indices, bootstrap approaches, sub-vector approach, additive models, models with allocative input, weight restrictions, window analysis approach (Haag et al. 1992, Färe et al. 1997, Millian and Aldaz 1998, Lansink et al. 2002, Thirtle et al. 2003, Kamruzzaman et al. 2006, Balcombe et al. 2006, Davidova and Latruffe 2007, Lilienfeld and Asmild 2007, Odeck

---

*Corresponding author: annakali@agro.auth.gr

2009, Monchuk et al. 2010, Garcia and Shively 2011, Vlontzos and Niavis 2014, Vlontzos and Pardalos 2017).

DEA approach at a regional level, evaluates efficiency or efficiency shifts, when regions or districts are considered as DMUs. Considerable amount of studies dealing with agricultural efficiency are performed at a regional level and both constant and variable returns to scale models were used (Aldaz and Millan 2003, Diaz et al. 2004, Zhang 2008, Monchuk et al. 2010, Ma and Feng 2013, Ray and Ghose 2014, Toma et al. 2015, You and Zhang 2016).

Among the DEA advantages is the handling of multiple inputs and outputs even if the measurement units differ, the capability of uncovering and quantification the inefficiencies and revealing hidden relationships. Some DEA drawbacks is that many DMUs are ranked fully efficient and the results are sensitive to the appropriate selection of variables. The problem of many DMUs on the efficiency frontier and low discrimination power is evident when small number of DMUs are compared.

In case of small number of DMUs, as happens in this study, the conventional DEA model is not able to discriminate effectively the efficiency performance of the seven prefectures. In order to improve the discrimination, we propose multiple criteria data envelopment analysis (MCDEA). In this study an MCDEA model was used in the framework of multiple objective linear programming (MOLP). The MCDEA approach was introduced by Li and Reeves (1999) to overcome the disadvantage of lack of discrimination. In conventional DEA models, the small number of DMUs, compared to the number of inputs and outputs, has as a drawback a large number of DMUs with maximum efficiency (Toloo and Tichy 2015, Toloo et al. 2015, Toloo and Babaee 2015). The MCDEA approach effectively addresses this problem.

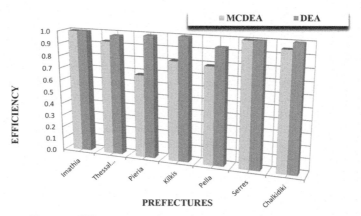

Figure 1. Efficiency results in the seven prefectures achieved by the MCDEA/DEA models.

Further developments of MCDEA model were carried out, aiming at optimizing its objectives (Bal and Orkcu 2007, Soares de Mello et al. 2009, Bal et al. 2010, Ghasemi et al. 2014, Chaves et al. 2016). In the MOLP framework, two additional objective functions are added to the original CCR DEA model. In this paper the Weighted Goal Programming (WGP) approach was used to solve the MCDEA model (Rubem et al. 2017) and was implemented in a real world problem in Northern Greece. The results from the proposed MCDEA model are compared with those achieved by the classic DEA CCR model.

2. Model description and data

In this work, the agricultural production efficiency is evaluated by means of a methodology that combines DEA and MOLP, known as MCDEA. Specifically, an MCDEA model of input orientation was developed, in its Constant Returns-to-Scale (CRS) form, and was employed to seven prefectures (DMUs) of the study region, namely Imathia, Pella, Thessaloniki, Serres, Pieria, Chalkidiki and Kilkis. The MCDEA model is composed by five inputs and two outputs. The proxies used for inputs are the land available in hectares, the variable costs in euro, the total labour used in hours, the total fertilizers in kgs and the number of tractors used. The outputs considered are gross margin, which is a good estimator of profit of farmers, and the bioenergy produced from the conversion of biomass of crops residues related to the main cultivated crops.

The selected inputs are the most important inputs in the agricultural production process and they are crucial in decision making of farmers (Tziolas et al. 2017, Kalioropoulou et al. 2018, Tarnanidis et al. 2018). The first output variable is gross margin which is a good estimator of profit of farmers. The second output variable refers to the concept of agro-energy districts and the bioenergy produced from crops residues (Manos et al. 2014, Fantozzi et al. 2014, Tziolas et al. 2017). Inputs and output data are reported in Table 1. The inputs and outputs refer to the year 2015 for both DEA models, the conventional model and the MCDEA model.

The data were extracted from different sources in Greece: from General Directorate of Rural Economy and Veterinary of each prefecture, from Ministry of Rural Development and Food, from Hellenic Statistical Authority and own calculation of inputs and outputs indices based on data available. Crops related to the largest percentage of cultivated land in each prefecture were considered. The thermal and electric energy produced from crops residues was estimated, based on the existing literature and includes the measurement of yield of crops residues, humidity percentage, dry residues and biomass (Di Blasi et al. 1997, Gemtos and Tsiricoglou 1999, Jolli and Giljum, 2005).The electric energy,

Table 1. Dataset (inputs and outputs) and efficiency results from MCDEA/DEA models

Variables	v_1	v_2	u_1	u_2	u_3	u_4	u_5	Efficiency scores	
Optimization values	0	7.7961E-09	0	6.376E-08	0	0	1.06E-06	DEA	MCDEA
DMUs	EE{O}	GM{O}	Hectares{I}	Labour{I}	VC{I}	Fer{I}	Tract{I}		
Imathia	138882	174765826	58748	21196725	45249284	25986222	10300	1.00	1.00
Thessaloniki	227812	54689668	110155	8094795	38840704	25582221	14479	0.98	0.93
Pieria	66291	68332083	38466	9893376	13459527	8532087	9876	0.99	0.68
Kilkis	159270	22970301	84139	3967271	18905586	15667430	6953	1.00	0.81
Pella	154997	140213392	66149	27847616	45584690	26532020	23615	0.93	0.79
Serres	261010	117554898	96068	14013591	40774692	25559516	21621	1.00	1.00
Chalkidiki	84685	122468083	66075	15561361	15421194	11684772	7320	1.00	0.95

as a variable in agricultural production, was also used in recent studies (Tziolas et al. 2017, Kalioropoulou et al. 2018). An example of electric energy calculations is presented in Appendix (Table A.1).

Equations (1) and (2) quantify the thermal and electric energy produced, when boiler efficiency is considered 90% and 20% respectively. The energy is measured in MJ and converted to MWh.

$$TE = 0.9 \times \text{Biomass (kg)} \times \text{LHV (MJ/kg)} \tag{1}$$

$$EE = 0.2 \times \text{Biomass (kg)} \times \text{LHV (MJ/kg)} \tag{2}$$

where TE is Thermal energy production, EE is Electric energy production and LHV are the Lower Heating Values.

In DEA problems the relation between the number of DMUs and variables of inputs and outputs tend to be decisive in calibrating a proper model since the relation between these properties determine consistent results. Several studies in DEA literature deal with the issue of increasing discriminative power, known as a rule of thumb in DEA (Banker et al. 1989, Golany and Roll 1989, Boussofiane et al. 1991, Dyson et al. 2001, Ramanathan, 2003, Cooper et al. 2006).

Golany and Roll (1989) establish a rule of thumb where the number of DMUs should be twice or greater than the number of inputs and outputs. According to Banker et al. (1989), when p is the number of inputs and q the number of outputs, the DMUs (n) should satisfy the condition $n \geq \max \{p \times q, 3(p + q)\}$. Dyson et al. (2001) suggest the full range of resources used and outputs produced to be covered. Cooper et al. (2006) propose the number of DMUs to be acceptable if the number of efficient DMUs is less than the one third of the sample size, greater than the product of inputs and outputs, and greater than or equal to three times the sum of inputs and outputs. Ramanathan (2003) differentiated the latter condition and stated that the number of DMUs should be greater than or equal to two or three times the sum of inputs and outputs. Boussofiane et al. (1991), stipulate that to get a good discriminatory power out of the CCR model, the number of DMUs should be at least the multiple of the number of inputs and the number of outputs.

The rough rules of thumb mentioned above, even though not compulsory, are helpful to get valid results by constructing a model with appropriate combination of inputs, outputs and DMUs. Often, the number of DMUs are small and cannot be increased, while it is not possible to consider less inputs and outputs to conform to the above rules suggested in conventional DEA models, because they all play a decisive role in decision making.

In this study, the MCDEA model was used because the rules of thumb, for good discriminatory power, proposed for conventional DEA models are not always feasible. In case of small number of DMUs when compared to the number of inputs and outputs, the MCDEA model can overcome the weak discriminating power and any inappropriate weights distribution.

The MCDEA model in this study was used in the framework of multiple objective linear programming (MOLP) and was solved by weighted goal programming (WGP) approach. The model suggested is the WGP-MCDEA-CCR model. This is a transformation of the conventional DEA CCR model and has the following formulation (Rubem et al. 2017):

$$\text{Min } \{\lambda_1 d_1^+ + \lambda_2 d_2^+ + \lambda_3 d_3^+\} \text{ Achievement function} \quad (3)$$

$$\text{s.t. } \sum_{i=1}^{r} v_i x_{io} = 1$$

$$\sum_{j=1}^{s} u_j y_{jk} - \sum_{j=1}^{r} v_j x_{jk} + d_k = 0, \forall k$$

$$M - d_k \geq 0, \forall k$$

$$d_0 + d_1^- - d_1^+ \leq g_1 \text{ Goal 1}$$

$$M + d_2^- - d_2^+ \leq g_2, \forall k \text{ Goal 2}$$

$$\sum_{k=1}^{n} d_k + d_3^- - d_3^+ \leq g_3, \text{ Goal 3}$$

$$u_j, v_i \geq 0, \forall j, i$$

$$d_k, d_1^-, d_1^+, d_2^-, d_2^+, d_3^-, d_2^+, \geq 0, \forall k$$

where x_{ik} and y_{ik} are the values of output j and input i for the DMU_k ($k = 1,..., n$), u_j and v_i the decision variables that denote the weights assigned to the output j and input i, d_k is the deviation for the DMU_k ($k = 1,..., n$), and M is the variable corresponding to the linearization of the objective function, λ_i is the weight related to the ith goal, g_i is the aspiration level of the ith goal and d_i^-, d_i^+ are deviations from the aspiration levels of the ith goal.

The MCDEA model has three objectives which are transformed to the three goals of the model. Table 2 presents the three objective functions of the MCDEA model, as they were introduced by Li and Reeves (1999) work, and their transformation to goals in the model of Rubem et al. (2017), by incorporation of positive and negative deviation variables. The aspiration values g_1, g_2 and g_3 are assigned respectively to each objective function and consist the target values to be achieved. In agreement with Bal et al. (2010) in their goal programming approach (GPDEA-CCR model) and Rubem et al. (2017), we consider in this study the values λ_1, λ_2 and λ_3 all equal to 1, so that the achievement function becomes Min $d_1^+ + d_2^+ + d_3^+$. More specifically, the first MCDEA objective function of seminal model is the measure of inefficiency of conventional CCR DEA model that is minimized. After the

Table 2. MCDEA and GP objective functions

Objective functions MCDEA	Corresponding goal
Minimization of f_1 = Min d_0	$d_0 + d_1^- - d_1^+ \leq g_1$
Minimization of f_2 = Min M	$M + d_2^- - d_2^+ \leq g_2$
Minimization of f_3 = Min $\sum_{k=1}^{n} d_k$	$\sum_{k=1}^{n} d_k + d_3^- - d_3^+ \leq g_3$

inclusion of the deviation variables and the assignment of aspiration level, it comprises the first goal of the proposed model (3) above. The second MCDEA objective function minimizes the maximum deviation, within the set of DMUs under evaluation. In the new proposed model (3), after the inclusion of deviation variables, the maximum deviation is set less or equal to the aspiration level and it comprises the second goal. And finally the third MCDEA objective function model is the minimization of the sum of the deviation of the other DMUs that is transformed to the third goal after the inclusion of deviation variables and the assignment of respective aspiration level.

To summarize the final objective function (achievement function) in WGP-MCDEA-CCR model 3 is presented in terms of deviations and minimizes the sum of the deviations d_i^+. The deviation variables represent the difference between the aspiration levels and the result achieved by the minimization of each objective function. When the transformed goals are set to be less than or equal to these aspiration levels, it is implied that the deviation variables are the ones that increase the aspiration levels. The purpose of the proposed model is to achieve multiple objectives at the same time, by setting aspiration levels and seeking a solution in terms of minimization of weighted sum of deviations from their respective goals.

3. Results

The results achieved from the MCDEA model are presented in Table 1. More specifically, the results refer to input-orientation CRS version. MCDEA solution, has improved the discrimination among the prefectures, as the number of efficient units falls from six in the conventional DEA analysis to only two in the MCDEA approach. Table 3 presents the efficiency results achieved by the two models, according to the number of fully efficient DMUs and the number of DMUs with efficiency scores above/below 0.90. More specifically, in MCDEA and conventional DEA models comparatively, the prefectures with full efficiency are 2 and 4 respectively, the prefectures with efficiency score above 0.90 are 4 and

Table 3. MCDEA and conventional DEA results compared

Efficiency score	Number of DMUs in conventional DEA	Number of DMUs in MCDEA
Fully efficient	4	2
Efficiency score above 0.90	7	4
Efficiency score below 0.90	0	3

7 respectively, and the prefectures with efficiency score below 0.90 are 3 and zero respectively. It is evident that the conventional DEA model has no discriminatory power and almost all 7 prefectures are fully efficient, while in MCDEA model only 2 prefectures present maximum efficiency (Imathia, Serres), 4 prefectures have efficiency scores above 0.90 (Thessaloniki, Chalkidiki, Imathia, Serres) and 3 prefectures have efficiency scores below 0.90 (Pieria, Kilkis, Pella). The above results indicate that the MCDEA model has better discrimination power, because there are less DMUs with maximum efficiency. In the conventional DEA model there is a large number of efficient units, and at the same time small number of DMUs compared to number of inputs and outputs, which result in low efficiency discrimination. The proposed MCDEA model has managed to capture some additional inefficiencies in input allocation, not evident in the conventional DEA model, due to lack of discrimination among DMUs. The results revealed that the proposed MCDEA approach and its implementation to a real world dataset, actually increases the discrimination, reducing considerably the number of DMUs with maximum efficiency.

Conclusions

In this study we reviewed the conventional DEA and MCDEA models and evaluated the efficiency performance of the 7 prefectures (7 DMUs) of the region of Central Macedonia in Greece. The proposed model for ranking the DMUs was the MCDEA model and the results obtained were compared with those achieved by the conventional DEA model. The reason MCDEA approach was selected is due to the weak discrimination power provided by the conventional DEA model, when the number of DMUs is small comparatively with the number of inputs/outputs considered. This limitation of conventional DEA, when it is not possible to conform to the rules of thumb suggested in DEA literature (concerning the number of DMUs and their relation to the number of output/input variables) is addressed by MCDEA approach.

The results verified the applicability of the MCDEA model and revealed that, with the use of MCDEA models, the number of efficient

DMUs decreased considerably. In more detail, the empirical results from the MCDEA model of constant returns-to-scale revealed that two prefectures achieved an efficiency score of 1 and five prefectures efficiency scores of less than 1. In the conventional DEA model four prefectures have achieved efficiency score of 1 and three prefectures efficiency score of less than 1. The benchmark DMUs in the proposed MCDEA model are the prefectures of Imathia and Serres and it can be inferred that they use best practices and techniques concerning the agricultural production processes. The efficient DMUs can obviously serve as best-practice benchmarking for the inefficient DMUs and a better allocation of inputs is necessary for inefficient DMUs to reach the efficient frontier. In this study, the prefectures with higher efficiency scores, in relation to the main factors of agricultural production and outputs considered, could serve as a benchmark DMU for the prefectures with lower efficiency scores.

The model used has two outputs criteria the gross margin and the electric energy produced from the biomass of crops residues. The use of sustainable energy sources is in accordance with world sustainability goals for less dependency on carbon based energy sources. The prefectures are considered agro-energy districts and the decision making is determined not only by profit but also by biomass potential. Sustainable management of agricultural regions in their economic, social and environmental dimensions through different benchmarking methodologies and multicriteria techniques is a supportive policy tool in order to capture hidden inefficiencies in agricultural productivity.

In future work, it would be interesting to test with real agricultural dataset also other models existing in the recent MCDEA literature that aim at addressing the problems of discrimination and weight dispersion simultaneously e.g. the super-efficiency model by Hatami-Marbini and Toloo (2017).

Appendix A

Table A.1. Thermal and electric energy produced by the available biomass production from crop residues in Pella prefecture for 2015

Crops	Cultivated area (ha)	Residue type	Yields (tn/ha)	Moisture %	Yields dry basis (tn)	Biomass production (tn)	LHV (MJ/kg)	Thermal energy (MWh)	Electric energy (MWh)
Cotton	11,950	Pruning and shells	4.226	40%	2.54	30,354	18	136,602	30,356
Peach trees (cling stones)	8,705	Pruning	2.9	40%	1.74	15,146	22	83,312	18,514
Maize	8,054	Stalks and cobs	10.5	55%	4.725	38,055	17	161,747	35,944
Cherry trees	9,185	Pruning	2.5	40%	1.5	13,778	22	75,784	16,841
Peach trees (free stones)	5,705	Pruning	2.9	40%	1.74	9,926	22	54,599	12,133
Hard wheat	4,874	Straw	1.6	15%	1.36	6,629	16	26,518	5,893
Lucerne (alfaalfa)	4,173	Straw	3	15%	2.55	10,641	16	42,568	9,460
Barley	4,221	Straw	2.7	15%	2.295	9,688	17	41,178	9,151
Soft wheat	3,972	Straw	2.5	15%	2.125	8,440	16	33,761	7,502
Nectarine trees	3,119	Pruning	2.9	40%	1.74	5,426	22	29,847	6,633
Apricot trees	2,192	Pruning	1.6	40%	0.96	2,104	22	11,573	2,572
Total	66,149					150,187		697,488	154,997

References

Aldaz, N. and J.A. Millán. 2003. Regional productivity of Spanish agriculture in a panel DEA framework. Applied Economics Letters 10(2), 87–90.

Bal, H. and H.H. Örkcü. 2007. A goal programming approach to weight dispersion in data envelopment analysis. Gazi University Journal of Science 20, 117–125.

Bal, H., H.H. Örkcü and S. Celebioglu. 2010. Improving the discrimination power and weights dispersion in the data envelopment analysis. Computers and Operations Research 37, 99–107.

Balcombe, K., I. Fraser and J.H. Kim. 2006. Estimating technical efficiency of Australian dairy farms using alternative frontier methodologies. Applied Economics 38(19), 2221–2236.

Banker, R.D., A. Charnes and W.W. Cooper. 1984. Some models for estimating technical and scale inefficiencies in data envelopment analysis. Management Science 30(9), 1078–1092.

Banker, R.D., A. Charnes, W.W. Cooper, W. Swarts and D. Thomas. 1989. An introduction to data envelopment analysis with some of its models and their uses. Research in Governmental and Nonprofit Accounting 5(1), 125–163.

Boussofiane, A., R.G. Dyson and E. Thanassoulis. 1991. Applied data envelopment analysis. European Journal of Operational Research 52(1991), 1–15.

Charnes, A., W.W. Cooper and E. Rhodes. 1978. Measuring the efficiency of decision making units. European Journal of Operational Research 2(6), 429–444. https://doi.org/10.1016/0377-2217(78)90138-8

Chaves, M.C.C., J.C.C.B. Soares de Mello and L. Angulo-Meza. 2016. Studies of some duality properties in the Li and Reeves model. Journal of the Operational Research Society 67, 474–482.

Cooper, W.W., L.M. Seiford and K. Tone. 2006. Introduction to DEA and Its uses with DEA-Solver Software and References. Springer, New York.

Davidova, S. and L. Latruffe. 2007. Relationships between Technical Efficiency and Financial Management for Czech Republic Farms. Journal of Agricultural Economics 58(2), 269–288.

Di Blasi, C., V. Tanzi and M. Lanzetta. 1997. A study on the production of agricultural residues in Italy. Biomass and Bioenergy 12, 321–331.

Díaz, J.A., E.C. Poyato and R.L. Luque. 2004. Applying benchmarking and data envelopment analysis (DEA) techniques to irrigation districts in Spain. Irrigation and Drainage 53(2), 135–143.

Dyson, R.G., R. Allen, A.S. Camanho, V.V. Podinovski, C.S. Sarrico and E.A. Shalea. 2001. Pitfalls and protocols in DEA. European Journal of Operational Research 132(2), 245–259, https://doi.org/10.1016/S0377-2217(00)00149-1

Fantozzi, F., P. Bartocci, D.A. Bruno, S. Arampatzis and B. Manos. 2014. Public-private partnerships value in bioenergy projects: Economic feasibility analysis based on two case studies. Biomass and Bioenergy 66, 387–397.

Färe, R., R. Grabowski, S. Grasskopf and S. Kraft. 1997. Efficiency of a fixed but allocatable input: A non-parametric approach. Economics Letters 56, 187–193.

Garcia, A.F. and G.E. Shively. 2011. How might shadow price restrictions reduce technical efficiency? Evidence from a restricted DEA analysis of coffee farms in Vietnam. Journal of Agricultural Economics 62(1), 47–58.

Gemtos, T. and Th. Tsiricoglou. 1999. Harvesting of cotton residue for energy production. Biomass and Bioenergy 16, 51–59.
Ghasemi, M.R., J. Ignatius and A. Emrouznejad. 2014. A bi-objective weighted model for improving the discrimination power in MCDEA. European Journal of Operational Research 233(3): 640–650. DOI: 10.1016/j.ejor.2013.08.041
Golany, B. and Y. Roll. 1989. An application procedure for DEA. Omega 1(3), 237–250.
Haag, S., P. Jaska and J. Semple. 1992. Assessing the relative efficiency of agricultural production units in the Blackland Prairie, Texas. Applied Economics 24, 559–565.
Hatami-Marbini, A. and M. Toloo. 2017. An extended multiple criteria data envelopment analysis model. Expert Systems with Applications 73, 201–219.
Jolli, D. and S. Giljum. 2005. Unused biomass extraction in agriculture, forestry and fishery. Sustainable Europe Research Institute (SERI), Vienna.
Kalioropoulou, A., B. Manos, Th. Bournaris and S. Nastis. 2018. Planning of agricultural production in agro-energy districts of Greece. Int. J. Sustainable Agricultural Management and Informatics 3(3), 181–195. DOI: 10.1504/IJSAMI.2017.10011403
Kamruzzaman, M., B. Manos and A. Begum. 2006. Evaluation of economic efficiency of wheat farms in a region of Bangladesh under input orientation model. Journal of the Asia PacificEconomy 11(1), 123–142.
Lansink, A.O., K. Pietola and S. Bäckman. 2002. Efficiency and productivity of conventional and organic farms in Finland 1994–1997. European Review of Agricultural Economics, 29(1), 51–65.
Li, X.B. and G.R. Reeves. 1999. A multiple criteria approach to data envelopment analysis. European Journal of Operational Research 115(3), 507–517. https://doi.org/10.1016/S0377-2217(98)00130-1
Lilienfeld, A.R. and M. Asmild. 2007. Estimation of excess water use in irrigated agriculture: A data envelopment approach. Agricultural Water Management 94, 73–82.
Ma, S. and H. Feng. 2013. Will the decline of efficiency in China's agriculture come to an end? An analysis based on opening and convergence. China Economic Review 27, 179–190.
Manos, B., P. Bartocci, M. Partalidou, F. Fantozzi and S. Arampatzis. 2014. Review of public–private partnerships in agro-energy districts in Southern Europe: The cases of Greece and Italy. Renewable and Sustainable Energy Reviews 39(C), 667–678.
Mello, J.C.C.B.S.D., J.C.N. Clímaco and L.A. Meza. 2009. Efficiency evaluation of a small number of DMUs: An approach based on Li and Reeves's model. Pesquisa Operacional 29(1), 97–110.
Millian, J.A. and N. Aldaz. 1998. Agricultural productivity of the Spanish regions: A non-parametric Malmquist analysis. Applied Economics 30, 875–884.
Monchuk, D.C., Z. Chen and Y. Bonaparte. 2010. Explaining production inefficiency in China's agriculture using data envelopment analysis and semi-parametric bootstrapping. China Economic Review 21, 346–354.
Odeck, J. 2009. Statistical precision of DEA and Malmquist indices: A bootstrap application to Norwegian grain producers. Omega 37, 1007–1017.

Ramanathan, R. 2003. An Introduction to Data Envelopment Analysis: A Tool for Performance Measurement. Sage Publications, New Delhi.

Ray, S.C. and A. Ghose. 2014. Production efficiency in Indian agriculture: An assessment of the post green revolution years. Omega 44, 58–69.

Rubem, A.P., S. dos, J.C.C.B. Soares de Mello and L. Angulo Meza. 2017. A goal programming approach to solve the multiple criteria DEA model. European Journal of Operational Research, Elsevier B.V. 260(1), 134–139. doi: 10.1016/j.ejor.2016.11.049.

Tarnanidis, T., J. Papathanasiou, M. Vlachopoulou, B. Manos and A. Kalioropoulou. 2018. A multicriteria approach for assessing agricultural productivity. Int. J. Sustainable Agricultural Management and Informatics 3(4), 314–324.

Thirtle, C., J. Piesse, A. Lusigi and K. Suhariyanto. 2003. Multi-factor agricultural productivity, efficiency and convergence in Botswana, 1981–1996. Journal of Development Economics 71, 605–624.

Toloo, M., M. Barat and A. Masoumzadeh. 2015. Selective measures in data envelopment analysis. Annals of Operations Research 226(1), 623–642.

Toloo, M. and S. Babaee. 2015. On variable reductions in data envelopment analysis with an illustrative application to a gas company. Applied Mathematics and Computation 270, 527–533.

Toloo, M. and T. Tichy. 2015. Two alternative approaches for selecting performance measures in data envelopment analysis. Measurement 65, 29–40.

Toma, E., C. Dobre, I. Dona and E. Cofas. 2015. DEA applicability in assessment of agriculture efficiency on areas with similar geographically patterns. Agriculture and Agricultural Science Procedia 6, 704–711.

Tziolas, E., B. Manos and T. Bournaris. 2017. Planning of agro-energy districts for optimum farm income and biomass energy from crops residues. Oper. Res. 17, 535–546.

Vlontzos, G. and S. Niavis. 2014. Assessing the evolution of technical efficiency of agriculture in EU countries: Is there a role for the agenda 2000? *In*: Zopounidis, C., Kalogeras, N., Mattas, K., van Dijk, G. and Baourakis, G. (eds.). Agricultural Cooperative Management and Policy. Cooperative Management, Springer, Cham.

Vlontzos, G. and P.M. Pardalos. 2017. Assess and prognosticate green house gas emissions from agricultural production of EU countries, by implementing, DEA Window Analysis and artificial neural networks. Renewable and Sustainable Energy Reviews 79, 155–162.

You, H. and X. Zhang. 2016. Ecoefficiency of intensive agricultural production and its influencing factors in China: An application of DEA-Tobit analysis. Discrete Dynamics in Nature and Society, vol. 2016, DOI:10.1155/2016/4786090

Zhang, T. 2008. Environmental performance in China's agricultural sector: A case study in corn production. Applied Economics Letters 15, 641–645.

Index

A

Agricultural ecosystems, 40, 42, 43, 52, 53, 56, 59, 65, 66
Agricultural knowledge, 203, 205, 207, 217
Agricultural production, 172-175, 183, 192
Agrotechnology, 18
Architecture, 201, 205, 207, 216-218, 225
Artificial intelligence, 122, 125, 127, 129, 130

C

Cartographic modelling, 43
Circular economy, 1-3, 14, 18, 20
Crop protection, 112, 113, 115, 118, 120, 121, 135, 145, 160
Crop yield modeling, 184, 185
Crop yield prediction, 38

D

Data envelopment analysis, 228
Data, 199-205, 207, 209, 210, 215-221, 223-225
Decision support systems, 113, 121, 123, 143
Decision-making, 98-101
Digital platform, 200, 201, 205, 216, 218, 222, 225

Dimension reduction, 33, 36, 38
Disease detection studies, 130

E

Environmental satellites, 175-178

F

Farm management information systems, 121
Farmers' satisfaction, 87, 89, 100
Fragmentation, 43, 49, 52, 53, 56, 65

G

Greece, 75, 78-80, 82, 83, 99

H

High dimensional data, 28, 29
High impact knowledge reservoir, 199-201, 204
Hyperspectral curves, 34

I

Internet of Things, 2

L

Land use-land cover change, 40
Local communities, 84, 96, 98, 101

Index

M

MCDEA-WGP-CCR, 229
Mediterranean landscape, 42
Meteorological satellites, 175, 179, 188
Multicriteria DEA, 227

O

Ontology, 200-202, 205, 209, 211, 212, 214, 216, 217, 224, 225

P

Plant protection products, 112, 139
Precision agriculture, 3, 9-11, 19

R

Relative efficiency, 227

Remote sensing in crop yield modeling, 172

S

Social cohesion, 74, 76, 90, 97, 101, 102
Southern Spain, 42
Sustainability, 3, 9, 10, 19

T

Thematic network, 199-212, 214-217, 219, 223-225

W

Wetland protected areas, 77, 78, 101